WORLD AND ISLAMIC TERRORISM

SPHERE AND RESPONSES

WORLD AND ISLAMIC TERRORISM

SPHERE AND RESPONSES

Sarah Jacobs

HOW
ACADEMICS
an imprint of Highlyy Publishing LLP

ISBN: 978-93-95522-84-7
First Published : 2025

Published by : HOW ACADEMICS
an imprint of Highlyy Publishing LLP

Correspondence Address :
4/30 A II Floor, Double Storey Buildings
Vijay Nagar, Delhi-110009
Editorial: +91 9811026449
Sales : +91 9999953412
Email: info@howacademics.com
Website: www.howacademics.com

Contents

Preface

In the intricate tapestry of global history, the phenomenon of terrorism has emerged as a persistent and evolving threat, influencing political landscapes, societal structures, and international relations. Among the various forms of terrorism, Islamic terrorism has garnered significant attention due to its profound impact on global security and its association with a particular religious and cultural framework. This book aims to unravel the complex relationship between the world and Islamic terrorism, providing a nuanced understanding through historical context, cultural references, and scholarly essays.

The origins of Islamic terrorism are deeply rooted in a confluence of historical events, ideological evolutions, and geopolitical dynamics. To comprehend its contemporary manifestations, one must delve into the annals of history, tracing the rise and spread of Islam, the socio-political conditions of Muslim-majority regions, and the external influences that have shaped these societies. This book endeavors to present a balanced narrative, exploring the intricate web of causes and consequences that have led to the emergence of terrorism under the banner of Islam.

Throughout this work, readers will encounter a diverse range of perspectives and analyses. Essays by renowned scholars and experts dissect the theological, cultural, and political dimensions of Islamic terrorism, offering insights into the motivations of its proponents and the strategies employed to combat it. The inclusion of cultural references serves to enrich the reader's understanding, highlighting the interplay between religion, culture, and violence.

While Islamic terrorism is a focal point, this book also situates it within the broader context of global terrorism. By comparing and contrasting different forms of terrorism, readers can appreciate the unique characteristics and commonalities that define these violent movements. The aim is not to single out Islam but to provide a comprehensive exploration of terrorism as a global phenomenon, emphasizing the need for informed and multifaceted approaches to address it.

In a world where misconceptions and prejudices often cloud our understanding, this book strives to foster a more informed and empathetic perspective. By examining the historical and cultural underpinnings of Islamic terrorism, we hope to contribute to a more nuanced discourse, one that acknowledges the complexity of the issue and seeks solutions grounded in knowledge and compassion.

This preface sets the stage for a journey through time and thought, encouraging readers to engage with the material critically and thoughtfully. The essays and analyses that follow are intended to provoke reflection, challenge assumptions, and ultimately, inspire a deeper commitment to understanding and addressing the roots of terrorism in all its forms.

Chapter 1
From Arab Spring to ISIS Dominance: Unraveling the Shift

In this chapter I will explain how the hope of the Arab Spring resulted in a new level of Islamic extremism as radicals took advantage of a vacuum in leadership to gain new ground for their cause.

During the whole year of 2011 one major topic dominated the world media: the so-called Arab Spring. A revolution crying out for freedom and democracy was spreading over the whole Middle East like a bush fire. Dictator regimes, which had been in power for decades, were overthrown in just a few days.

On December 18, 2010, in Tunisia a young Tunisian man in an economically desperate situation committed suicide by setting fire on himself. This was the first spark that later created a big fire that covered the whole region of the Middle East, including Egypt, Libya, Syria, Yemen, and Bahrein.

As a result of this revolution:

- The Tunisian president Ben Ali fled his country, and his government was overthrown.
- Egyptian president Mubarak resigned and was put in jail and on trial along with his two sons and six top officials of his regime.
- The Libyan dictator Qaddafi was killed after a civil war with foreign military intervention, and his regime was overthrown.
- The president of Yemen, Ali Abdullah Saleh, was kicked out of his position and the power was handed over to a national unity government.
- In the kingdom of Bahrain a civil uprising took place that forced the king to do some government changes. However, the changes didn't stop the uprising.
- In Jordan, Morocco, Lebanon, Oman, Kuwait, Iraq, and Algeria protestors forced the governments to make constitutional reforms and governmental changes.

- In Syria the corrupted dictator president refused to leave his position and continued killing his own people. Consequently a civil war started which would keep burning for years.

In the same way a huge forest fire caused by just one little match, the overwhelming fire of the revolution in the Arab world was caused by one individual incident.

A fire, however, only will spread that much if the land is very dry. The region of the Arab world was exactly like a dry forest in a very hot summer. It was dried out by the heat of corruption, dictatorship, and economical distress. The region was heated by the misery, torture, and all the unjust trials against innocent people that were done by the corrupt dictator regimes. People were suffering from the lack of freedom and justice. The abuse of basic human rights by the secret services and the corrupt, vicious police departments had heated up the moods. The Arab region of the world was so dry, heated, and ready to get burned that the smallest spark could light a huge fire.

Eventually millions of people went to the streets to demonstrate for bread, freedom, and social justice. The world was just watching and could hardly believe what they saw. One dictatorship after the other was overthrown. The situation in the Middle East was turned upside down within a few weeks, and it seemed that the whole world was full of hope that finally peace and democracy would lead the way. Indeed, Egypt experienced a free democratic election for the first time in its history.

When the revolution that had started in Tunisia reached Egypt in the beginning of 2011, I was watching the news almost day and night. My heart was dancing inside me when the old regime finally stepped back. I was so happy to witness the end of this corrupted dictator regime that I myself had been suffering under. However, at the same time I had the strange feeling that this revolution, which had been started by the moderate young generation, might be hijacked and the country might be taken into an even deeper and darker kind of dictatorship and abuse of human rights than before. Before the revolution the people suffered corrupt regimes and corrupt politics. But now the people might fall under the dictatorship of the radical Islamic religious ideology, which can violate the basic human rights even more.

Catching the Wave: The Muslim Brotherhood's Opportunistic Rise

A few months later my concerns became reality. The revolution had been stolen from the young generation, who had started the revolution, calling for bread, freedom, and social justice. In Egypt Muslim Brotherhood and Salafists won the parliamentarian election and a new president, who was a member of Muslim Brotherhood, came to power. The new parliament was on its way to implement Islamic law step by step.

While various radical groups come and go, Muslim Brotherhood is the most mature and well-organized powerful Islamic radical movement in our modern history. It was established by the well-educated Egyptian Sheikh Hassan Al-Banna in 1928 as a result of the collapse and the fall of the Islamic Caliphate. The main purpose of the establishment of the Muslim Brotherhood was to restore Islam in the Muslim world in every single area of life—politics, social affairs, economy, education, jurisdiction, and military.

A brief review of their history will help you understand their strategy and position today. In the first years after their establishment during the 1930s and 1940s Muslim Brotherhood was very actively engaged in fighting against the Jews in Palestine. Later their focus turned to Egyptian internal affairs, and so in the 1950s they turned aggressively against all politicians whom they deemed too secular. They assassinated the Egyptian prime minister al-Nuqrashi in 1948 and later attempted to assassinate president Gamal Abdel Nasser. Their very radical behavior triggered, however, a very harsh reaction: President Nasser went after them with resoluteness. He killed many of them and put many of them in prison for many, many years. Muslim Brotherhood was officially banned for the following decades. Nevertheless, the organization continued their work underground.

When the powerful wind of change started to shake the whole Middle East during the Arab Spring and spread the hope that this revolution would bring true democracy and liberty to the Middle East, many signs very soon showed how well prepared the political ground was for Muslim Brotherhood to take power and how well prepared the organization was to jump in and use this unique opportunity. They had learned from their past and were well prepared for a better future. They changed their strategy and adapted a peaceful approach. Having the long-term goal in mind, they presented themselves as modern, peaceful, and in favor of democracy. This way they were able to gain international support and win the democratic elections. Their strategy was quite successful as previously mentioned. They won both the majority in the parliament as well as the presidential elections.

Their success, however, didn't last long, and it would soon provide justification for the new level of extremism we see in ISIS, the Islamic State in Iraq and Syria. After just a few months the democratically elected president Mohamed Morsi was kicked out of his position through a military coup under the leadership of Abdel Fattah al-Sisi, who shortly later became the new president. Many Egyptians considered this coup as a great liberation and al-Sisi was viewed by many as a messiah. And indeed, under al-Sisi the country recovered economically, and peace in the country was reestablished. However, the way this new government radically wiped out all its political opponents soon revealed that with this new president returned the same kind of dictatorship as before the revolution. Again all political opponents were wiped out with extreme harshness.

Egypt can be considered the heart of the Middle East. Whatever happens there has a great influence on the rest of the Middle East. This is why the development there is crucial and kind of representative for the entire Middle East.

For Muslim Brotherhood and all the other Islamic groups that had been dreaming to get rid of this kind of corrupt and secular regimes, the Egyptian backlash was a real trauma. I strongly believe that the failure of the peaceful approach of Muslim Brotherhood in Egypt has greatly contributed to the fast spread of the extremely violent group of ISIS.

Tracing Paths to Power: The Ascendancy of ISIS:

ISIS can be seen as the grandchild of Muslim Brotherhood. In June 2014 the militant group declared it is establishing a caliphate spanning across Iraq and Syria. The Egyptian military crushing Muslim Brotherhood after the Arab Spring gave ISIS an excuse for their extremism. They could look to Egypt and say that gaining power through politics doesn't work; peaceful change is not possible. The only way is the extreme way.

Setting up a caliphate ruled by the strict Islamic law has long been a goal of many jihadists, who complain that Islam has been taken out of society and who demand for Islam to rule again—in every area of life. They go to Islamic history and point to Muhammad's example of war—aggression and terrorism and the use of fear and terror. You will read these stories in detail in this book.

ISIS is operating under the premise that they are living in the house of war and therefore must use all means at their disposal to conquer territory for their cause. The concept of house of war and house of peace has been discussed for centuries in Islamic law, and an understanding of it is essential to make sense of what is happening in the Islamic world today.

These terms do not come directly from the Quran or hadith, but the early scholars of Islam created these terms in order to describe the environment of a place where a Muslim may be living. For example, Mecca during the time of Muhammad's weakness and persecution would have been a house of war (Dar-ul-Harb). As a result, after he was prepared, Muhammad declared war on Mecca and established Islamic authority there. Medina, when it was governed and ruled by Muslims, would be considered a house of peace (Dar-ul-Islam).

Abu Hanifa, one of the founders of the four Muslim legal schools, had a moderate standard for these two terms. He said the most important issue is the security of Muslims. If Muslims are in a secure place, it is Dar-ul-Islam; if not, then they are in Dar-ul-Harb. By these standards, a nation where Islam could be practiced freely (such as the United States or England) would be considered Dar-ul-Islam. However, another group of Muslim scholars reject this definition. They say that Dar-ul-Harb is any place not ruled by Islam and not submitting to Islamic law.

Sayyid Qutb popularized the strict interpretation in his most influential book, Milestones Along the Road. Qutb declared:

1. Dar-ul-Islam is that place where the Islamic state is established and Sharia is the highest authority and God's limits are observed and where all the Muslims administer the affairs of the state with mutual consultation.
2. The rest of the world is the home of hostility (Dar-ul-Harb). A Muslim can have only two possible relations with Dar-ul- Harb: peace with a contractual agreement or war. A country with which there is a treaty will not be considered the home of Islam.

A Muslim must only declare loyalty to Dar-ul-Islam, not to a particular nationality. Qutb wrote:

> *A Muslim has no country except that part of the earth where the Sharia of God is established.... ; a Muslim has no nationality except his belief... ; a Muslim has no relatives except those who share the belief in God.*

A committed Muslim will have only one defining characteristic—his faith. All other identity not based in his faith is irrelevant, including lineage, race, nationality, and family. These relationships were from the time of ignorance before Islam, says the radical.

The Prospects of ISIS

ISIS has written a new powerful chapter in the story of Islamic radicalism. They have recruited twenty thousand fighters from ninety nations, including France, Morocco, Russia, Saudi Arabia, Tunisia, the United States, and Canada.They have taken control of portions of Iraq's Anbar Province and oil-rich areas in Syria and are operating transnationally.The United States and its allies have been carrying out air strikes against ISIS targets, and officials claim thousands of militants have been killed.Even if ISIS will eventually be defeated, the world must be prepared for others who will take their place. This is because the philosophy that drives groups such as Muslim Brotherhood and ISIS needs to be understood and addressed in the Islamic world.

Chapter 2
Core Principles of Islamic Extremism

Even though each radical group is different, they all share some core beliefs, and these beliefs are strong enough to draw in new waves of radicals. These ideas did not stay inside a single country. They are sent all over the world through internet, which helps them win the hearts and minds of more Muslims.

I call these guiding principles the "Five Pillars of Radical Islamic Philosophy." They are:

1. Obey no law but Islamic law.
2. Infidels are all around.
3. Islam must rule.
4. Jihad is the only way to win.
5. Faith is the reason.

In my first book, Journey into the Mind of an Islamic Terrorist, I talked about these ideas. If you can understand these five ideas, you will have a good idea of how an Islamic radical who fights because of his religion and not because of politics thinks.

Islamic Law Above Al

The only thing that sets the extreme Muslim apart from everyone else is Islamic law. Since the start of the modern Islamic terrorism resurgence, the extreme leaders have been begging their governments to follow Islamic law.

The difference between terrorists who are religious and terrorists who are not religious is the law of Islam. I put it as Pillar 1 because without it, fanatics would have no reason to criticize secular governments and call for jihad.

Because Islamic law is seen as a clear order from Allah, it is a very powerful idea. Even worse, the most extreme thinkers tied it to the worship of Allah in a way that couldn't be separated.

How did the laws of Islam come to be? And who today follows Islamic law? Muhammad was the first person to use Islamic law to settle disagreements in the new Muslim government state. When a problem came up, he would either get a message from Allah or decide on his own. For example, after military victories, the people asked Muhammad how to divide the spoils of war. In answer, Muhammad said that Allah had told him how to divide the spoils of war. Once the new discovery was made public, Muslims had to agree with his decision.

Ubiquity of Non-Believers

The radical thinks that people who don't believe in God are against him and his word of faith. Radicals spend a lot of time and energy in their writings claiming that almost all societies, including those who call themselves Muslims, are infidel.

Islam means submission, and to be a Muslim you must submit to Islamic law, the radicals say. They repeatedly appeal to this Quranic verse:

> *But no, by your Lord, they can have no Faith, until they make you (O Muhammad) judge in all disputes between them, and find in themselves no resistance against your decisions, and accept (them) with full submission.*

Radicals use these verses to sweepingly condemn nearly the whole world as infidel.

The radicals see Islam as an all-or-nothing faith. An individual must follow all of the regulations of Islam (according to the radical's understanding), or that person is an infidel. You cannot accept some and reject some. For example, during Muhammad's time a group of new Muslim converts wanted to keep charging interest (usury) for loans, even though the Quran prohibited it. At this point Muhammad received the following revelation from Allah:

> *"The Exalted said 'O ye who believe! Fear Allah, and give up what remains of your demand for usury, if ye are indeed believers. If ye do it not, Take notice of war from Allah and His Messenger'".*

In other words, Allah required Muhammad to go to war against those who would not give up usury (charging interest), even though they were following other teachings of Islam. This is known in Islamic teaching as "accepting some, rejecting some." The Quran says:

> *Surely those who disbelieve in Allah and His apostles and (those who) desire to make a distinction between Allah and His apostles and say: We believe in some and disbelieve in others, and desire to take a course between (this and) that. These it is that are truly the unbelievers, and we have prepared for the unbelievers a disgraceful chastisement.*

When Abu Bakr took over after Muhammad died, a group of people who had just become Muslims refused to pay the tax to the Islamic state. This is another example of this philosophy. Abu Bakr sent his best general to fight them, and in three terrible months, he killed 80,000 people. Abu Bakr was Muhammad's best friend, so this shows the radicals that they can't let people obey only some of the rules.

In the end, the radical is sure that he is surrounded by non-Muslims who must be fought in order to protect Islam. His main goal is to bring back the kingdom. He says, "Islam must rule." This is what the third part, which you will read about next, is all about.

Supremacy of Islamic Rule

People in the West hear about bombs and other acts of terrorism in both Muslim countries and the West. They often throw their hands up in anger and ask, "What do these people want?" What are they looking for?"

The answer is that these attackers want the caliphate back and want Islam to rule the whole world in the end.

In general, Muslims are very proud of the past of the Islamic caliphate. The caliphate was a government and spiritual union for Muslim lands for 1300 years.

When Turkey ended the caliphate in 1924, it caused Muslim people a lot of mental pain. The radical thinks that setting up the kingdom is a way to show that you are willing to obey Allah. The caliphate is given to those who believe (Muslims) in the Quran:

> *Allah has promised, to those among you who believe and work righteous deeds, that He will, of a surety, grant them in the land, inheritance (of power), as He granted it to those before them...*

The verse goes on to describe the characteristics of the caliphate—that it will make it easy for Muslims to practice their religion and will give them security in place of fear.

> *He will grant them the authority to practise their religion which He has chosen for them (i.e. Islam). And He will surely give them in exchange a safe security after their fear (provided) they (believers) worship Me.*

Islam is a religion and a state. After Muhammad emigrated from Mecca to Medina, he set up a political government, established laws, and established Islam as a system of belief that covers every aspect of life.

Blueprint for Worldwide Islamic Authority

The radical plans to restore the caliphate by accomplishing three goals:

1. Establish Islamic states.
2. Join these states together under the caliphate.
3. Use the caliphate to submit the entire world to Islamic authority.

To a committed radical who is fighting for his faith, the caliphate means everything and nationality means nothing. His nationality is now belief in Islam.

Jihad: The Sole Route to Success

The Islamic radical is a fundamentalist—he wants to practice Islam the way Muhammad practiced Islam. So his definition of jihad is based on Muhammad's—both in word and by example.

The Quran contains a tremendous amount of teaching about jihad. In fact, I estimate that 60 percent of the Quran is related to the concept of jihad.

Radicals believe non-Muslims who oppress them cause all their problems. Therefore, they readily identify with verses such as these:

> *And what is wrong with you that you fight not in the Cause of Allah, and for those weak, ill-treated and oppressed among men, women, and children, whose cry is: "Our Lord! Rescue us from this town whose people are oppressors; and raise for us from You one who will protect, and raise for us from You one who will help."*

> *March forth, whether you are light (being healthy, young and wealthy) or heavy (being ill, old and poor), strive hard with your wealth and your lives in the Cause of Allah. This is better for you, if you but knew.*

> *O you who believe! What (excuse) have you that when it is said to you: Go forth in Allah's way, you should incline heavily to earth; are you contented with this world's life instead of the hereafter? But the provision of this world's life compared with the hereafter is but little. If you do not go forth, He will chastise you with a painful chastisement and bring in your place a people other than you, and you will do Him no harm; and Allah has power over all things.*

This verse was revealed while Muhammad was preparing his people to go fight in the Campaign of Tabuk. Some Muslims hesitated to go and fight, so this verse warned them that Allah would punish the ones who refused to go and replace them with better people.

Decisive Blows in Battle

The world was horrified by videotapes of beheadings in Iraq. People wondered why religious radicals would commit this grisly act. The answer is in the Quran:

> *Therefore, when you meet the Unbelievers (in fight), smite at their necks; at length, when you have thoroughly subdued them, bind a bond firmly (on them)...*

Faith Underpins the Purpose

You will never understand what a Muslim terrorist is thinking until you realize that their main motive is their religion. In the modern West, talking about a person's religion is generally considered rude and, in some cases, illegal. But it is pointless to try to understand a Muslim extremist if you don't fully accept that he is acting because of his faith.

I could be accused of making radicals' reasons sound too simple by saying that they are all based on their faith. So, I'll agree that things other than a person's faith can push them toward anarchy. In other words, if someone is jobless and suffering under a corrupt government that says it is Islamic, radicalism will look like the answer to his problems. But these outside reasons won't be enough to make him strap a bomb to his body and blow himself up in the name of the cause. It comes down to hope.

As extreme groups are brought under control or broken up, it is their faith that gives birth to new groups all over the Islamic world. Here are the main ideas that guide their actions so you can understand why they do what they do.

Faith in Allah Requires Obedience

The Quran says, "Therefore fear not men, but fear Me". If you believe in Allah, then you are obligated to follow the command of jihad, the radicals say, even if it means jail, loss of your job, or worse. If you don't follow the commands of Allah, then you don't believe in Allah.

If you Believe in Fate, You will Obey

One of the most important ideas in Islam is about how things turn out. Islam says that Allah decides whether a person will have good or bad things happen to them and when they will die. No amount of work can change what will happen. The Quran says, "No one can die except with Allah's permission and at the right time." So, the radicals say, death is nothing to be afraid of because Allah is in charge of it.

Belief in the Final Day Compels Obedience

Radicals use Muslims' fear of the Last Day, or the Day of Judgment, to get them to join war. Islamic doctrine says that after judgment comes "eternal fire or eternal bliss." Radicals say that if a Muslim thinks hell is as bad as Allah says it is, then the Muslim will do anything the Quran says to do to stay out of hell.

Martyrdom is the Path to Paradise

Martyrdom is a source of comfort; those who make the ultimate effort get the ultimate reward. Islam says that on the Day of Judgment, a person's actions will be weighed, and then Allah will decide if that person can go to Paradise. As the quote from the Quran said, if you live as an unbeliever, you might be sure to go to hell, but if you try to be the best Muslim you can be, you're still not sure you'll get into paradise. There is only one sure thing, and that is death.

The Prophet Muhammad said, "Whoever fights in (Holy battles) for Allah's cause, and nothing forces him to do so except belief in Allah and His Apostles, will be rewarded by Allah either with a reward or booty (if he survives) or will be allowed into Paradise (if he dies in the battle as a martyr)."

To a radical, dying as a martyr is not a sign of failure; it is a way to get to heaven.

Your Faith Elevates You Above Others

The idea that the believer is better than the rest of society is a common theme in radical teaching. This is true in terms of faith, understanding and concept of the nature of the world, values and standards, morality and understanding, law and life. Radicals think that people are against them because of their religion. So, when a country in the West uses armed force against an Islamic country, many Muslims see it as an attack on Allah and the Islamic faith.

Conclusion

From what we've learned in this chapter, it's easy to see what kind of faith makes radical Muslims do crazy things. It is a call for morals to be restored and a defense of Islam, along with a fear of hell and the belief that the only way to get to heaven is to die as a martyr.

In the next part of this book, you'll learn about the lives of Muhammad and his followers, which is where the terrorists got their Five Pillars of Radical Philosophy.

Chapter 3
Basic doctrines of Islam

In 1980, when I was a first-year student at Al-Azhar University, I took a class called "Interpretation of the Quran." We would get together twice a month to hear a blind sheikh talk about Islam. The kids liked him because he was so passionate about Islam.

But it was clear that he was a radical. Whenever the Quran mentioned Christians or Jews, he loved to call Christians "infidels" and Jews "the children of pigs." He made it clear that he wanted to use jihad to bring the Islamic kingdom back to its glory days.

One day, he gave us the chance to ask him questions. I stood up and asked him a question I had been thinking about for a long time: "Why do you always teach us about jihad?" What about the other parts of the Quran that talk about being kind and forgiving?"

His face turned red right away. I could see that he was angry, but I also saw that he decided to keep it in check. He could have yelled at me, but instead he used the chance to make his point in front of 500 students who were listening. "My brother," he said, "there is a whole surah called 'Spoils of War.'" There's no surah called 'Peace.' Islam is all about jihad and killing. If you get rid of them, you'll cut off the top of Islam."

Today, that man is locked up in an American jail. Omar Abdel Rahman is his name, and he was found guilty of planning the first bombing of the World Trade Center in 1993.

Before he moved to the United States, he was the spiritual leader of the radical Egyptian group al-Jihad, which killed the president of Egypt, Anwar al-Sadat. Later in this book, I will tell the amazing story of how Sheikh Abdel Rahman talked the Egyptian Supreme Court into letting him go, which allowed him to go to the United States and perform jihad there.

Understanding the mindset

From this story and what I've said, you can see that I've been close to terrorists for most of my life. Terrorists are hard for people in the West to understand. "Are they all just crazy?" they wonder.

I can tell you for sure that these people are not crazy. They are also not psychopaths who get joy from hurting other people. No, they are following a set of rules, and once you understand these rules, you won't be surprised by anything they do.

In this chapter, I'll explain the basics of Islam, but we'll move on quickly to talk about the specific religious beliefs that drive an Islamic bomber. I will also talk about how radicals get rid of the parts of the Quran that say people should live together in peace.

Complying with Allah's commandments

The word Islam means "submission"; the word Muslim means "one who submits to Allah." The Quran says you cannot be a true Muslim unless you submit.

> *O you who believe! Obey Allah and obey the Messenger (Muhammad) and those of you (Muslims) who are in authority.*

Now, if you want to bow to Allah, you need to know what Allah wants from you. The solutions are in the Quran and the hadith, which are the holy books of Islam. Sharia, which is the name for Islamic law, is also based on these beliefs.

The Holy Book of Islam

Muhammad, the founder of Islam, said that the angel Gabriel spoke to him while he was sitting in a cave near Mecca in the year 610. This is when the Quran was written. Muhammad said that these words came from Allah, the one true god. Over a period of about twenty-two years, Muhammad's twelve friends wrote down these words from God as Muhammad heard them. In short, the Quran is thought to be what God says. As we'll see later, the fact that not all of the discoveries happened at the same time is important.

Recorded Traditions of the Prophet: The Hadith

Another set of holy works is the books of hadith. The things that Muhammad said and did are written about in these books. In other words, the books of hadith show both what Muhammad said and how he did it. Muslims look up to Muhammad as the best model, so the hadiths, which are also called the record of the Sunnah, are about as important to them as the Quran.

Here is how the hadith books came to be. People who knew Muhammad well, like his friends or wives, watched and wrote down what he did. Scholars gathered these writings, checked to see if they were real, and put the hadith that they thought were true and trustworthy into six sets of books called the right books (sahih) of hadith. Hadith by Sahih Al-Bukhari is an example of how to refer to one of these books by the name of the person who put the stories in it.

Most Muslims around the world believe that these six books of hadith are true. Sunni Muslims accept all six of these books. Shiite Muslims accept most hadith, but they don't accept the hadith that was written down by Muhammad's second wife.

Foundations and Development of Sharia

Sharia, or Islamic law, is based on what's in the Quran and hadith. Sharia says what Muslims should do for the God of Islam.

There are different Sunni and Shiite schools of thinking, but they all agree that the Quran is the most important source of Islamic law. So any decision in the Quran must be accepted, and no other source can change it. When the Quran doesn't say what to do, the law experts look to the example of Muhammad. When Muhammad's life doesn't answer a question, legal experts look to the lives of Muhammad's friends. When the companions didn't talk about something, the experts use different ways to figure out what it means. This method is called ishtihad. The views about the law that Islamic jurists come up with (called fatwas) become part of Islamic law.

The books that explain Islamic law are called Qutb al-Fiqh. These aren't particular books like the books of hadith. Some of these books are very old and some are written recently.

Basic Obligations of a Muslim

So what does the Quran and hadith say that Allah wants people to do? There are five key requirements that must be met in order to be a Muslim. These requirements are known as the five pillars of Islam:

1. Statement of belief. There must be acceptance of the Muslim statement of faith: "There is no god but Allah, and Muhammad is his prophet."
2. Prayer. Muslims are to pray five times a day while facing Mecca, the birthplace of Muhammad. Prayers are at dawn, afternoon, late afternoon, after sunset and night. Special prayers are on Fridays.
3. Giving alms. This is similar to a tax. It is paid at the end of the year and distributed to those in need.
4. Fasting. This takes place during the Islamic month of Ramadan, which starts at the first visual sighting of the ninth crescent moon according to

the Islamic calendar. During this fast Muslims do not eat or drink during daylight hours. A light meal and a large amount of water are taken in before daybreak. After the sun sets, a heavier meal is eaten, and a large amount of liquid is consumed.

5. Pilgrimage. Muslims are encouraged to make a pilgrimage at least once in their lifetimes to Mecca where a five-day ritual is followed.

Why does it matter so much that Muslims do what Allah wants? Because Islam is a faith based on doing things. To get into Paradise (heaven), you have to work for it. The sad thing is that Muslims can never be sure they will go to heaven. They think that when they die, they go to the grave and wait for their sentence on the day of the resurrection.

When the day of judgment comes, Allah weighs the good and bad things people have done and chooses what will happen to them.

> *Then as for him whose balance (of good deeds) will be heavy, he will live a pleasant life (in Paradise). But as for him whose balance (of good deeds) will be light, he will have his home in Hawiyah (pit, i.e., Hell).*

Even if you do good things your whole life, it doesn't mean you'll go to Paradise. All of it depends on what Allah says.

Secured Place in Heaven

There is only one way to be sure of getting into Paradise, which is why suicide bombers and jihad fighters do what they do. The only way to know for sure that you will go to Paradise is to die in war, which means to die while fighting for Allah's cause and against Islam's enemies.

Jihad just means working for Allah's cause, and radicals usually take it to mean that Muslims have to fight Allah's enemies until they die or the Muslims do. The real meaning of the word "jihad" is "struggle." Islamic fiqh has even given a formal definition of jihad, which says the following:

> *[Jihad] is fighting anybody who stands in the way of spreading Islam. Or fighting anyone who refuses to enter into Islam.*

If you die in jihad, you don't even have to go to the grave and wait for judgment; you go directly to Paradise.

Jihad is really a contract between Allah and the Muslim. If the Muslim fights, Allah rewards him in the afterlife.

Let those (believers) who sell the life of this world for the Hereafter fight in the Cause of Allah, and whoso fights in the Cause of Allah, and is killed or gets victory, We shall bestow on him a great reward.

In reference to those who fight jihad, the Quran also says:

For them Allah has got ready Gardens (Paradise) under which rivers flow, to dwell therein forever. That is the supreme success.

When someone dies in war, they are buried in a different way. Normal people's bodies are cleaned and dressed up as if they were going to the mosque after they die. When someone dies in war, his body is not washed or given clean clothes. This person is put in the box right after he dies. The blood is a sign of respect and a witness for him in front of Allah. Muslims think that the angels will treat him like he is important to God.

Western media have made fun of the Muslim view of Paradise (heaven)—virgins for men to enjoy, etc.—but it is much more important to realize that a Muslim can only be sure of going to Paradise if he or she dies in war. Because of this, Muslims leave their own countries to fight war in other places. Religion is what drives them, which is a much more dangerous reason than politics.

All Muslims are told to do jihad in the Quran, but let's answer an important question that many people ask right now: "What about all the "nice" verses in the Quran?"

Understanding Quranic Contradictions: Abrogation and Its Impact

You have probably seen or read about verses in the Quran that say nice things about Christians or that support kindness or even religious freedom. You may have asked, "Are those verses really there?"

The answer to the riddle is that the Quran is full of conflicts. You can find lines that praise Christians and verses that tell Christians they are going to hell.

There are also differences in ideas about other things. During Muhammad's time, there was a lot of drinking of booze, for example. Arabs were told in one revelation not to drink alcohol when they went to the mosque to pray, but they could drink again when the prayers were over. Later, another phrase came out that said people should never drink.

Another example is how Muslims and Christians treat each other. Some verses say that Muslims can get along well with them, while other verses say that Muslims must turn them to Islam.

In the beginning of Islam, women did not have to wear a hijab. However, later texts told women to stay inside and wear a cover.

So, Islamic scholars had to figure out which texts to follow when they seemed to go against each other. The concept of abrogation (naskh) was used to do this.

The fact that the Quran was given to Muhammad at different times over a period of about twenty-two years is the basis for the concept of abrogation. Some parts of the Quran were written before others. To get rid of a contradiction, they agreed that new revelations would take the place of or cancel out the old ones.

There are at least 114 verses in the Quran that speak of kindness and forgiveness, especially in the surah titled "The Heifer". But when Surah 9:5 was revealed later, it canceled out those previous verses. This verse states:

> *Fight and slay the Pagans wherever you find them, and seize them, beleaguer them, and lie in wait for them in every strategem (of war); but if they repent, and establish regular prayers and practise regular charity, then open the way for them: for Allah is Oft-forgiving, Most Merciful.*

This part of the Quran is called the "verse of the sword," and it says that Muslims must fight anyone who doesn't turn to Islam, no matter where they are in the world. It is seen as the last step in the evolution of war in Islam.

Abrogation is a very strong concept. If a word is abrogated, it is as if it had never been written before.

You might wonder, "Why does the Quran have contradictions in the first place?" Why did the facts change as time went on?" If you look at the life of Muhammad, the founder of Islam, you can find the answer to that question.

At first, the lessons that were given to Muhammad were kind and peaceful so that people would listen. But then things changed.

In Mecca, where he first shared his message, Muhammad ran into a lot of trouble, so he left in the year 622. He went to Yathrib, which is now called Medina, where he built up his army and got more people to follow him. (Both Mecca and Medina are in Saudi Arabia, which is where we live now.) Later, when Muhammad had more power, he was able to go back and take over Mecca and the places around it. This is a big step toward making Islam a political movement instead of just a spiritual religion.

In his early years in Mecca, the prophet Muhammad spent a lot of time praying and thinking. This is why the Quranic teachings from that time talk about peace and working with others. But in Medina, Muhammad became a military leader and attacker, so the revelations from Medina talk about military power and invasion in the name of Islam (jihad).

About 60% of the lines in the Quran are about jihad, which makes sense since Muhammad got most of the Quran after he left Mecca. Jihad became Islam's main force and source of power.

It would be nice if the surahs in the Quran were put in the order in which they were given, but they are not. Some versions of the Quran say whether a word was revealed in Mecca or Medina. However, to find out the exact order of the revelations, you need to look at more scholarly sources.

Conclusion

- In this chapter you have learned some very necessary concepts that will help you to understand the mind-set of an Islamic terrorist. In summary this is what they believe:
- Islam requires submission to Allah, whose words are written in the Quran.
- On Judgment Day Allah weighs your good and bad works and decides whether you go to Paradise or hell.
- Allah stated in the Quran that if you die in jihad, then you are spared judgment and automatically go to Paradise.
- The verses in the Quran that speak of jihad abrogate (cancel out) the verses that speak of love and kindness.
- Jihad is the motivation behind almost every act of terrorism that is done in the name of Islam.

Because war was such an important part of Muhammad's life in Medina, the Quran has a lot to say about how to do it. In the next chapter, we'll look at texts from the Quran that talk about jihad, and we'll also talk about whether or not all Muslims believe this.

Chapter 4
Armed Conflict in Islamic Teachings

The Quran says that all Muslims must take part in war. The goal of war is to beat those who don't believe in Islam. During Muhammad's time, jihad was often used against Christians, Jews, people who worshipped idols, and anyone else who did not turn to Islam.Let's let the Quran do the talking.

> *Those who reject Islam must be killed. If they turn back (from Islam), take (hold of) them and kill them wherever you find them...*

> *So, when you meet (in fight—Jihad in Allah's Cause) those who disbelieve, smite (their) necks till when you have killed and wounded many of them, then bind a bond firmly (on them, i.e. take them as captives).*

> *O you who believe! Fight those of the disbelievers who are close to you, and let them find harshness in you; and know that Allah is with those who are Al-Muttaqun (the pious).*

Allah commanded the prophet Muhammad to enforce killing rather than taking prisoners.

> *It is not for a Prophet that he should have prisoners of war (and free them with ransom) until he had made a great slaughter (among his enemies) in the land.*

Muslims were told to prepare themselves to fight against the unbelievers.

> *Let not the Unbelievers think that they can get the better (of the godly): they will never frustrate them. Against them make ready your strength to the utmost of your power, including steeds of war, to strike terror into (the hearts of) the enemies, of Allah and your enemies, and others besides, whom you may not know, but whom Allah knows.*

Adversarial relations with Jews and Christians in Islam

Christians and Jews are called "People of the Book" in the Quran because they believe in and follow the Bible. At first, the things that were revealed in the Quran made Muslims want to get along with Christians. But after Muhammad moved to Medina, all of the "People of the Book" were shown to be very bad.

The next verse is thought to be the last thing that Allah has to say about Christians and Jews, so it is thought to take precedence over all other teachings. It says :

> *And fight them until there is no more Fitnah (disbelief and polytheism, i.e., worshipping others besides Allah) and the religion (worship) will all be for Allah Alone [in the whole of the world]. But if they cease (worshipping others besides Allah), then certainly, Allah is All-Seer of what they do.*

In other words, this text says, "Fight those who reject Islam until all worship is for Allah alone." The Quran also says that Muslims can't be friends with Christians or Jews.

> *Take not the Jews and the Christians as Auliya (friends, protectors, helpers), they are but Auliya of each other. And if any amongst you takes them (as Auliya), then surely he is one of them.*

This is also made clear in Surahs 5:52–57 and 4:89. The Quran tells Muslims that when they fight Christians, they should hurt them very badly so that the Christians will scatter.

In very strong and clear words, the Quran tells Muslims to force Christians and Jews to become Muslims. This is from The Noble Quran, which is written in English. There are notes in the brackets.

> *O you who have been given the Scripture (Jews and Christians)! Believe in what We have revealed (to Muhammad) confirming what is (already) with you, before We efface faces (by making them like the back of necks; without nose, mouth, eyes) and turn them hindwards, or curse them as We cursed the Sabbath-breakers. And the commandment of Allah is always executed.*

In case the meaning isn't clear, there is a footnote at the bottom of the page that says, "This Verse is a strong warning to Jews and Christians, and they must believe in Allah's Messenger Muhammad, his Message of Islamic Monotheism, and this Quran."

Rallying Muslims to engage in warfare

When you read these Quranic verses, it is helpful to think of them in their historical context. Allah told Muhammad to go out and conquer the world, so many Quranic verses were given that encouraged the people to fight jihad. Here are some examples:

> *Allah has preferred in grades those who strive hard and fight with their wealth and their lives above those who sit (at home). Unto each, Allah has promised good (Paradise), but Allah has preferred those who strive hard and fight above those who sit (at home) by a huge reward.*

Those who did not participate in jihad were threatened with hell fire.

> *... they hated to strive and fight, with their goods and their persons, in the cause of Allah: they said, "Do not go forth in the heat." Say, "The fire of Hell is fiercer in heat." If only they could understand!*

Those who retreat would incur Allah's wrath.

> *If any do turn his back to them on such a day—unless it be in a stratagem of war, or to retreat to a troop (of his own)— he draws on himself the wrath of Allah, and his abode is Hell —an evil refuge (indeed)!*

Killing, or jihad, is not a choice, as you can see. It must be done because Allah says so. Every Muslim must take part in order to live out his faith. The only people who don't have to pay are those who are blind, disabled, or unable to walk.

The Ultimate Aspiration of Islam

Jihad is done so that Islam can reach its final goal, which is to rule the whole world under Islamic law. Islam is a government as well as a religion. Because of this, everything always comes down to politics. Islam says that Allah is the only authority, so political systems must be built only on what Allah says.

The Quran states:

> *If any do fail to judge by (the light of) what Allah has revealed, they are (no better than) Unbelievers.... If they fail to judge by (the light of) what Allah has revealed, they are (no better than) those who rebel.*

People who are fighting jihad think they have won when a country says that Islam is both its faith and its form of government. This has happened in

Afghanistan (during the time of the Taliban), Iran (during the time of Ayatollah Khomeini's revolution), and Sudan (during the time of Hasan al-Turabi). In 2015, the extreme Islamic army known as ISIS took control of some parts of the world, but not whole countries.

All political systems made by people, including democracies and dictatorships, are thought to be wrong. Not all moderate Muslims, though, agree with this. Anwar al-Sadat, who used to be president of Egypt, is a good model. He said that there would be "no politics in Islam and no Islam in politics."

Sheikh Omar Abdel Rahman, who used to be my university professor and was now the spiritual leader of the Egyptian terrorist group al-Jihad, didn't agree with this comment. Sheikh Abdel Rahman said that President Sadat was an infidel and apostate who should be killed after he said those things. Islamic law says that al-Jihad had to do what its master said, so they shot the president to death. In the 1980s, Egypt's President Sadat paid the final price—his life—to stop Islam from taking over the government.

In the 1980s, radical Islamic groups attacked their own states most of the time. Now, these groups are making direct attacks on the West. I'll explain why in the next part of this book.

Chapter 5
Duped by Media Spin

One secondary effect of the events of September 11, 2001, was that the media paid a lot of attention to Islam. Most of the time, Islam was shown to be a faith of peace. It was made to sound good to people in the West.

The experts who were asked tried to separate the religious side of Islam from its political side, but that can't be done. When a Muslim says that Islam is a faith of peace on TV or in the newspaper, it can be explained in one of two ways:

1. Wishful thinking. Although this is not the Islam taught in the Quran, this person really wishes that it were. He sincerely believes he can explain away the unpalatable parts.
2. Deceit with the intent to attract converts. This is jihad practiced a different way. Instead of killing the enemy, you convert them with lies.

Rosy outlook

The show that Oprah Winfrey, a famous talk show host, puts on is a great example of wishing about Islam. The first airing of "Islam 101" was on October 5, 2001. This was after the attack on the United States, but before the U.S. took action in Afghanistan.

A few Muslim guests came on Oprah's show to tell people about the basics of Islam. Queen Rania, the modern, Westernized queen of Jordan, was one of the guests on the show that day. She is 31 years old. Oprah asked her what she thought about whether or not women and men are equal in Islam.

First of all, asking Queen Rania about Islam is like asking Michael Jackson about his Christianity and what the Bible really says. Still, the queen and the other Muslim women on the show acted like they were the most knowledgeable people about Islam. "Islam views women as full and equal partners to men, so [women's] rights are guaranteed by Islam," the queen said with a lot of conviction.

Her answers made Western viewers feel good, but they do not accurately reflect the teachings of the Quran regarding women. If women are equal to men, why does the Quran say:

1. A Muslim man can be married to four women at the same time, but a Muslim woman can only be married to one man. "Marry (other) women of your choice, two or three, or four".
2. Men have the right to ask for a divorce, but not women.
3. Women only inherit half of what men inherit.
4. Women may not serve as imams, and they are not allowed to lead prayer in the presence of men.
5. A woman is not allowed to answer the door at home if her husband is not there, even if it's her brother or a relative at the door. (This is derived from Surah 33:53, where Muhammad was giving instructions to people who visited his home. He said that if he wasn't home, they had to speak to his wives through a screen.)
6. Women should stay in their houses. Many Muslim women cannot travel without the permission of their fathers or husbands.
7. If a wife refuses to have sexual relations with her husband, it is permissible for the husband to physically beat her until she submits.
8. During jihad, when a man dies, he goes to heaven and Allah rewards him with incredible energy to enjoy sex with seventy virgins the first night. What happens if a woman dies in jihad? What is her reward—to be one of the seventy?

I don't know if the queen was trying to persuade herself or everyone else. "If there is a bad sign in anything, it is in the house, the woman, and the horse," said the prophet Muhammad.

Oprah also asked Queen Rania about the hijab, which is a veil worn by some Muslim women. "It's up to each person," the queen said. Some people are more hesitant to change than others." She made the point that she doesn't wear one herself.

Here are the lines from the Quran that say women should cover themselves when it comes to the veil in Islam.

> *O Prophet! Tell your wives and your daughters and the women of the believers to draw their cloaks (veils) all over their bodies (i.e. screen themselves completely except the eyes or one eye to see that way).*

> *And stay in your houses, and do not display yourselves like that of the times of ignorance...*

The only people allowed to see a woman's face are her husband, children, siblings, and parents:

It is no sin on them (the Prophet's wives, if they appear unveiled) before their fathers, or their sons, or their brothers, or their brother's sons, or the sons of their sisters, or their own (believing) women, or their (female) slaves.

By making these rules for Muhammad's wives part of Islamic law, they now apply to all women.Queen Rania and other wishful minds don't realize that they can't make the Quran say what they want it to say.

Oprah Winfrey's show was just another chance for these Muslim women to show a version of Islam that is not backed by the Quran and Islamic teaching: one that is secular, Westernized, compromised, and Christianized. I hope that Oprah will learn the truth about Islam and talk about it in the right way.

Smoke and Mirrors

In August of 1998, when I was in the United States, I stayed with a family friend near Los Angeles. We were flipping through TV channels when we saw a show about Islam that interested us. I was surprised to hear the announcer say, "In a minute, Brother Paul will take us on a spiritual journey through the life of the prophet Muhammad."

I didn't get up from the couch until I saw Brother Paul on TV. When I first saw him, I almost fell over. He was a dark man with black hair and a thick, long, black beard. He wore a long white robe and a small head covering. Paul possibly got his degree from an Islamic school in the Middle East. He then became a missionary and went to the United States to spread Islam in the West.

I'm asking myself, "Paul? Paul is now a name for a Muslim? He was born and raised in the Middle East, just like I was. It's impossible that's his real name." What surprised me was how Brother Paul said things like, "The Lord bless you; the grace of our Lord be with you; God bless you." He talked about how people can have a connection with God the Creator, how we can hear His voice and He can hear our prayers, and how we should let God's Spirit work in us.

When I was listening to this show from California, it made my head spin. I thought, "Now I understand how they are spreading Islam in the US and Europe." I jumped out of my chair and cried out, "O God, have mercy on America! God, please watch over America and the people who live there. Please let everyone know about this great lie! "Save this country from this great lie!"

My friend and his family tried to make me feel better by telling me, "God's hand of protection has always been on America, and it always will be."

"Why does this man lie to Americans about his name?" I asked my friend. Why would he bring a new version of Islam to America that is so different from the one I've known for most of my life? Why would he show an Islam that is much more like Christianity than the real Islam I learned for so many years?" I told my friend, "This man should tell America what his real name is. Most likely, it is Muhammad, Ahmed, Mahmoud, Mustaffa, Omar, or Osama, and not Paul."

This was the first time I saw Muslims show the West a whole new side of Islam. The normal Muslim from the Middle East would never recognize it as Islam.

Now, it's clear that many Islamic leaders are doing their part for war by trying to change the way the Western media reports things. Yes, they are doing their part when they trick most people into thinking that Islam is not about killing, that it is only a faith and not a political system, and that it is about peace, love, forgiveness, and so on. This will keep Islam the faith that is growing the fastest around the world. It is just a different way to put the same ideas of war into action.

Remember that Muslims launched jihad all over the world, but each Muslim has a different plan. One uses guns and bombs, and the other uses words and lies, to get more Muslims around the world. No matter how they do it, they are both true Muslims, and the Quran says that there is only one kind of jihad: jihad against Allah's enemies who try to stop the spread of Islam around the world.

I can't believe how bold these people are. They put the American flag on top of their centers, schools, churches, and other Islamic places of learning. They put up signs that said "God Bless America" or "United We Stand." In the meantime, their fellow Muslims in the Middle East were burning American flags and putting up signs backing bin Laden and his terrorist attack on America.

To be fair, some "wishful thinking" Muslims did help the U.S. at this time. But some Muslims did what they thought was best at the time. They are a good example of how Islamic politics work in places that are not Islamic. As long as it helps Islam, these Muslims will lie and say things they don't believe at any time. They are loyal to Islam, not to the country in which they live.

True-Blue Allegiance

I know that if I say, "There are many American and European Muslims who are loyal and sincere to their countries," many people will disagree with me. After all, they have lived in these places for a long time." I would like to respond to this comment by saying that Islam does not believe in the national organization of non-Islamic peoples or any countries that do not follow Islamic law.

Under Islamic law, there are only two kinds of countries: those that belong to the "house of Islam" and those that belong to the "house of war." We all know that the United States and most of Europe are not part of "the house of Islam," which means they don't follow Islamic law. Because of this, they are the "house of war."

Any good Muslim who lives by Allah's rules and the Quran will never choose to be loyal to their country over Islam. This is not a matter of opinion; it is the rule according to Islam.

One good example of this is how Egyptians, Algerians, Sudanese, Saudis, and many others who joined one of the fundamentalist groups denied their citizenship and loyalty to their home countries. These groups tell their members, "Islam is your flesh and blood."

All fundamentalist movements in Arabic countries forbid their members from joining the military or protecting their countries. They think that they shouldn't help countries that have turned away from Islam and don't follow Islamic rule everywhere.

This idea was taken even further by Shokri Moustafa, a guy you will learn a lot more about later in the book. His organization said that its members couldn't work for the government.

Muslims who care about Islam will have a hard time defending their loyalty to a country that is not Islamic. The real Muslim thinks that the whole world is his home and that Islam tells him to make the whole world obey its rules. A true Muslim won't die for a small piece of land called "homeland," but he will die for Islam and its holy places.

When you see Palestinians fighting and dying, know that non-Muslim or shallow Muslim Palestinians are fighting for the land, but true Muslim Palestinians (Hamas) are fighting the enemies of Allah and defending an Islamic holy place, the Dome of the Rock in Jerusalem.

Muslims think that the Dome of the Rock is the third most important holy place in Islam. The prophet Muhammad told his followers that Allah miraculously brought him from the Arabian Desert to this spot in Jerusalem and made him the imam so that he could lead prayers for all of Allah's preachers and prophets who came from heaven that day. After the prayer, the prophet Muhammad said that he went to heaven to meet with Allah. (This is called "Al-Asrah waal MahRag," which means "The Miraculous Night Journey.")

There are different reasons why different groups of Palestinians fight the same enemy. One group is fighting for a piece of land where they can live and set up a government. According to George Habash's guidance, this could be a communist government. Habash has a Christian name, but he is not a Christian.

It's just his name. Another group wants the land so it can set up a socialist government based on the ideas of Yasser Arafat, a former businessman and repair engineer.

The third group is made up of Palestinians who are Muslim to the core. They see the other two groups as traitors who use the name of Palestinians to get power. Sheikh Ahmed Yassin started this group, which is called the Hamas organization.

Chapter 6
Rights and Liberties in Islam

Muslim extremists are always fighting with writers, authors, and other media people who say what they think in the free world. A lot of people have died because they didn't agree with what Muslim fundamentalists thought.

For example, on January 7, 2015, radical Muslims attacked the French satirical magazine Charlie Hebdo and killed 12 writers because of the magazine's funny pictures of the prophet Muhammad.

I am very sure that the free world, including Muslims, should not self-censor in response to threats and bullying from any group in the world. People who are free shouldn't limit human rights because some people want to force their version of Islamic law on everyone else. Freedom of speech doesn't mean anything if it isn't used. But I think we should have enough respect not to carelessly hurt sacred feelings. What people in the West see as freedom of speech, people in the Islamic world see as an insult to their beliefs, and even the most peaceful Muslims will often get angry when this happens.

I was very sad when I saw how the French president, millions of people in France, and important leaders from all over the world reacted to the actions of the magazine. They all joined the protests to show their support. I didn't hear any of them say sorry for hurting Muslims, Jews, and Christians' holy feelings. People would only defend the freedom of speech, and they wouldn't even talk about the freedom of religion.

When Charlie Hebdo kept putting out cartoons that made fun of Muhammad, the Muslim world was furious, and over the course of a weekend of protests, 45 churches were burned down in Niger. This kind of response from the Muslim world could have been expected and avoided.

Please keep in mind that the real problem isn't making a picture of Muhammad. The real problem is disrespecting Muhammad. The Muslim world wasn't exactly upset about the picture; they were upset about how it made them feel. In fact, the cover of my book, Coffee With the Prophet, is a picture of Muhammad by an artist. Muslim sources say that the picture was a good and true representation of what Muhammad looked like. This picture is neither insulting nor offensive, and it didn't get any more attention from Muslims than the many other historical pictures of Muhammad that are shown every day in texts and on the Internet.

Suppressing speech among Muslims

Even Muslims can be judged and punished for having ideas that are different from those of radicals. This is shown by the fact that Dr. Naguib Mahfouz won the Nobel Prize in writing in 1988. Dr. Mahfouz is an Egyptian Muslim, but in 1994, some Muslim extremists tried to kill him. He was walking home from work at a university when a group of guys with knives attacked him. They left him lying in a pool of blood on a street in Cairo. When this happened, Dr. Mahfouz was 83 years old. I am glad he lived.

Another victim of one of the Islamic movements was Dr. Farag Foda, a moderate Muslim who cared about the country's political survival. He decided to fight the Islamic movement through his writing. He warned Egypt, the Arabic countries, and the world about the dangers of fundamentalist Islam. He wrote:

> *What kind of time in our history is this? This is the time when if someone asks a question the other party answers him with bullets. Many times I asked myself, What is this that we are going through in our Egyptian history? Are we ever going to snap out of it? Is this the time that if you have an opinion, or something to say, you had better get to know how to use a machine gun first or get your black belt in the martial arts? If they think that this will make us back off or stop, they are terribly mistaken. If they think their actions will scare us, they are wrong! If they think for a second that we will rest our pens from writing or our mouths from voicing opinions, they are expecting the impossible. This is not about courage; it's about logic.*

Dr. Foda lost his life because of what he thought. He was killed by the groups he warned against, and they shot him to death in 1992. However, his life and work have been a great inspiration to many Egyptian artists.

Contrasting a Muslim Convert with a Christian Convert

In the winter of 2000, when I was in Washington, DC, I heard that the Islamic Society at Georgetown University was holding a gathering for American college students. An ex-Baptist pastor from Texas who had switched from Christianity to Islam was the rally's main speaker. Like this, I had never heard of anything before.

I thought right away, "What in the world could happen to an American Baptist pastor that would cause him to make a decision like that?"

I went to this class with a friend. We sat in the middle of the room, which had about 300 kids in it. A little less than half of the students came from other countries and were faithful Muslims. Young men had long beards, and girls wore a head covering called a hijab.

I couldn't believe what I saw when I saw this man walk into the room. He was dressed in the clothes that Islamic extremists in Egypt always wear. He had everything, including the long, white dress and the long, thick beard. The last thing they said was that he used to be a preacher. He was known as Sheikh Yusef.

I listened to this man talk for almost an hour as he gave a very dry speech that showed how little he knew about Islam and Islamic history. You could almost tell from the look on his face that he didn't know where he was. He worked hard to show a group of young, interested people that Islam is the answer to all the problems in the world today. He painted a picture of Islam that was completely different from the truth. It was the same picture that the Islamic group used to trick him, and it is the same picture that Islamic groups use to lure Westerners.

After he was done talking, he let people say what they thought and ask questions. My hand was the first one to go up. After he told me I could talk, I began to ask him questions.

"How long has it been since you converted to Islam?"

He replied, "Eight years."

"Good," I said. "Have you faced any type of persecution here in the US since you made this decision?"

"Not at all," he said.

"Did your church or other churches commit their members to go after you and never stop until they killed you because you betrayed Christianity?"

"None of that happened," he said.

"Are there any verses in the Bible that say Christian apostates should be killed?"

"No, there are no verses in the Bible that talk about that."

Now you could see the interest building among the students, but you could see the fear on the face of this ex-pastor. At that moment I introduced myself by saying, "I am a former professor of Al-Azhar University. I taught Islamic history and culture. Eight years ago I left Islam and became a Christian. Do you know what consequences I suffered for leaving Islam? I lost my job at the university.

I was put in prison by the secret police who tortured me almost to death. Even my own family pursued me and tried to kill me and several times I suffered attempts of assassination.

"Now it has been eight years exactly, just like you, but the difference between you and me is that I lost everything I ever had or lived for. I lost my family, job, home country, and right to live. Now I am constantly on the run. The sword of Islam is on my neck all the time because the Quran and the prophet Muhammad made it this way.

"My question for you, pastor, is, what was the price you paid for leaving Christianity? When you made that decision, did anyone start persecuting you? No one tried to kill you or put you in prison. The FBI did not arrest you as if you had committed a terrible crime against your country and your people. No church sentenced you to death or sent out someone to kill you with a sword.

"You, Sheikh Yusef, are still living in your country, secure and protected by great laws. You're free to travel from state to state to share about what you believe, but I can no longer walk along the Nile or set a foot on the soil of my country.

"You grew up free in a free country to make any decision you like until you made this one, to become a Muslim. Sadly, with this decision, you gave up your freedom. I hope you realize that you are no longer free, because the day you think of leaving Islam again, you will be killed by the sword of Islam and will not be able to escape."

Sheikh Yusef had just learned a hard truth about Islam: when you become a slave of Allah, you give up your right to change your religion again.

Religious Liberty

If you've read this far in the book, you already know that Islam doesn't believe in freedom of belief. In fact, the Quran tells people to hurt other religions. At this point, all I can add to that understanding is a story from Holland. In this case, Muslim writers criticized a foreign government for letting people who used to be Muslims practice their religion freely.

The Dutch government passed a law that lets people who have left Islam and turned to other religions, like Christianity, get political asylum. In the Muslim World League Journal, a magazine that comes out in Mecca, Saudi Arabia, there was a very angry protest. In a story called "The Right of Political Asylum for Muslim Apostates in Holland," the magazine complained that this decision was made by two Christian political parties in Holland who "acted as if becoming a Christian is a reason to be persecuted." What an odd thing to say, since Islamic law says that people who leave Islam must be killed.

The story said that Christian parties in Holland were trying to get Muslims to give up their religion so they could get Dutch citizenship.

> *This wicked decision is designed to take advantage of the situation of the Muslims that live in Holland. It is about manipulating the thousands of Muslims struggling to stay legally in Holland. They are pressuring these Muslims to change their religion so that they can get legal status.*

The article continued to insult and accuse the church by saying:

> *This law is just legalizing the agenda of the Christians and the church which did not succeed in the past to entice the Muslims by all kind of financial and material prizes to get them to change their religion. Now they are using stronger methods [citizenship].*

When I read a story like this, my heart goes out to the Muslim world and the terrible situation of human rights in these countries. Leaving Islam is the most dangerous thing a Muslim can do, no matter why. I really care about people who are brave enough to leave Islam. The sword of Islam hangs around these people's necks for the rest of their lives.

Chapter 7
Bedouin Culture

When you're learning about a historical person, it's important to know where and how he lived. Jesus, for instance, lived in a Jewish society that was run by the Romans. His deeds and teachings were shaped by the times He lived in. For example, when it came to paying taxes to Rome, He said, "Give back to Caesar what is Caesar's and to God what is God's."

So, if we want to understand Muhammad and Islam, we need to look at the culture of the place where Islam began. We will learn that terrorism has its roots in Arabia in the seventh century. Arabia is the peninsula where the current countries of Yemen, Oman, the United Arab Emirates, Saudi Arabia, Kuwait, and Jordan are located. During this time before Islam, the tribes can be put into three main groups based on how they lived.

The Tribal Mentality

Before Islam, there were no separate states or countries in southwest Asia, which is also known as the Arabian Desert. People did not have to follow any laws or follow the rules of any government. The only person with power over his people was the tribe head. People knew that these groups stayed true to their own cultures. What outsiders think of as unusual loyalty in modern Islamic history has its roots in the Arabic society before Islam.

Extremism in Pre-Islamic and Early Islamic Arab Culture

Arabs in Muhammad's time were known for being extreme in everything, including how much they loved, how much they hated, and how they treated people who were different from them. They were not likely to be open to different ideas or views. Only they knew how to do things.

During this time in Arab history and society, many poets were very good. One of the older writers said this about extremism: "We are people with no middle ground, and tolerance is not the way we live." We get what we want, or we'll die trying." They were very proud of how extreme they were, and they wrote songs about it.

After Islam, this extreme way of thinking didn't change at all. In fact, Islam took on many of the most important parts of this Arabic culture. There was neither compromise nor making peace with other people. No one would ever leave a fight between two people. They didn't have the mindset to sit down, talk about it, and figure out a solution. "Give me my way or give me death!" was their attitude. As a result, there has been a lot of killing in Islamic history.

Many Muslims who are not Arab, like Iranians, Afghans, Pakistanis, Indians, and others, have learned to adapt to and follow these rules as part of their religion.

Perpetual Conflict and Strife

Being courageous and violent was a sign of manhood in seventh-century Arabia. The people of this culture considered being quick to fight as a necessity for survival. Only the strongest survived; therefore, these tribes fought constantly as a way of existence. This mentality was manifested into a basic lifestyle.

- Defend your own tribe and its territory.
- Plunder the possessions of those you defeat. Many individuals and groups would invade others to gain position and wealth.

Islam did not change any of these things about Arabs or change how they behaved. Instead, Islam took on the Arab way of thinking and used it to get what it wanted. Jihad, which means "striving for Allah's cause," is a central part of Islam. For the Arabs, this was not a new way of acting, but one they were very used to. Islam told the Arabs to show how brave and violent they were.

Most Arabs converted to Islam so that they could get the things that people who didn't convert to Islam gave them. In the early days of Islam, Arab Muslims often disagreed about how to split the spoils. This is something we know from the history of Islam.

So, we can see that Muhammad was born into a society where war and killing were common. Now, let's look at how these rules became part of Islam through the idea of war.

Chapter 8
Muhammad Proclaims Holy War

Muhammad's move from Mecca to Medina was one of the most important events in the history of Islam. Everything about how the founder of Islam thought changed, especially how he felt about the people around him who didn't believe.

In Mecca, Muhammad didn't talk about war at all. No one talked about holy war because he didn't have a strong army and his group was small and weak in society. But in Medina, where he built an army, jihad and fighting the enemy were the main things that the Quran said. Revelations gave Muslims more and more reasons to fight.

Let's look at how Muhammad's life in Mecca was different from his life in Medina:

- **Mecca**: He invited people to be a part of Islam by preaching.
- **Medina**: He persuaded people to convert by the sword.
- **Mecca**: He acted as a priest, living a life of prayer, fasting, and worship.
- **Medina**: He behaved as a military commander, personally leading twenty-seven attacks.
- **Mecca**: He had only one wife, Khadija, for those twelve years.
- **Medina**: He married twelve more women in ten years.
- **Mecca**: He fought against idol worship.
- **Medina**: He fought against People of the Book (Jews and Christians).

Muhammad's move from Mecca to Medina changed Islam into a political movement. Dr. Omar Farouk wrote in his book The Arabs and Islam:

> *The immigration of the prophet of Islam from Mecca to Medina is of great importance in Islamic history. It marks a great revolution in the nature of Islam. Islam went from a religious and spiritual revelation to a political agenda.*

I'm going to tell you about the history of jihad as it grew and changed during the time of Muhammad. Remember that for about twenty-two years, the angel

Gabriel gave Muhammad words from the Quran. Just like Muhammad's political views changed over time, so did the idea of jihad. As Muhammad's status in society grew, the things he said about war got bigger and more important.

Why Muhammad Left Mecca: Struggles and Determination

People must ask, "Why did Muhammad leave Mecca?" Muhammad spent ten to twelve years in Mecca trying to get people to convert to Islam. He didn't kill anyone or make them pay taxes. His lesson was to turn away from wrongdoing, be patient, and forgive. But he and the group he was from had a lot of trouble getting along. The Quraysh were the largest tribe in the area. The tribe leaders didn't like how many people stopped worshiping idols and started following Islam.

At first, they tried to talk to Muhammad about a deal. "We'll make you king," the tribe leaders told him, "but stop talking about Islam. Or, if you want to be rich, we'll give you money and make you the richest man in Arabia."

Muhammad was standing next to his uncle when they said this. He told his uncle, "Oh, my uncle, if they bring the sun and put it in my right hand and bring the moon and put it in my left hand, I will not give up my revelation."

From AD 620 to AD 622, Muhammad talked with the leaders, but they never came to a deal.

The people from the tribe of Quraysh began to hurt him. They spat on him and threw dirt on his head while he was praying. Several times, they tried to kill him. Once, a woman invited him to dinner, but the lamb she served him was poisoned. The Quran talks about the problems Muhammad was having at this time:

> *And (remember) when the disbelievers plotted against you (O Muhammad) to imprison you, or to kill you, or to get you out (from your home, i.e., Makkah); they were plotting and Allah too was plotting; and Allah is the Best of those who plot.*

Muhammad did not just rush out of Mecca, though. He knew what he was going to do after he left.

Ephiphanies of Jihad

First revelation of Jihad: Repay those who mistreat You

Muhammad spent the first year of his time in Medina building up his army. His first jihad, or holy war, was meant to get back at the tribe of Quraysh, which had hurt him. This isn't surprising because Muhammad was still affected by the Arab way of thinking I talked about before. ("If you make me upset, I'll make you upset twice as much.")

Trade helped the Quraysh tribe get rich. Every year, they went to Yemen once and Syria once. They had a big caravan full of things to sell at their goal, and they also brought things home to sell there. They had a lot of money and valuable things with them.

Muhammad had a plan to attack one of the groups coming back to Mecca. In the Valley of Badr, he and his troops waited for them. But the leader of the caravan heard about the plan and went home safely by taking a different road.

The tribe leaders were very happy that the caravan made it home, but they were very angry with Muhammad. They decided to teach him a lesson so that everyone in Arabia would know that the Quraysh tribe shouldn't be messed with. Mecca sent its troops to Badr to fight Muhammad. They were surprised when Muhammad won a big battle and killed most of the enemy army.

Everyone in Arabia heard about the battle, and they all knew that Muhammad was now the most powerful person in Arabia because he had won against the most powerful tribe.

Number 2: Assert control over your area

After this win, Muhammad said that the angel Gabriel told him something new: he had to fight every tribe in Arabia and force them all to accept Islam. Muhammad said, "In Arabia, there will not be two religions." Only Islam will rule in Arabia." So, Muhammad no longer spent most of his time trying to convert heathens or people who worshipped idols. Now the Jews and Christians were being tried to convince.

This change in war came about because of the following verse in the Quran:

> *Fight against those who (1) believe not in Allah, (2) nor in the Last Day, (3) nor forbid that which has been forbidden by Allah and His Messenger (Muhammad) (4) and those who acknowledge not the religion of truth (i.e. Islam) among the people of the Scripture (Jews and Christians), until they pay the Jizyah [tax] with willing submission, and feel themselves subdued.*

At first glance this verse is a little hard to understand in English, but it will be very clear after I explain it. This verse says Muslims must fight four kinds of people:

1. Those who don't believe in Allah
2. Those who don't believe in the last day

3. Those who do things that Allah and Muhammad have forbidden
4. Those who don't acknowledge Islam as the truth, i.e., "people of the Scripture," who are the Jews and Christians

Muhammad gave people three options:

1. They could accept the message of Islam.
2. They could remain Jews or Christians but pay a special tax (jizyah), which is traditionally levied once a year.
3. They could die. (The phrase "and feel themselves subdued" is much stronger in Arabic than in this English translation. The Arabic word means something like "abject subjection." It carries the idea of someone cowering in fear before a greater power. If abject subjection is not achieved, then death follows.)

As a result of Muhammad's choices, most people accepted Islam, rich people who didn't believe paid high taxes, and the rest were forced to go to war.

Taxing Christians, Today

The tax on Christians is not just something that happened in the past. Fanatic groups still go to Christians in Egypt and ask them to pay the tax. They'll talk to the Christian and say, "You're a Christian. We follow Islam. This country is ruled by Muslims. Our job is to follow the Islamic rule. The rule says that you can either become Muslim or stay with your own faith. We don't mind if you stay true to your faith, but you must pay taxes to the Islamic government every year."

The Egyptian government isn't trying to collect the tax, so these private groups are doing it on their own.

So the tax is given to the Christian, which is generally a large amount of money based on how much he makes. The Christian might say, "Right now, I don't have the money. Give me a few days to work on it." So the rebels will leave for a few days and then come back.

The Christian may say again, "Please, give me another week." So they'll leave and come back a week later. But the Christian has no more chances if he or she still doesn't have the money. They will definitely come back and kill him, probably by shooting him.

A Christian friend of mine from Egypt is now a professor at a university in the United States. His two Christian brothers, a doctor and a chemist, were living in Egypt when the radicals came and asked for the tax. These Christians said no, so both of them were killed.

Bankrolling Jihad

Muhammad got some of his money from a tax on people who didn't believe in him. However, stealing was his main source of income. This was his main source of income, just like oil is the main source of income for the Gulf states today. They didn't farm, do trade work, or run a business. They battled.

Part of the money they made came from selling slaves. When they went into a country that was against them, they killed all the men and took the women and children as slaves. At that time, the Arabian Desert became known for selling slaves.

Of his plundering, Muhammad said:

> *All income that comes by the hooves of horses and the point of the sword is a gift from Allah. Allah provides for those who fight. But if they go back to their old trades, they will just earn a living the normal way.*

Muhammad made a deal with his army about what to do with the things they took from enemies they beat. Muhammad got to keep 20%, and the army got to split the other 80% between themselves. This sounds good, but his army could have up to 10,000 people in it. So each man in the army got.008% of the money, while Muhammad got 20%.

Muhammad's men started to rebel against him and complain that they didn't get to keep enough of the loot. Things looked like they were going to get out of hand until Muhammad got a new vision.

> *And know that out of all the booty that you may acquire (in war), a fifth share is assigned to Allah,—and to the Messenger, and to near relatives, orphans, the needy, and the wayfarer...*

The name of this whole surah was "The Spoils of War." It talks about the Battle of Badr in particular. Read this part to get a good idea of how Muhammad thought as a soldier.

Battles and Divide

Number 1: Uhud

This was the second war that the prophet Muhammad and new Muslims fought against Arabs who did not accept Islam. After the battle, there was a big fight between the military chiefs and Muhammad's guards. The dispute was about taking the enemy's things. The chiefs of the military told Muhammad's guards that they should take part in stealing things. "If we didn't fight, there would be no victory," they said. After this fight, Muhammad had to solve the problem by telling the military leaders and his personal guard to divide the loot in half.

Number 2. Hunayn

Ibn Hisham was a historian who wrote a lot about the attack of Hunayn. The Muslim army lost because they were too eager to take the enemy's things before the fight was over. When the Muslims went to get the things, their enemies set a trap for them and beat them. Prophet Muhammad inspired his army by saying, "Whoever kills someone has the right to steal his stuff."

Enlisting Aid for Battle

Dr. Solomon Basheer mentions that Muhammad even hired other tribes to help him fight, motivating them with a share of the plunder:

> *Sometimes the Arabic tribes agreed to get involved with Muhammad and support him in the battles. These tribes made contracts with the Muslim leaders regarding what percentage of the plunder they could take.*

This method of fund-raising continued after Muhammad's death. The second leader of Islam (Umar ibn al-Khattab) is credited with many conquests for Islam. This leader also made agreements with other tribes to fight for Islam.

> *Jarir Bin Abdullah came and asked the second Muslim leader after the death of Muhammad (Umar ibn al-Khattab), "If I go to Iraq with my people to fight for Islam, can we keep 25 percent of the plunder?" Umar agreed.*

Umar promised Muslims that they would profit from the people they conquered.

> *Allah brought Muslims to the world to conquer and rule and populate the world. If any nation opposes the will of Allah and refuses to be Muslim, they will be the slaves of Muslims and pay tax to the Islamic authority. These nations are going to work hard, and you will benefit.*

The Last Jihad Decree: World Conquest

The last step in the development of jihad was when jihad stopped being regional and went worldwide. This change was based on a new Quranic verse received by Muhammad:

Fight them until there is no more Fitnah (disbelief and polytheism, i.e. worshipping others besides Allah) and the religion (worship) will be for Allah Alone [in the whole of the world].

As a result, Muhammad told his followers:

I heard the messenger of Allah say, "Allah tells me to fight everyone until they say there is no god but Allah and I am his messenger." And whoever says that is just going to waste his time and money.

The Muslims started to use these new ideas right away. They took war outside of Arabia and attacked many countries in Asia, Africa, and Europe. At the time, this was the whole world that was known.

Twenty-seven fights were led by Muhammad himself. Also, he sent his men out without him 47 times, which is about seven times a year. Muhammad's rule came to an end when he died in AD 632. Even though he was in the service, he did not die in a battle. His death was actually caused by a long fever, according to history.

Summary

After looking at the society and some of the traits of the Arabic people before Muhammad, we know more about Islam's violent past. Due to their tendency to act emotionally and violently as a whole, the Arabic people before Islam often did terrorist acts when they disagreed or didn't understand each other.

Because Islam gave them the right to take the things of their defeated enemies, Arab groups fought harder and harder for power. Not only did they fight with people who weren't Muslim, but the first Muslim groups also fought with each other. The ongoing fighting between the Ammoweyeen and the Hashemite, who were both from the tribe of Quraysh, was an example of this. The idea of jihad, which was given to Muhammad, was quickly accepted by this society. These words from the Quran were revealed one by one over the course of about twenty-two years. The steps in order were:

1. Fight those who persecuted you (in Medina).
2. Conquer those who reject Islam in your region (the Arabian Desert).
3. Conquer the world in the name of Islam.

No Quranic revelation contradicted this final command of jihad, so it is still the goal of Islam today.

Chapter 9
The Apex of Islamic Aspiration

Like when Muhammad was alive, the fanatical Muslims of today want to take over the whole world. The best way for me to explain this way of thinking is to let one of the leaders say it.

Mawlana Abul Ala Mawdudi, who started Pakistan's fundamentalist movement, has written and thought about modern war in a way that makes a lot of sense. He is one of the most famous Islamic teachers and has written many books. The whole Islamic world sees him as a great leader who will always be remembered. He says the following about Islam's goal:

> *Islam is not a normal religion like the other religions in the world, and Muslim nations are not like normal nations. Muslim nations are very special because they have a command from Allah to rule the entire world and to be over every nation in the world.*

He points out that the purpose of the strive is not about land, but about the religion—the goal is to subdue the world to the rule of Islam:

> *Islam is a revolutionary faith that comes to destroy any government made by man. Islam doesn't look for a nation to be in better condition than another nation. Islam doesn't care about the land or who owns the land. The goal of Islam is to rule the entire world and submit all of mankind to the faith of Islam. Any nation or power in this world that tries to get in the way of that goal, Islam will fight and destroy.*
>
> *In order for Islam to fulfill that goal, Islam can use every power available every way it can be used to bring worldwide revolution. This is jihad.2*

Mawdudi also expressed the idea that Islam is a political system and way of life that must replace all other ways of life:

> *Islam is not just a spiritual religion; Islam is a way of life. It is a heavenly system revealed to our world through the angel Gabriel, and the responsibility of*

> *Muslims is to destroy any other system in the world and to replace it with the Islamic system.*
>
> *Everyone who believes in Islam in this manner can be a member of Jamaat-i-Islami [the Pakistani fundamentalist movement founded by the author]. I don't want anybody to think that Muslims who join the party of God are just normal Muslim missionaries or normal preachers in the mosque or people who write articles. The party of God is a group established by Allah himself to take the truth of Islam in one hand and to take the sword in the other hand and destroy the kingdoms of evil and the kingdoms of mankind and to replace them with the Islamic system. This group is going to destroy the false gods and make Allah the only God.*

When the author talks about "false gods," he or she means government leaders who are not controlled by Islam, like the presidents or prime ministers of Western countries.

As you can see, Islam is a religion of battle, war, and revolution. Islam doesn't just want a small part of the world; it wants the whole thing.

Christians in the Crosshairs

Christians are a target in the plan to take over the world because they don't want to be converted. This point of view isn't just assumed. It says so straight out.

The Muslim International World Society met in Lehore, Pakistan, in 1980. Le Vigaro, a well-known French newspaper, said that the meeting talked about how the Muslim world could get rid of the Christian minority or force them to become Muslim. Their plan was to do this by the end of the second thousand years.

In 1984, the head of this group sued a French newspaper because it said something that was not true. But I think the newspaper told the truth, because that is what Islam really wants to do.

During the Lebanese Civil War, there was another case of the idea that Christians should become Muslims. This war between Christians and Muslims went on for twenty years, and neither the UN nor the other Arab countries could figure out how to stop it.

Muammar Qaddafi, the late leader of Libya, thought he was a great thinker, and one day he said he knew how to solve the problem. His answer was for the Christians to become Muslim, which would make them brothers and sisters with the Muslims and stop the fighting. Qaddafi told us:

> *I hope there is a new generation of Lebanese Christians who will wake up one day and realize Arabs cannot be Christians and Christians cannot be Arabs, so then they will convert to Islam and be true Arabs.*

Approaches to Jihad

The establishment of jihad in the Quran and its association with the pursuit of global dominance have been observed. The concept of jihad has become a prevalent imperative among Muslims. Now, let us examine the contemporary implementation of jihad using a three-stage framework.

Chapter 10
The Triphasic Approach to Jihad

When examining Muslim nations globally, it becomes apparent that they can be categorized into one of three distinct phases of jihad.

Stage of Vulnerability

When Muslims are a small, weak group in a culture that is not Islamic, they are in this stage. In this situation, overt war is not what is needed. Muslims follow the laws of the country they live in, but they also try to grow their numbers.

At this point, Muslims follow what Muhammad was told in Mecca: "There is no force in religion." People in the media have possibly used this verse to show that Islam doesn't force anyone to become a Muslim.

Another key verse Muhammad received at this time was Surah 5:105:

> *O you who believe! Take care of your ownselves. If you follow the (right) guidance [and enjoin what is right (Islamic Monotheism and all that Islam orders one to do) and forbid what is wrong (polytheism, disbelief and all that Islam has forbidden)] no hurt can come to you from those who are in error. The return of you all is to Allah, then He will inform you about (all) that which you used to do.*

This verse was a reaction to the Muslims in Mecca who didn't know what to do about all the people who didn't believe. It basically said, "You have to take care of yourself. Don't worry about the people who don't believe in God. One day, you and they will all stand before Allah and be judged by what you have done.

These texts talk about how to live peacefully and quietly with people who don't believe. However, we should remember that Muhammad heard these words when Muslims were a small, weak group in Mecca. After his movement grew, Muhammad got new words that said these texts were no longer true.

Preparatory Phase

At this point, Muslims are a group that has a fair amount of power. Because their goal is to fight directly with the enemy in the future, they prepare in every way possible: financially, physically, militarily, mentally, and in any other way.

> *Let not the Unbelievers think that they can get the better (of the godly): they will never frustrate (them). Against them make ready your strength to the utmost of your power, including steeds of war, to strike terror into (the hearts of) the enemies, of Allah and your enemies, and others besides whom you may not know, but whom Allah knows.*

The Noble Quran includes some interesting commentary. Notice the words in parentheses:

> *And make ready against them all you can of power, including steeds of war (tanks, planes, missiles, artillery) to threaten the enemy of Allah...*

This explanation should prove to the reader that Muslims still follow this verse today.

The Call to Jihad

At this time, Muslims are a small group, but they are strong, influential, and powerful. At this point, it is the duty of every Muslim to fight the enemy, overthrow the government in the non-Muslim country, and set up Islamic rule.

This stage is based on Surah 9:5, which is the last message that Allah got about war. Even though I've already mentioned this verse, it's so important in Islamic thought that it's worth saying again:

> *Fight and slay the Pagans wherever you find them, and seize them, beleaguer them, and lie in wait for them in every strategem (of war)...*

Muslims are told to kill anyone who doesn't choose to become a Muslim. It says in the poem, "Wherever you find them." There are no limits on where it can be done.

Emulating Muhammad's Legacy

The prophet Muhammad went through all three of these steps. At first (Phase 1), he didn't show any anger toward his enemies. After he left Mecca, he moved to Medina and spent his first year there getting his army ready (Phase 2). Then he called for jihad, went back to fight his enemies, fully took over Mecca, and made it a part of his empire (Phase 3).

Lebanon

The recent past of Lebanon, which is now a country, is a good example of how the three stages work in real life.

Stage 1: Muslim-Christian Collaboration

If you had gone to Lebanon before their civil war, you would have seen the Hawaii of the Middle East. People used to call the city, Beirut, the Paris of the Middle East. Lebanon had the most beautiful scenery anywhere.

The Muslim minority and the Christian majority lived together in peace. That was because Muslims were a small group that didn't have much power. In those days, no one in Lebanon talked about jihad, or holy war.

Stage 2: Seeking External Support for Military Readiness

In the 1970s, the Islamic minority slowly started getting ready by getting help from Libya on one side and Iran on the other. Not long after that, a civil war broke out in Lebanon.

Stage 3: Muslims engage in conflict against non-believers

The beautiful country of Lebanon was cut up into many pieces while the whole world watched. Muslims said that they didn't care about their Christian brothers and sisters. They formed violent groups whose only goal was to overthrow the government and turn the country into an Islamic one.

The leader of the Islamic group Amal was Nabih Bary. The leader of the Shiite group Hizbollah was Sheikh Hassan Nasrallah.

After that, there was war for twenty years, but the Muslims did not achieve their goal.

Returning to Negotiation

Lebanon has a democratic government right now, but the country hasn't had a president in two years. Michel Suleiman, a Christian, was the country's president until May 2014. Since then, Tammam Salam, a Muslim, has been running the country in his place. Lebanon had peace because all the fighting groups worked together to form a government. They even made the founder of Amal president of the parliament and let Hizbollah exist in South Lebanon because they said, "We need them there to defend against Israel." But now the whole world is watching to see if the government stays true to democracy or keeps moving toward monarchy, where a few men make decisions for the whole country.

Rationalizing Deception

The three steps of jihad show how situations can be used to decide what is the right thing to do. This is also true of the Islamic way of thinking when it comes to lying. In some situations, Islam says it's okay to lie. In the next chapter, you'll find out what these situations are and how they relate to war.

Chapter 11
Bending the Truth when Necessary

Muslims think that war is all about lying, so lying is a big part of war in Islam. In this chapter, we'll talk about the specific times when Muslims are allowed to lie.

Tactical Deception in Non-Muslim Lands

Ibn Taymiyah was a philosopher who lived from 1263 to 1328. He wrote a book called The Sword on the Neck of the One Who Accuses Muhammad. In It, he talked about how Muslims should act when they are weak.

> *Believers when in a weakened stage in a non-Muslim country should forgive and be patient with people of the book [i.e., Jews and Christians] when they insult Allah and his prophet by any means. Believers should lie to people of the book to protect their lives and religion.*

In other words, if you are a minority in a country, it is okay to lie to non-Muslims to protect yourself.

A simple Islamic proverb says, "If you can't cut your enemies' hand, kiss it." This is clear from the way the prophet Muhammad lived his life and taught in Mecca and other places. After moving from Mecca to Medina, the calm lamb turned into a roaring lion that was a threat to the whole Arabian Desert.

I never knew what it was like to live in a weak state because there are a lot of Muslims in Egypt, where I grew up. We Muslims did our religious things in any way we wanted. The Christians were the group with the least power. I never had a reason to lie to Christians, but I saw every day how hard it was for them to live in an Islamic country as a minority group.

On the other hand, Islam is in the weaker stage in the United States, Canada, Europe, Australia, and South Africa. These Muslims are very good at making it seem like they are kind, loving, and forgiving people who support freedom. They make up for any difference between how they want to be seen and what they really think.

Christians and Jews get along with them as if they were brothers. They tell these countries that Islam is the answer to all of the world's issues. These Muslims who have become more like people in the West talk about their religion as if it stands for mercy, freedom, justice, and peace. They show Islam as a faith that doesn't care about any race or culture more than another.

Misrepresenting Peace Agreements

Muslim groups will use peace talks or peace deals to buy time so they can make new plans, get ready, and set themselves up for victory. Muslim military leaders will tell the other side whatever it wants to hear to buy time, but when it comes time to do what was agreed upon, you will see a different story.

Many of these peace deals have been made in recent times, but nothing has come of them. I think of all the deals that were made between the Hizbollah and Amal groups, which are Muslim groups in South Lebanon. Another great example is how Iraq and Iran tried to make peace for nine years but ended up fighting instead.

I remember very well what happened in Egypt when the government and al-Gama'a al Islamiyya were fighting. The chiefs of the Islamic Group said that they had stopped fighting and were ready to sit down and talk. That was just a way to buy time so they could get back together and go after the government even more than before. Based on what they knew about the Quran, Muhammad's life, and history, the Islamic Group told lies and used tricks.

People might not agree with how I talk about Islam, but these things are very clear in Islamic law. Let's look at how Muhammad lied, since what he did is a big part of what Islamic law is based on.

Renouncing Islamic Faith

Amar Ben Yasser was the first person the prophet Muhammad let say they didn't believe in Islam or that he wasn't a prophet. Yasser was one of Muhammad's friends. The tribe of Quraysh took him and held him as a slave. Yasser was tortured by his group, so he lied about Muhammad and Islam to get away from them.

As soon as they let him go, he went back to Muhammad and told him what had happened. Prophet Muhammad told Yasser that if something like that happened to him again, he should do what he did without feeling bad about it.

At another time, the prophet Muhammad heard that one of his enemies, Sha'ban Bin Khalid Al-Hindi, was getting his troops ready to fight the Muslims. Abdullah bin Anis Aljohani was sent by Muhammad to kill this enemy. Aljohani asked the prophet Muhammad to tell him about the person he had to kill.

Muhammad told him to join the enemy's army, say bad things about Islam and Muhammad, and he would find Al-Hindi that way.

The servant of Prophet Muhammad went to the camp of the enemy. When he found the boss, he started talking to him and said bad things about Muhammad and his people. In short, Aljohani got close enough to his target while he was sleeping to cut off his head while he was sleeping. He gave the prophet the head.

Here, we can see that the messenger of the prophet Muhammad lied, rejecting the faith and cursing the prophet Muhammad, in order to do his job.

Pulling the wool over fellow Muslims' eyes

Muslims will even lie to other Muslims if they have to when it comes to war. This is what happened between Saddam Hussein, the president of Iraq, and Hosni Mubarak, the president of Egypt. Mubarak went to Baghdad to see Hussein the day before Iraq attacked Kuwait. Hussein told Mubarak that he wouldn't attack Kuwait, but as soon as Mubarak got back to Cairo, he heard that it had happened.

Hussein lied to a fellow Muslim, and he didn't even keep his word for 24 hours. That really upset the president of Egypt.

Common Perception of Deception

As you can see, Islam agrees with and encourages lies during war. A story about Aiysha, one of Muhammad's favorite wives, shows how most people feel about lies.

Justified Deception to Avert Harm

Abi Hamid Al Gahazali (the founder of Sufism) states:

> *Know this that lying is not sin by itself, but if it brings harm to you it could be ugly. However, you can lie if that will keep you from evil or if it will result in prosperity.*

We know that Aiysha and Zeneb, two of Muhammad's wives, were very jealous of each other because of Islamic history and the prophet Muhammad's account. Zeneb's sister started a story that Aiysha was seeing someone else.Her goal was to help her sister because adultery is a crime in Islam and the sentence is to be stoned.

Even though people who knew her well, like Muhammad's best friend, were sure she had done it, Aiysha said she hadn't. It was okay to lie because it kept people from getting stoned.

Summary

As you can see, the Islamic way of thinking includes lies and being dishonest. This fact can be hard for people in the West to understand. Another thing that is hard for people in the West to understand is that a mosque is not just a place for religion. Mosques are used to help fund war, and this was clear when the US bombed Afghanistan.

Chapter 12
Muhammad's Mosque Strategy

On October 23, 2001, during the US bombing operation in Afghanistan, the US military bombed a mosque. "People who were inside praying were killed and hurt," the Lebanese News Center said. On the other hand, the Washington Post reported that recent refugees said that the Taliban had started moving military weapons and people to mosques, schools, and other places where they wouldn't be attacked.

This shows two things: how lies are used during war, and how a mosque is used for war work.

A Mosque is Not Equivalent to a Christian Church

The majority of Muslims mentioned by Western media only talk about Islam as a religion. They say that the heart is the most important part of Islam and that the mosque is the place where Muslims pray, just like a church or synagogue.

But during the time of the prophet Muhammad, the mosque was more than just a place to pray. It was also used to keep weapons and make plans for war. When Muhammad was in Medina, he ran all of his wars from the mosque. Even after he died, those who came after him still used the churches for the same things.

In Islam, a mosque is where people go to pray, get justice, plan for war, and run the government. Islam is both a faith and a government, so this makes sense. Islam is both a book and a weapon.

Prophet Muhammad told Muslims that the mosque is not like a church or a temple. At his mosque in Medina, which is the second holiest place in Islam today, he made plans for war, held court, and met with local leaders who came to visit. It was like having the Pentagon, the White House, and the Supreme Court all in one place. The mosque was the center of power in the Islamic world.

When it was time to fight, people were told to do so at the mosque. The kings who came after Muhammad kept doing this. Throughout the history of Islam, you can see that every war movement started in a mosque.

Utilization of Mosques by Egyptian Militants

Mosques are still used as war hubs in the present day. One good example is the Islamic groups in Egypt. In 1986, Zaki Bedr, who was the prime minister of national security, told the Egyptian police to attack different mosques in southern Egypt where radical Islamic groups were meeting.

Moderate Muslims were very angry about the attack on the churches. Bedr, who directed the strikes, and Mohammed Mahfouz Helmy, a member of the other party, had the following conversation in the Egyptian Parliament. Helmy explained why he thought Bedr's acts were strange:

> *The motive of my questions is not to accuse you of doing wrong, but as a representative of the people, we demand an explanation of the action of the administration of security in southern Egypt. The way that your administration surprised Muslim worshipers inside of the mosque and arrested them was an insult to Islam.*

Bedr answered by saying:

> *We had accurate information that these radical Islamic groups used the mosque to plan and operate an attack on the citizens and the police. To be more specific, on Friday, October 31, 1986, we monitored the members of these groups taking weapons and people to the mosque to prepare for a major attack on the citizens of Assout and the police force. As a result of these attacks, six high-ranking officers and seventeen soldiers were wounded. However, we confiscated from the mosque many illegal handguns, and we found dead bodies of the citizens. We arrested fifty-seven members of these groups. After a short investigation we released two of these fifty-seven and jailed the other fifty- five.*

The prime minister of national security told the Egyptian parliament that this wasn't the first time a mosque had been used as a military station. Another attack took place five days before this one.

> *October 26, 1986, we received accurate information about a major plan for the Islamic radicals to destroy and attack the police and the citizens right after the Friday prayer. This information was enough for us to send out some of our best forces to stop these plans and keep national security under control. Moments after the arrival of the forces they discovered the gathering of 120 members of the Islamic Group inside the mosque. These members did not allow general worshipers to enter the mosque to pray that day. We monitored them carefully and stood by to see how they would act. As soon as they made their first step to come out of the mosque and carry out their plans, we immediately attacked the mosque and arrested 121 people.*

The prime minister of national security addressed the parliament by saying:

> *What these two incidents mean to me and my administration is that mosques are the gathering place and the centers for these radical Muslims. As long as I am in position, I will not tolerate it. We should stand together and unite in opinion to fight the threat of terrorism to our country even if they are raising the banner of Islam. I do not attempt to deny my responsibility for these attacks as my opponent's party claimed, but as a citizen of this great nation of Egypt I call the opponent's party to unite with our government and stand strong in the face of these threats of terrorism to keep our nation secure.*

In this written history of modern times, we saw that the Islamic Group movement (al-Gama'a al Islamiyya) used the mosque to plan strikes and hide weapons, just like the prophet Muhammad did.

Chapter 13
The masterminds behind the mayhem: The Terrorism Instigators

You are about to start a walk through 1200 years of Islamic history with a guide. Along the way, you will learn about the events and actions that led to the current principles of jihad.

From the time of Muhammad to the 1800s, this chapter will explain:

- The logic behind attacking leaders and governments who reject Islam, Muhammad, or the Quran
- Justification for killing women and children
- The belief that you should fight even if you know you will lose
- The suicide mission by Muhammad's grandson
- Eleventh-century terrorists who got high on marijuana before going to attack their enemies

Compelling Grounds for Lethal Decisions

Let's start our tour by looking at a few pictures from Muhammad's life. As you think about these parts of Muhammad's life, it might be interesting to think about what it would have been like if Jesus had done the same things.

In AD 622, when Muhammad went to Medina, he found a lot of strong Jewish clans who were against him. The head of a clan called Beni Nadir spoke out against what was happening. He was very good at writing poems, which he used to criticize Muhammad and his ideas.

This poetry got him into trouble with a strong Jewish clan (al-Aus) that had converted to Islam and was very competitive. (It's true; they did change.) When they heard this poem, they decided to kill the poet, Ka'b ibn al-Ashraf, so that Muhammad would like them. They talked the poet's brother into killing him. (Their father was Arab and their mother was Jewish.)

Because the clans were all trying to get on Muhammad's good side, al-

Khazraj, a rival Jewish clan that had also turned to Islam, looked for someone else Muhammad didn't like and killed him. Abbah Rafah Salam was the second person who was killed to stay in Muhammad's good graces.

In the meantime, Muhammad told someone else to go kill a woman named Osama, who was the daughter of Marawan. She had also used her poetry to criticize Muhammad and his beliefs.

Arabs didn't like the fact that a Jewish artist was killed. Ali ibn Abi Talib, who was Muhammad's first cousin and one of his first followers, took on the job of supporting Muhammad's orders to kill. He told the people that God told Muhammad to kill this man through the angel Gabriel. Then he wrote a song to prove that God had told him to kill.

A basic rule of behavior was set by these three killings.

Muhammad Paves the Way for Killing Women and Children

Let's see what the Islamic master said about killing the enemy's women and children.

Someone once asked the Prophet Muhammad if it was OK to kill the women and children of people who believed in many gods or were not Muslim. He said, "I think of them as if they were my own." In other words, it was okay to kill their children if their parents were not Muslims. This is what radical Muslims think about killing women and children because this is what the leader of Islam thought.

Dealing Death to Leaders Who Transgress Islamic Law

According to history, Muhammad died in the year 632 AD after having a fever for a long time. When Uthman ibn Affan became the third leader after him, there were many complaints about how he led and ruled the people. He was charged of being bad with money, having moral problems, and doing other wrong things. Muslims from many different countries gathered around his house and asked him to step down. He swore by Allah that he wouldn't do what was asked of him, and he refused to give up his position as boss.

When they went back to the house a few days later, they found him relaxing and reading the Quran. He was killed there.

After he died, Islam would never be the same again. This was the place where the Islamic faith split in two for good.

Fraudulent Agreement Splits Muslim Community

After the death of Islam's third leader, Ali ibn Abi Talib, Muhammad's first cousin, was picked to be Islam's fourth leader. Ali was looked up to by a lot of people because he was Muhammad's greatest helper, like his right arm.

The governor of El-Sham, which is in Syria, was against this choice. He came from the same family as Uthman, the leader before him who was killed. So, the governor of El-Sham asked Ali to find and judge the people who had killed Uthman. Ali said, "There are a lot of them. Who am I going to arrest?" Whom do I have the right to judge?"

This made war start. Ali was in many fights with the ruler, Muawiya ibn Abi Sufyan.

Ali's group fell apart. Part of them didn't want to fight, so they asked Ali to stop the war. They wanted to talk about how to solve the problem and chose someone from each side who knew the Quran to represent them.

To make a long story short, Muawiya's agent offered Ali's representative a deal to end the dispute. The deal was that if Ali's fans got rid of him as leader, Muawiya's followers would get rid of Ali. Muslims could then vote for anyone they thought was right, based on what the Quran said.

Ali's followers kept their word and got rid of him as leader, but Muawiya's representative didn't. Instead, he told the Muslims that Muawiya was their only boss.

El Kharij's Fatal Attack on Ali

By the year 660, there were two groups in the Islamic world: those who followed Ali and those who followed Muawiya. The people who followed Ali were called Shiites, and those who followed Muawiya were called Sunnis.

The Shiites broke up into a new group. el Kharij was its name. El Kharij called for change, just like terror groups do today. They wanted to follow Islam in the same way that Muhammad did.

El Kharij decided that the best way to deal with Ali, Muawiya, and Muawiya's agent was to kill them all. They thought that if they killed these three leaders, Muslims could go back to having just one head, like in Muhammad's time.

Ali was very respected by Muslims, but one person was able to kill him. Right away, el Kharij's spiritual leader used a verse from the Quran to explain what they had done.

Ali's killing is a good example of what many extreme groups think.

This is another thing in Islamic past that led to terrorism.

Since then, the ideas and beliefs of El Kharij have been a threat to terrorism in every kingdom, dynasty, society, or country. The Islamic militias we see around the world today are the same thing as el Kharij. Since this old group had so much power, let's look at what they thought.

El Kharij: The Revolutionary Sect and Its Controversial Beliefs

The Arabic word El Kharij means "one who goes out." During this time in Islamic history, the el Kharij rebelled against a leader or government that they thought was not following God's laws and the Quran. Here are a few of their most important ideas:

- They believed that there is no law but God's law. They declared many imams (prayer leaders or Muslim preachers) to be infidels, including some of Muhammad's friends.
- They expected all Muslims to obey the call of jihad against rulers (Muslim or non-Muslim) who did not comply with the Quran. Anyone who did not participate in jihad was labeled an infidel.
- They believed in the right to kill children and women of infidels.
- They believed Muslims have the right to and control over women, children, and all material possessions of infidels.
- They made assassination, dishonesty, mistrust, and unfaithfulness a strong part of the Islamic faith.

Their beliefs have been demonstrated throughout the history of Islam.3

Muhammad's Grandson's Final, Fateful Mission

In AD 680, Muawiya died, and his son Yazid took over as leader of the Islamic kingdom. Ali's son al-Husayn, who was in charge of the Shiites at the time, did not accept him. This was to be expected.

Al-Husayn thought he should lead the Islamic kingdom next. His mother was Muhammad's daughter, and his father was Muhammad's right arm and first cousin.

Al-Husayn knew that he didn't have enough people or tools to beat Yazid. But he still went to Iraq to fight him. In the same year that his father died, Al-Husayn was killed in a place called Kabala. The death of their master taught the Shiites a new lesson.

From this point of view, al-Husayn died for Islam. Even now, especially among Shiite Muslims, he is respected and seen as a great example of selflessness.

These views help us figure out why some Muslims are willing to take part in suicide attacks. They may not be able to change much, but they get to die as heroes of Islam and as martyrs.

Marijuana Warriors

The name of this group from the 1100s comes from the Arabic word for people who smoke or eat hashish, which comes from marijuana. El-Hashashen was a group of very religious Shiite Muslims who thought that killing the enemy was an order from Islam and that being a martyr meant killing the enemy. In the 11th century, a guy named Hassan El-Sabaah started this group.

Before going on suicide missions, the soldiers in this group would get high on hashish. While they were high, they saw themselves in a garden with a lot of beautiful women. When they were high, they got a taste of what heaven would be like, so they worked quickly to finish their tasks and get to the real thing.

This group grew quickly and was responsible for a lot of killings and attacks all over Iran and Iraq. Many military leaders and government figures of the Sunni Muslims were killed by people in this group. Nearly the whole Middle East was almost part of the El-Hashashen movement at the start of the 12th century. They bothered every king and governor they could find.

Ibn Taymiyah's Zero Tolerance Approach

Ibn Taymiyah was a powerful Sunni leader who came to power at the start of the 14th century. He was born in 1263 in a city in Syria called Haran. He fought against the Mongolian attack of Syria. Ibn Taymiyah taught that Mongolian Muslims were not real Muslims and that people from his country shouldn't listen to them. He also said that anyone who gave in to them, helped them, or did business with them was the same as them: they were all "infidels." From then on, Ibn Taymiyah acted like he was in charge of a force. He called a lot of Muslims "infidels" and attacked them.

Ibn Taymiyah set up the idea that there should be no mercy. He reaffirmed ideas that had been used for hundreds of years.

In the last two hundred years, most of the Islamic groups have had a lot to do with Ibn Taymiyah's ideas. This way of thinking has led to the attacks we see today.

The Evolution from Ibn Taymiyah to Saudi Arabia: Wahhabi Movement

Muhammad ibn Abd al-Wahhab (1703–1792) led the Wahhabi movement. He did this by building on what Ibn Taymiyah had done. This group stood up to the Turkish government, fought against it, and overthrew it. Abd al-Wahhab started a new country that was 100% Islamic. This country later became Saudi Arabia.

Saudi Arabia's current ruling family is made up of the descendants of Abdul Aziz Bin Saud, the political leader who helped Wahhab create the country of Saudi Arabia. At the same time, the Saudi government has to deal with the el Kharij movement, which is made up of people who want to return to the original rules. One person from that group was Osama bin Laden.

The way Ibn Taymiyah thought has had a big effect on the world we live in now. Now, a lot of groups are trying to get rid of their governments and go back to what Muhammad taught, without any mercy or compromise. They are using armed force to get what they want. History is definitely going over and over again.

Summary

Now that you've learned about the history of terrorism, from Muhammad to the 1800s, we can talk about the man I call the "founding father of modern jihad." The government of Egypt put him to death because of what he taught, and many of his books are banned in Egypt and other places, like Libya and Iraq. Still, his impact lasts. Sayyid Qutb is his name.

Chapter 14
The Pioneer of Modern Jihadism

In the past of many Middle Eastern countries, the 1920s were an exciting time. Many people were fully freed from European rule, some by the British, some by the French, some by the Italians, and some by the Turks. Others were on their way to being freed. Egypt was one of these places.

Egypt had a leader for the first time in its history. People in Egypt were finally seeing the light of freedom again, and for many of them, it was the first time in their lives.

When things happen in Turkey, Egypt will soon move toward Islamic fanaticism. In 1924, Mustafa Kemal Ataturk, a military leader in Turkey, set up a state that was completely free of religion. By doing this, he changed the Islamic ruling system, which had been in place for 600 years and ruled the Islamic world. In fact, he got rid of the Muslim system and put in a military system that was more like the West.

Muslims, including Muslims in Egypt, didn't like this. In reaction, a religious leader named Sheikh Hassan al-Banna started the Muslim Brotherhood Movement in Egypt. We'll keep calling this el Kharij all over again. His ideas were a mix of those of early el Kharij, El-Hashashen, and Ibn Taymiyah. His goal for Egypt was to bring back Islamic law and a method for deciding who should rule next.

The Muslim Brotherhood was very violent and hateful toward the country's leaders and anyone else who didn't follow Islamic law. They used terrorism to shake up society and get what they wanted, which was to bring Islam back to its former greatness.

In 1948, when Israel became a country, extreme fundamentalist groups grew even stronger. When Israel was made, it was the start of many wars between Jews and Arabs.

The fundamentalist groups made many groups of rebellious, hateful Muslims who were ready to die for their cause. Their hatred did not just go toward Jews. They told their followers that the leaders of Egypt and the rest of the Arabic world were not real Muslims.

They taught very strongly that Islamic law should be followed, and that neither the government nor people of any other faith should be allowed to get in the way. The main thing these radical and extreme terrorist groups did was kill people. They thought that killing was the only way to get Islamic countries to follow the Quran and Islamic rule again.

In 1948, the Egyptian Prime Minister Mahmoud Nokrashy Pasha was killed by the Muslim Brotherhood. They tried to kill Egypt's new prime minister, Ibrahim Abdel Hadi, in 1949, but ended up killing Supreme Court Judge Moustashar Ahmad El-Kazendari instead.

In this setting, a smart young Egyptian got his degree and started a promising job as a teacher. Sayyid Qutb was born in Southern Egypt in 1906. In 1948, the government sent him to the United States to learn different ways to teach. After his trip to the United States, he went back to Egypt and joined the Muslim Brotherhood.

The Duality of America: Qutb's Conflicted Impressions

Qutb had never been anywhere but Egypt before. When he got back from America, he was both jealous of and angry at the country. Here's a line from a letter he wrote to a friend while he was in the U.S.

> *Nowhere else on earth could I find people that excel in education, knowledge, technology, business and civilization like the Americans. However, the American values, ethics and beliefs are below the standard of a human being.*

When Qutb was in the United States, he spent time in Washington, DC, California, and Colorado. He was very impressed by America's natural beauty, great size, educational institutions, and diversity of population. Yet he felt that America's resources were wasted on materialism.

> *It seems to me that there is no relation between greatness of culture and greatness of the people that create this culture. It is obvious that Americans have focused all of their ingenuity on the production of materialism, but they don't have much to offer as to what makes humans great.*

He was disgusted with what he saw as a lack of religious conviction.

> *No one else in the world has built more churches than the Americans.... You will find Americans in church on Sundays, Christmas, Easter and special religious occasions, yet they are so empty and do not have a spiritual life. The last thing that an American would think about in everyday life is their religion.*

Qutb was also angry because American influence had led the Muslim world astray from the ways of Islam.

> *Not only the non-Muslim world is pagan and heathen but also the existing Muslim world is so influenced by the rest of the world.1*

Fundamental Tenets of Qutb

Sayyid Qutb wrote more than seven books. He is known as the founder of modern revolution. But the book that got him sentenced to death at age 59 by the Egyptian government can only be bought on the black market. Signs Along the Road (Ma'alim fi el- Tareek) is the name of that book. In 1965, when Gamal Abdel Nasser was in charge of Egypt, Qutb was arrested and given a death sentence. The Egyptian government thought that killing Qutb would stop him from spreading his dangerous ideas.

The Egyptian government told the cops to take any copies of his book and burn them. Some copies did get away, though. Before I left Egypt, I read this book. The content of the book is still being spread by extreme Muslims in Egypt and all over the Islamic world.

Sayyid Qutb and his book Signs Along the Road are now at the center of radical Islamic groups. Al-Jihad, al-Takfir wal-Hijra (Repentance and Holy Flight), El Najune Min El-Narr (Rescued from Hell), and many other terrorist groups in Egypt follow his teachings. The Islamic terrorist groups of today look to Qutb as their spiritual leader and teacher.

Let's look at Qutb's ideas in more depth.

Qutb thought that the world had gone back to being pagan and full of idols, like it was before Muhammad's lessons.

> *Today we are living like heathens—just like the days before Islam in the way people act, the world's culture and what they believe and think. It is all heathenism. Even in the Islamic world, Muslims' education, their philosophies, their culture, their thinking and their laws are all far from the true Islam.*

Qutb believed that Allah is the only ruler over earth and that no human should rule or govern the earth. Therefore, he rejected all man-made systems of government, including democracy, socialism, dictatorships, and communism. He wrote:

> *The way that life is lived today is an insult to Allah and his authority on earth. It contradicts godly principles. This idolatrous world gives the authority of*

> *Allah to humans as if they were God. We have become our own gods. These heathens are not like the ones before Islam, but far worse. Today's heathens reverence and honor man-made constitutions, laws, principles, systems and humanistic methods. They disregard Allah's law and his constitution for life.*

Qutb believed Muslims should rebel and resist any human power on earth until they overturn all man-made governments. This is the ultimate calling for a Muslim, and it is not to be compromised, deviated from, or stopped.

> *We should immediately eliminate this pagan influence and the heathen pressure on our world. We must overturn this current society with its culture and leadership of infidels. This is our first priority: to shake and change the foundations of heathens. We must destroy whatever conflicts with true Islam. We should get out from under the bondage of what keeps us from living in the ways that Allah wants us to live.*

His logic was as follows: good and evil cannot live together, truth and false are not the same, and people cannot live under the authority of both man and God. And to please God, people should destroy the ways of man. He wrote:

> *Demolish all governments and organizations that are established by man. Eliminate human racism that exalts one over the other. The return of God's kingdom can only be established by a movement of power and the sword.*

Following what Ibn Taymiyah had said, Qutb went so far as to call some Islamic leaders "apostate infidels." He thought that other Muslims and Allah were behind him because he made this statement.

Qutb didn't just use these means in his own country; he also started a movement to spread his beliefs around the world.

Jihadist Group Overview

In his book, Qutb asked a very important question: How can this change happen? He didn't say exactly what needs to be done to make this happen. He might have been afraid that the Egyptian government would see this book as a plan for a new Islamic revolt to overthrow their government.

Or maybe he thought the government would be mad at him because his ideas were so close to those of Sheikh Mawlana Abul Ala Mawdudi, the leader of the Islamic movement in Pakistan. (This is the author whose words I used to explain what war is earlier.)

However, an average reader who can read between the lines would conclude that Qutb envisioned the following type of group to carry out the call of Islam:

- This group would be purified from any and all inclination to lean toward the pagan world. They would eliminate all sources of spiritual beliefs that would compete with Allah and the Quran. This includes destroying books and man-made Islamic commentaries.
- They would accept no authority but Allah for beliefs, worship, systems, laws, and constitution.
- They would experience tremendous resistance from the rest of the world. Existing governments and authorities would cause them financial difficulties. Their families and society would reject them.
- They would claim that the new Islamic world could exist only if their group obtained a great deal of power and force to gain the respect and submission of the pagan world. They would use armed forces to overthrow governments, just as Muhammad did.
- There would be no mercy or compromise in this war.
- This Muslim group may have a difficult start, but as soon as true believers hear the call, the numbers will multiply to hundreds, thousands, tens of thousands, and then throughout the world.

Qutb's Critique of Complacent Muslims

Qutb was very frustrated with Muslims who questioned the call to jihad as a command to be followed by all Muslims of all time. Qutb asserted:

> *The order in which Allah gave Islam to Muhammad was gradual and progressive to maximize positive results toward Islam. Many Muslims take the early verses of this progression of teaching out of context as if they are Allah's final and complete instructions. These Muslims strip Islam of its power and build their own theory on these verses.*
>
> *The results of this type of interpretation of Islam are Muslims who are living a defeated life spiritually and mentally. They are under the pressure of the hopelessness that they cannot spread Islam any longer.*
>
> *These people are only Muslims by name. They only have the title of Islam but not the power. They only fight to defend their beliefs.*
>
> *These are the same Muslims who like to carry the title of Islam without the responsibility of overturning the entire earth with all of its politics and earthly governments. These Muslims choose to compromise the message of Islam by not forcing high taxes on people who refuse the message of Islam.*

Qutb expressed deep frustration about the people whom he described as "defeated Muslims, spiritually and mentally." He complained about them distorting the meaning of jihad. "These Muslims write about jihad in Islam as just a spiritual jihad against evil." He said that the truth is:

> *Islam is nothing but Allah declaring his liberation to the human race on earth from slavery. Allah declares his lordship over the entire earth. This means that Allah greatly protests all man-made government and authorities. Absolute rebellion is a must against anything on earth that conflicts with Islam. We should eliminate and destroy with great power anything that stops Allah's revolution.*

Walk the talk

Following Qutb's ideas, the Muslim Brotherhood tried to kill Egyptian President Gamal Abdel Nasser twice, in 1954 and 1965. These terrorists put bombs in a lot of places where people meet. The Cairo Bab El-Kalk Court and many police stations were both bombed. They killed a lot of Egyptian police officers.

In order to protect itself, the Egyptian government put many of these groups' leaders in jail. Many of them got out of jail in their coffins without being tried. The guards were told to just shoot them by President Nasser.

Sayyid Qutb's works became very important in the Islamic world after the Egyptian government had him killed. Radical Muslims all over the world know and admire him. He is respected by Muslims in the same way that Christians respect John Calvin or Martin Luther. Long-term effects were felt not only in Egypt but all over the world.

Chapter 15
The Minds Shaping Jihad

There is a trend to what people who think about jihad say. The author will write a book about war and how he thinks it should be done. People will follow him. Then the government of that author's own country kills him. The author who died is a hero, and the power of his work grows.

Then the next author takes the same ideas and makes them even more bold. After three or four of these rounds, we got the idea of jihad, which led to al-Qaeda and the September 11, 2001 attack on the United States.

Pioneer of Egypt's Islamic Liberation

Qutb's teaching and philosophy captured a large number of Muslims, though many of his followers were imprisoned at the time of his hanging. Following this period of time a man named Dr. Salah Serea led a new radical movement called the Islamic Liberation Movement (Hezb al-Tarir). He based his movement on the mind-set of Qutb's teaching. His goal was to overturn the Egyptian government and declare a new Islamic nation. Let's look at what Dr. Serea had to say:

- Muslims are nothing but talk. They make commitments but do not follow through. Throughout the last few centuries, Islam changed from a religion of action to a religion of just talk.
- The priority of the Islamic nations should be to carry on the message of Islam and apply it internally and externally in all ways.
- Jihad should be enforced. It is the way of paying a price for what you stand for and keeping the message alive. It should be practiced inside the nation and carried out to the world.
- Our goal is to find out the most effective way to overturn and destroy any governments that do not completely comply with Islamic law, including existing Muslim countries.
- We will establish a great Islamic nation that will stretch across the world. The only political system will be Islamic law.

Serea felt that leaders of the Muslim world are corrupted because they enforce fasting and prayer but not jihad:

> *Many of the rulers of the Islamic world today are people of prayer. They have built mosques. They have reinforced fasting and prayer, and they do whatever it takes to have the appearance of good Muslims. Their ulterior motive is to gain popularity using the religious sincerity of the Muslims. Meanwhile they carefully keep true Islam away from the hearts of the people. They persecute anyone who stands for true Islam with physical violence. These rulers are infidels, and anyone who stands behind them or supports them is also an infidel.*

Dr. Serea continued to complain about what he saw as the corruption of the existing Islamic governments by saying that Islam is one of the laws they use to govern the land when it should be the only law used to govern. Dr. Serea stated:

> *They are building mosques, but they are also building places of secular entertainment. They are broadcasting the Quran and also music and dancing. They give to charities and are also gambling. What is popular among these Muslims is only the worship part of Islam, and they leave out jihad, the heartbeat of Islam. These Muslims carefully read the Quran daily, and many of them cry in their prayers, but they do not go out and carry on the mission of Islam through jihad. These are hypocrite infidels. They are the shame of Islam.*

Dr. Serea did what he said he would do. Dr. Serea and his group began their attack on the Egyptian government on April 19, 1974. They broke into a military school in Cairo in order to set up a base from which to try to overthrow the government.

The Egyptian government reacted with a lot of force and arrested him and everyone in his group. In October 1975, the Egyptian government sentenced Dr. Serea and many of his followers to death. Twenty-nine followers of the movement were still in jail.

Egypt and the rest of the Islamic world were just starting a new round of radical Islamic groups and attacks. Egypt had a new radical group before Dr. Serea was even convicted.

Al-Takfir wal-Hijra: Moustafa's Vision

The next armed group to carry on Dr. Serea's goals was called Al-Takfir wal-Hijra (Repentance and Holy Flight). Shokri Ahmad Moustafa started it. He came from the same part of Egypt as Sayyid Qutb. Shokri Moustafa, who was born in 1942, was only 24 years old when Qutb, the man who started modern jihad, was killed. When he was given a death sentence, Dr. Serea was 33 years old.

Shokri Moustafa knew exactly what he wanted to do and what was most important to him. In his speech to the Egyptian federal court on November 7, 1977, he said the following:

> *My greatest priority, for which I am willing to pay whatever price is required to accomplish it, is to see a true Islamic movement take off. I must find fertile ground to plant a great Islamic nation worldwide. I will revive Islam and bring it to its original state.*

The danger that the Egyptian court faced with Moustafa was that he had a large number of members in his organization who would obey him at a moment's notice. Moustafa said:

> *Each member of our movement would be willing to sacrifice his own life to fulfill the responsibility that Allah has put on our shoulders. That responsibility is to spread the message of Islam across the earth and reinforce it with the sword. My group of people will fight with me to the end to accomplish the great mission.*

Shokri Moustafa wrote songs in his own handwriting and put them in a book. The court used this book to find him guilty. Poetry is an important part of Islamic society. The poem "Before the Flood," which was written in 1967, can be found in Moustafa's most famous journal, The Battle (El-Maalhamma). In it, Moustafa talked about how sad and angry he was about the way Muslims lived now. He told himself that he needed to get ready for his life's calling and purpose, and that in doing so, he should get ready to meet Allah.

In another song called "Immigration" ("El-Hejhera"), he shows that he thinks everything on earth is pointless and that he just wants to do his job and leave.

In another book called Expectation (El-Tawaseemat), he asked, "Where is the mother of the villages?" During the time of Islam, this is what Mecca was called. Mecca is seen as bad because it is where Muhammad was tormented, which is why he died there. Moustafa was saying that Egypt was the new Mecca and that it was the new country that was against Islam. He said that Egypt was the place that brought in evil, slander, and wrong thinking. He wrote, "It is the country of non-believers."

Moustafa tried to calm himself down by telling himself, "Just like Muhammad left Mecca and moved to Medina to start the first Islamic nation, I'll leave Mecca in my mind and go to my Medina to start over."

Moustafa wanted to start an Islamic country that would spread all over the world. He planned to do this from Egypt. First, he planned to win over a lot of people in his home country. This would be the basis for building an Islamic nation all over the world. From this new base, he would spread Islam to the rest of the world.

One of Moustafa's most scary ideas was that his efforts to spread Islam would cause a lot of friction between the East and the West, which would lead to a nuclear war on the whole planet.He thought that most of the world would be destroyed in this war, but that his followers would not be killed because they would hide in caves in remote, isolated mountains. His people would come out of the caves after the destruction, take over the world, and rule it with the sword.

He thought that the sword would be used as the main weapon again, like it was during the time of Muhammad, if there was a nuclear war that wiped out all current technology and weapons.

Moustafa's Vision: The Path to Islamic Revolution

The movement started by Shokri Moustafa wanted to make Qutb's ideas come true. The people in this group planned to start by living completely separate from the rest of society. They planned to work hard to get more people to join them and get ready for when they would have enough power to overthrow the government and start an Islamic country. They thought that their goal would be done in two steps:

- **Phase I**—The absolute destruction of the heathen world
- **Phase II**—Muslims would inherit the earth and everything on it

During the prosecution of Moustafa, the Egyptian court asked him from what source he drew his philosophy. Moustafa replied, "It is from the clearcut source of the Quran and Allah's word. We don't know anything, but Allah knows everything. We must learn only from Allah, and Allah only speaks from the Quran." He based this on the Quranic verse:

Allah knows but you do not know.

Other books than the Quran are not allowed.

Moustafa said that this is what Allah said, and he asked the Egyptian Islamic leaders if they were going to ignore what the Quran says. Shokri Moustafa and his group were put on trial for kidnapping and killing Dr. Hussein El-Thehaby, a professor at Al-Azhar University and one of the school's most famous people. He was attacked because he led a group of teachers who spoke out against

Moustafa and tried to stop his movement. Moustafa thought he was an enemy of Allah and one of the non-believers who supported the government.

Moustafa told the Egyptian court that they had carried out Allah's ruling against Dr. El-Thehaby because he had given in to the pressure of the Egyptian government and changed Allah's word to please people.

After the Egyptian media and a new team from Al-Azhar University met, Shokri Moustafa's cause got more support. This new group was led by Dr. Sayed El-Tawhel, a professor of Islamic studies at Al-Azhar. He said, "Don't judge this group. They are true Muslims who just want to restore Islam's glory. We only need to sit down with them and talk." This statement was made to clear up the situation in Egypt after a news report said Moustafa's group was trying to spread a new kind of Islam that wasn't based on the Quran.

In a message to the main Egyptian newspaper, Dr. El-Tawhel told Al-Azhar University officials not to say or judge anything bad about Moustafa in the name of Islam. He told them to go back to the Quran and read it with fresh eyes. Then they would see that Moustafa's group was made up of true Muslims who were loyal to the call of Islam. Dr. El-Tawhel praised Moustafa and his group and said that he wished there were more young people like them. He said that the Islamic world needed people like them to bring it back to true Islam.

The Verdict and the Volume

Shokri Moustafa got the death sentence. He left behind a group of radicals who didn't believe in any kind of guidance or respect for the government in Egypt or anywhere else in the world.

When he died, they knew for sure that these countries were evil. When he said that these countries were infidels and that anyone who gave in to them would be just like them, they believed every word.

Moustafa wrote down all of his ideas and thoughts in a book that he left behind. The Leader (Al-Kalafa) is the name of the book. The Egyptian government took all of the copies it could find and burned them all. The government's actions made this book more valuable to people who follow radical Muslim groups, which still spread his ideas and views to this day.

Moustafa's Revised Approach

This book was full of Qutb's ideas about how to think. Moustafa was more dangerous than Qutb because he wanted to start by fighting religious, police, and military institutions. This was the only new thing about him.

Moustafa told them that they should attack the holy institutions because they had given in to a pagan government, which is against Islamic law. He said to attack the police and the military because they defend and enforce the laws of heathen governments. The cops and the military are the ones who hunt down, jail, and kill real Muslims.

In his book, Moustafa said that the governments of Israel, the United States, and European countries were not that different from each other. Moustafa said that they are all heathens and enemies of Allah, and that war should be used to fight them until they all accept Islam.

When the Egyptian government put Moustafa and some of his top leaders to death in 1977, they thought that would be the end of the movement. This did not happen. Egypt had a lot of radical groups in the 1970s and 1980s for a number of different reasons. All of this led to a new attempt to take over the country.

Chapter 16
Calling for Holy Combat

At the beginning of the 1970s, the Egyptian government let out of jail many people who were part of the Muslim Brotherhood Movement. President Sadat thought that their work would counter the impact of the Soviets and communism in Egypt, which it did. But at the same time, the movement grew, gained power, and became a threat to the Egyptian government.

A new group called al-Gama'a al-Islamiyya, which in English is called the Islamic Group Movement or IGM, came together. Its plan was to get young guys from high schools and colleges to join and learn from them.

When they got out of jail, many of the older people worked as teachers for the younger people. These teachers used to teach at Al-Azhar University.

Inside the Islamic Group Movement: Campus Recruitment

The leaders of the new Islamic Group Movement followed the first two steps of Qutb's plan. They set up camps all over to prepare the spiritual and mental lives of their followers. They brought in people from the universities of Egypt to fill their camps. These groups were in charge of everything on the campuses of Egypt's top colleges.

New members would come to the camps for three to seven days to pray, fast, study the Quran, and learn about the past of Islam. They studied Muhammad's life and how he led war and put Islamic law into practice. The leaders of these groups made the students think that they were the only ones who could save Islam and that now was the time to get Islam back on the right track to making the whole world an Islamic country.

At the time, I was living in Cairo's Nasser City in the Al-Azhar dorm. There were 3500 kids from all over the country living in this dorm.

Members of the Islamic Group Movement prayed every day in the school mosque, and in the time between prayers, they worked hard to find and train new students to join the movement. One day, we were all praying at the mosque when an IGM leader stood up and said, "There is a secret Christian group that rents flats near the dorms. They don't like Islam, and they make female students sleep with Christian guys. Then he told them the numbers of the apartments. The kids were shocked, and their feelings were on fire.

He went on to say, "There is also a small store near the door to the girls' dorm. It's selling food, pens, and paper. The Muslim girls can get free pornographic magazines from this shop. This Christian group wants the girls to leave Islam.

Every student's heart was set on fire. "You Christians! Putting our girls through this? We'll go there and kill them!"

Hundreds of students rushed to the store all at once. They filled it with gasoline and set it on fire. Then they went to the houses and destroyed them as well.

The group of students went back to their dorms for lunch, but they wouldn't eat. They threw away 35,000 meals and told the workers to leave the building. Then they locked the doors and ran around the building screaming, "Allah is the greatest!" (God is wonderful!)

The shared room was locked for three days. There was nothing to eat and no school. Some students, however, did not agree with this trend. They had to climb over the wall around the school and run back to their homes to get out. One of those kids was me. The standoff didn't end until the head of IGM met with the president of the university and a government secretary at the university.

Later, the minister of national security came to school and said that no Christian group was trying to woo the female students. This helped a lot of students see that aggressive people in groups like the IGM were just trying to make an enemy to fight. They only wanted to show how strong they were.

Faith-Based Leadership

The movement held protests across the country once a year. Different college sites came together to hear people like Sheikh Abed Al-Hamid Kishk, Sheikh Omar Abdel Rahman, and other leaders and icons of Islam talk about how to start a movement. Every year, this movement spread to more and more countries, including Sudan, Tunisia, Algeria, Yemen, Syria, Iraq, Lebanon, and many others.

During that time, Sheikh Kishk and Sheikh Abdel Rahman had a huge effect on the minds of young guys.

Sheikh Kishk: Orator and Radical

Sheikh Abed Al-Hamid Kishk was one of the most articulate Islamic figures in Egypt and the Arab world as a whole. Sheikh Kishk had a very loud voice and a special way of holding the attention of his audience by using old classical Arabic. He used his skills to share many political ideas with thousands of young people who were eager to hear them. He made people cry and laugh in the same breath. It was almost like he could read their minds.

Kishk was known for having a rude and sassy mouth, and he often spoke out against the government and people in high places. Sheikh Kishk spread his radical ideas all over the Arabic world by using cassette tapes to spread his words.

Sheikh Abdel Rahman: From Scholar to Jihadist

At Al- Azhar, my "freshman Quran" class was taught by Sheikh Abdel Rahman. For bombing the World Trade Center in 1993, he is now serving a life term in the United States. But he had an even bigger effect on the Middle East before he came to the U.S.

As a member of Al-Azhar University and a professor there, he has a Ph.D. in how to understand the Quran and Islamic law. Sheikh Abdel Rahman became the radical groups' spiritual head and leader of the faith.

His way of running things was the best example for these radical terrorist groups, as shown by the following:

- He did not compromise the Quran.
- He did not have any relationship with the government and did not submit to its laws and authority.
- He was a teacher of the Quran and Islamic law, which made many young Muslims trust him and obey his commands, even to kill.
- He led jihad according to the Quran and believed in building an Islamic nation according to Islamic law. He was willing to give his life for the cause.

While these two men were trying to get people to join their plan to overthrow Egypt, another country in the Middle East did it. It would give a lot of rebels ideas and strength. Iran was this country.

Chapter 17
The Rise of the Shiite Revolution in Iran

Iran's Shiite Muslims began their Islamic movement in 1979. They were against the government of Muhammad Reza Shah Pahlavi. The country's religious leaders backed this effort to overthrow the government.

Before this, conservative Iranian Muslims didn't talk about what they believed. People were very afraid of the government. They tried to hide their faith by using the Al-Tokiya method: "Inside I hate you, but on the outside I pretend to be your friend." Al-Tokiya meant that Muslims acted in a way that the government liked, not in a way that was true to their views.

Many Shiite Muslims rediscovered the spirit of martyrdom that had been buried inside them, which led to the start of the uprising. They remembered how al-Husayn, who was Muhammad's grandson and the son of Ali ibn Abi Talib, went to fight his enemy even though he knew he would die. The religious leaders of Iran reminded the Shiites of the past of people dying for their faith. Right away, Iranian Muslims began to leave Al-Tokiya and take on the Shiite martyrdom spirit.

At the same time, Ayatollah Khomeini was leading this effort from afar through cassettes. Khomeini sent cassette tapes to the people of Iran with his teachings, views, and plans for the new Islamic revolution. He did this from a town in France called Le Chateau. Millions of people were brainwashed by these tapes. The book was called The War of Cassettes, and it was written by an Italian author.

During this movement, thousands of people in Iran were killed. Iran's past had never seen a revolution with so much power.

The revolution got rid of the government and set up an Islamic government in its place. Ayatollah Khomeini was brought back to Iran from France by plane. Before the flight to Tehran, he bowed down twice outside the plane and thanked Allah. He told the Shiites in Iran and the rest of the world through reporters and media that "no one can beat a nation that listens to Allah and does what he says."

When he got to the airport in Tehran, millions of Iranians were there to greet him. The sound of them screaming "Allah is greater!" shook the city. God is very good. They took Khomeini on their shoulders all the way to Al-Ferdose, a cemetery where all the revolution's dead were buried. Khomeini said, "No more Al-Tokiya after today." He meant that Shiite Muslims could now follow their religion without worrying about the government or any other power in the world.

Iranian Influence: The Islamic Group Movement's Uprising in Egypt

Those important times in history had a big effect on Islam and the rest of the world. Members of the Islamic Group Movement at the university used what was going on in Iran as a reason to fight against the Egyptian government. They disrupted classes at every university in Egypt, including Al-Azhar University, by using violence.

Thousands of students yelled in Khomeini's favor. A lot of students who had never been part of the Islamic Group Movement before joined this protest. This was a great chance for new people to join.

The protest spread like wildfire all over Egypt. The number of marchers got so big that it became a big problem for the government of Egypt.

Members of the Islamic Group got a lot of people to yell against the government. They said that, just like in Iran, Islam should take over Egypt. "Oh Sadat, you coward, you are the puppet of the Americans," they yelled.

"Patience, patience, all you Jews! Muhammad's army is on its way back to you," they said about the country of Israel.

The Global Reach of Iran's Revolution

Many extreme Islamic groups in the Arab world and around the world got help from the Iranian revolution. The leaders of the Iranian revolution said they were starting a new business. They planned to sell the real Islamic law and revolution to the whole world as their best offering.

Iran has helped all of the Islamic extremist groups that have terrorized the world in the years since the revolution. Hizbollah was one of the first groups that Iran set up and helped. This was a Shiite group in Lebanon whose goal was to topple the government and turn the country into an Islamic state. Lebanon was a country where most of the people in charge were Christians.

Iran also helped get the Islamic nation started in Sudan. Hasan al-Turabi, who was in charge of Al-Jepha Al-Islamia, overthrew the government of Sudan and turned it into an Islamic country. Iran helped Islamic groups in a lot of places, like Egypt, Algeria, Tunisia, and many other Arab countries.

The Iran-Iraq War: Defending Against Revolution

Arab countries in the Gulf were hit with fear and terror. The Iranian plan to bring change to their countries was a threat to them. Saddam Hussein, who was in charge of Iraq, didn't want fanatical Muslims or anyone else to share his power. He led the defense of the area against the Iranian Revolution and went to Iran to fight against it. He had the backing of every Arab country and the rest of the world.

The Iraqi forces moved into 30% of Iran's territory. The Iranians used this chance to protect their country and die as heroes in the name of Allah. It took the Iranians two years of fighting to get the Iraqi military to leave their land. At the crossing, the Iranians did not stop. They continued the war in Iraq for another six years.

Almost a million Muslims on both sides of the Iran-Iraq war died, and two million more were hurt. The goal of this war was to stop Iran's plan to spread their movement to Arab countries. But the goal grew stronger, and the plan to spread Islam all over the world never stopped.

All Islamic groups around the world got new hope from the Iranian revolution. This new hope was that Islam would take over the world and be in charge of everything.

Chapter 18
Betrayal Among Extremists

In Egypt in 1980, something was going on that would be a big loss for those who were trying to do jihad. Egyptian leaders of the Islamic Group Movement (IGM) thought it was time to stop preparing spiritually and mentally and take action to overthrow the Egyptian government. They also thought it was time to join forces with Sudan and Iran, which had already set up Islamic states, to finish the attack of the Arab world and move on to the global vision.

The IGM split Egypt into areas and gave each region a strong leader. These areas and the people who ran them were:

- Al-Minya region: Karim Zohdi, Fouad Al-Dolabi, Assim Abdul-Majed, Ayman al-Zawahiri (later he became the right-hand man of Osama bin Laden), and Essam Dirbala
- Asyut region: Najeh Ibrahim and Osama Hafez
- Sohaj region: Hamdi Abdul Rahman
- Nagh Hamadi region: Ali Sharif and Talat Qusam

General Prince Halmmi Al-Gazar and his assistant, Essam Al-Aryan, were in charge of all of these leaders from the area.

Merging Alliances

The Muslim Brotherhood's leaders were worried about this newly formed Islamic Group Movement. The head of the Muslim Brotherhood Movement, Omar Al-Talmasani, also didn't agree with their plans for when to do things. He told all Muslims, "The time for jihad is not yet right." He told the leaders of IGM to slow down and be more patient.

He also said that having two different groups of Muslims was bad for their unity. He said that they should work together better if they put their trust in him.

The head of IGM, his assistant, and the leaders of the Al-Minya region welcomed the call for unity right away, citing the Quranic verse, "Verily, Allah loves those who fight in His Cause in rows (ranks) as if they were a solid structure." He said that this verse was about how Muslims should be united.

The leaders of the IGM asked the leader of the Muslim Brotherhood to attend the event of unity in the south of Egypt. But there were a lot of people at the IGM who didn't agree with the call for unity. As soon as the Muslim Brotherhood's group got there, the IGM members got very angry. Those who didn't like the idea of working together tried to hurt the boss of the Muslim Brotherhood. Members who were for unity stood up for him by killing members who didn't agree with them.

Internal Terror in the Community

After that, people fought each other with knives and swords. People from Egypt who lived in the areas of Asyut and Al Minya were afraid of this war. People in the group who were against unity went to the homes of other people in the group and knocked on their doors. When they opened the doors, they killed the people inside by stabbing them. Before the victim died, he was told that he had betrayed Allah and Islam, so he was getting the punishment that the Quran says should happen to people who put off fighting.

Even when the IGM members of the house were not there, the attackers still broke in. They told the wives and children that they were going to be killed. Hundreds of people from all over the country took trains to get to this troubled area to stop the violence and save their cause.

IGM members who were against unity took over through violence and fear. They gave up control of the rest of both moves to them. The IGM was almost wiped out by this terrible storm.

Rise of the Jihadists

A new group called al-Jihad split off from IGM, the Muslim Brotherhood, and a few other smaller groups. Mohammed Abdul-Salam Farag was in charge of it. In the middle of the 1980s, they killed several people, including thinkers, journalists, and the head of the Egyptian Parliament.

Al-Jihad in Egypt got a big boost from a chance meeting that happened when Farag went to the home of Tarek Al-Zomor, a member of the movement. At the time, Zomor was also receiving his brother-in-law, Abod Al- Zomor, who was a high-ranking officer in the Egyptian military intelligence.

There was real friendship between these three guys. They promised each other that they would do whatever it took to overthrow the Egyptian government and free Egypt from its apostate and non-religious leaders.

In the summer of 1980, this happened. Abod Al-Zomor said, "I often wished I could get out from under the control of the government and start fighting it.

Now that we've met Farag, we have the same ideas about how to set up the right plan to reach the goal of an Islamic government.

Soon after that important meeting, the leaders of al-Jihad (Abod Al-Zomor, Karim Zohdi, Fouad Al-Dolabi, and Nabil Al-Magrabi) got together to set up an operating system and organize the movement. After a lot of talking, they agreed to put together a group of counselors.

The committee agreed to focus on appointing, managing, and making the necessary decisions. They also agreed to spin off from the committee three minor committees:

- Preparation committee—its responsibility was to organize and prepare weapons and transportation.
- Economic committee—its responsibility was to raise the necessary finances to accomplish the mission.
- Distribution and awareness committee—it was in charge of preparing and distributing literature to those involved in upcoming jihad.
- The committee of counselors divided the country into regions and set up the committee members as princes over these regions.

The group told all of the leaders that they could choose their own assistants for these areas. Each region had to train and pay for its own troops on its own. Now, the al-Jihad movement was a real thing in Egypt. In the future, it would spread to the rest of the Islamic world.

Al-Jihad in Palestine is the most well-known child. Egyptian Islamists taught its leaders how to run the group, and their ways are similar. For example, al-Jihad in Egypt had two men put bombs on their bodies and blow themselves up in an attempt to kill the Egyptian minister of national security. Al-Jihad in Palestine sends people on suicide missions in the same way.

Al-Jihad: A Theoretical Perspective

Al-Jihad was put together. Now, the group needed a strong set of beliefs to keep its members together. This idea came from a book by an engineer named Mohammed Abed al-Salem called The Missing Commitments (Al-Fareda Al-Gaaba).

The author of this book met with Karim Zohdi, the boss of the southern Egypt region. Zohdi turned the book into the bylaws of al-Jihad.

I'd like to tell you what the book is about in three sentences. The book talks a lot about how war is the only way for Islam to come back to power. But the author goes one step further than any other author by saying, "The Islamic invasion is coming to Rome." Muslim writers before al-Salem had mostly written about the Arab world and some African countries. In this book, however, he started talking about taking over Europe and the West. Here are a few examples of what al-Salem thinks:

Denouncing the Compromised Faithful

It doesn't matter if Muslims like it or not, but fundamentalist Islamic power must be set up in every country. Allah told us to do it, so we have to do it. Al-Salem said that the most important question is, "Are we living in a true Islamic nation?"

He asked the leaders of many Muslim countries, "How can they be true Muslims?" They were brought up with Judaism, Christianity, and Communism. He thought that these people were only Muslim in name. He said that they were all apostates, non-believers, and heathens who should all be killed.

He also said that these Muslims should be punished more harshly than the other people. He agreed with Ibn Taymiyah, a thinker from the 1400s, and wrote, "Muslims should not mix with anyone else, and if they do, they should be killed as well."

Jihad takes Precedence

He said that all of Islam's other religious practices, like fasting, prayer, and doing good deeds, were wrong because they kept Muslims so busy that they didn't hear the call to war.

Killing as a Sacred Duty for Muslims

Killing is the main thing that sets Islam apart from all other faiths. Abed Al-Salem wrote that before Islam, when people didn't believe in God, God would sometimes punish them with fires or floods or other things. But when Islam was founded, Allah told Muslims to take the law into their own hands. It became their job to torture and kill people who were against Allah.

The Aggressive Nature of Jihad

Abed al-Salem went after the Muslims who thought that war was the only way to protect Islam. He was very clear that war is not up for discussion and can't be compromised. All Muslims are called to Jihad. He used the prophet Muhammad's letters to the kings of different countries, how the first Muslims fought, and how Islam spread by the sword to prove his point. He said that this is how Islam should be spread now.

Enemy Reinterpreted

He also defined the enemies in a new way. They were:

- Heathens
- Muslims not governed according to Allah's law and the Quran

Abed al-Salem supported fighting those Muslims who did not live according to his interpretation of Islam.

Strategic Frameworks for War

Al-Salem spent a lot of his book talking about how Muslims fight wars and do jihad. He talked about attacks, killings, lies, betrayal, foul play, treachery, and breaking faith. He also said that the enemy's women, children, and other things belong to the Muslims and their troops, and that Muslims should kill anyone who fights back.

Building the Next Islamic State

Al-Jihad already had a strong base. It wanted to do what Iran did and become the next true Islamic state. Al-Jihad needed money, so its members chose to use the same methods as Muhammad. What they did will be explained in the next part.

Chapter 19
Al-Jihad: Readying and Striking

In the 1980s, when al-Jihad was getting ready for war, they needed guns, bombs, weapons, and ways to get around. They were put under a lot of pressure to come up with a lot of money quickly. The Muslims did not care enough about the cause to give this much help.

An investigation, according to court records in Egypt, found that Abod Al-Zomor gave the movement 4,000 Egyptian pounds, several automatic machine guns, six tear gas bombs, four RBG bombs, seven Russian bombs, Russian Kalashnikov guns, and several hand guns. These were given away from his own stash. But these and other donations were not enough to keep the cause going. They had to find a different way to make money.

Fear Tactics Against Christians

Ali Sharif, the leader of Quna and Nagh Hamadi, came up with an Islamic answer that was illegal. He said that the movement should take the things owned by the 15–17 percent of Egyptians who are Christians and use them as support. It wasn't a new idea. In the seventh century, the el Kharij movement had the same idea: "Their women and all of their possessions are our rights." The idea goes back to when Muhammad killed his enemies and took their towns.

This horrible idea raised not a question of right or wrong, but of how to carry it out. How can we get the things that the Christians have? Should we rob them, make them pay the jizyah (a special tax for non-Muslims), or threaten them? Should we only go after the things that Christians own, or should we also go after the churches?

In Egypt, Christians ran a lot of different businesses. One of these was the business of making gemstones and jewelry. The plan was to attack the shops, kill the Christians, and steal all of the money and goods.

When this idea was told to the group, there was a long period of silence. The leader of the Asyut area, Najeh Ibrahim, broke the silence by saying, "This is nothing but a heavenly inspiration."

The head of the Al Minya region, Karim Zohdi, then said, "We should start with any business that helps the churches do their work." The group agreed, so Ali Sharif was put in charge of planning the first attack.

From the records of the court's sessions we can hear the testimony from one man who witnessed an attack:

> *On July 26, 1981 at noon I was in the jewelry store of Nabi Masud Askaros, in the city of Nagh Hamadi. The owner, his workers and a few customers were in the store. I heard several shots at the door of the store. I immediately hid under a table. I saw two men carrying automatic machine guns. They were wearing facemasks and gloves. They fired at the owner and also at Zarif Shinooda. They took all of the merchandise and money and, while fleeing, continued firing their guns. In the meantime, I found out that they did the same thing to Fouad and his brother, Fah'iz, Masud's jewelry store. Six men were killed and two were injured in that store. The two robbers got in a Peugot and took off.*

During this time, many Christians were killed, and people were very scared because they didn't know who would be next.

The court record shows that Egyptian Muslims who worked in oil-producing countries helped the cause a lot. There were 21,000 dollars, 10,400 German marks, 26,000 Egyptian pounds, and a lot more among the gifts that were found. All of this money wasn't enough, so they started taking cars from people who worked at Christian churches. So the cops wouldn't be able to find them, these cars were taken to the desert, taken apart, and sold as used parts.

Al-Jihad killed, robbed, and stole from Christians, just like the Quran told them to do with Jews and Christians, who are called "People of the Book."

> *Fight against... those who acknowledge not the religion of truth (i.e. Islam) among the people of the Scripture (Jews and Christians), until they pay the Jizyah [tax] with willing submission, and feel themselves subdued.*

Because there were so many Christians in Egypt, it would have been hard to follow this verse. There were too many Christians to kill them all. But this was still the goal of the movement: to force Christians to live by Islamic rule and pay a high tax to Muslims or be killed.

Now al-Jihad was ready and able to start the first big fight with the Egyptian government and its system. They planned to overthrow the government and make Egypt the center of a revolt in all Islamic countries.

During this time, eleven new people joined the committee of counselors, but they felt they needed one person to lead them through this important historical process. After a lot of thought, they chose Sheikh Omar Abdel Rahman, the Quranic science professor at Al-Azhar University that I had. Even though he was blind, he was more than able to lead a movement like this.

Sadat: The Fatal Attack

Sheikh Abdel Rahman issued a fatwa that President Sadat and his government were apostate infidels who all must die.

The plan to overturn the country included these steps:

1. Kill the president.
2. Gain control over strategic places in Cairo, such as the defense department, national security department, and the national radio and TV stations.
3. Take over the Asyut region in South Egypt and call the Muslim Egyptians to come out for a new Islamic revolution.

Khaled al-Islambouli, an Egyptian soldier and the best long-range shot in the country, was hired by al-Jihad to be their sharpshooter. He was also a part of al-Jihad and worked with them.

At first, everything went as planned. On October 6, 1981, the president was shot and killed during a yearly military party to celebrate winning the 1973 Israeli war. The force took over the area of Asyut, but they were not able to take over Cairo.

After Sadat was killed, Vice President Mubarak told the troops to go and take back control of the Asyut region from the movement. Sheikh Omar Abdel Rahman, who was in charge of al-Jihad, was among those who were arrested by the government. All of them went before the highest military court in Egypt.

How could the legal system in an Arabic country that was meant to be Islamic deal with these Muslims who followed the Quran's orders? Let's look at the court record of what might be the most important case in the history of Egypt.

Chapter 20
The Quran's Conquest of Justicè

It was time for Sheikh Omar Abdel Rahman to show the court what he could do.

He defended the ideas of the al-Jihad movement in front of the court. He spoke twice: once to explain to the jury how jihadists think, and again to answer the attorney general's questions. If you read the court record and his answers carefully, you will see Islam for what it really is. Sheikh Abdel Rahman, who knew a lot about the Quran and Islamic law, used his skills in a way that no one expected to help the cause.

He got the attorney general to play the game he had been good at his whole life. He was able to put the attorney general on the side of the people who were being accused. In the first round, Sheikh Omar Abdel Rahman set the stage for himself. He told the court about the following Islamic ideas:

- Justice should be according to what Allah has set for the Muslims only. Allah's lordship should be acknowledged by all Muslims, and no one can deny it because Allah created everything and everyone. He has the absolute right to his creation.
- The people who carry out Islamic justice should be faithful believers who obey Allah's commands and the prophet Muhammad's teaching. If the justice system is not run according to the Quran, Muslim believers should not submit themselves to its laws.
- The imported laws from infidel countries, "USA and Europe," are man-made and not according to Allah's laws. The existing law of Egypt is influenced by men who compromise Allah's law in many areas such as adultery, gambling, homosexuality, alcoholism, and theft. Anyone who modifies Allah's laws is an apostate infidel. Anyone who submits to these laws is also an apostate infidel.

Sheikh Abdel Rahman proved that what he was saying was true by saying, "What I'm saying is not my opinion or someone else's spiritual ideas. It's what Allah's book says."

Here is a part of the court record from the last court session, when the sheikh was being questioned by the attorney general.

In Islamic history we find many Muslims who claimed that Allah is the ultimate judge Attorney but acted any way they pleased. Islam called them el-Kharij. Islamic society rejects them.

General:

Sheikh Kharij are those who rebelled against or disobeyed the Islamic successor, so who is the Rahman: Islamic successor today? Where is Ali ibn Abi Talib today? And if you call us Kharij , it means that we disobeyed or rebelled from the successor, the Muslim leader. So who is today's successor and leader of Muslims? Is he the friend of Jews, the supporter of Israel and Begin's buddy? [He referred to peace talks between President Sadat, Menachem Begin, prime minister of Israel, and Jimmy Carter, US president. Sadat was the recipient of the Nobel Peace Prize at this time.] Is our successor the man who abandoned Allah's law and commanded compliance with the laws of heathens and infidels?

The belief that Allah is the lawmaker and the only judge does not mean that if our Attorney Islamic society finds solutions according to our social and mental standards of living General: today that so doing makes it an apostate, infidel society.

Sheikh Disobeying Allah and his law in the name of convenience has only one meaning—these Rahman: are sinful, lost infidels who have made their own laws and abandoned Allah's laws. They are the ones whom Allah commanded the Muslims to kill in jihad.

Jihad is not killing. This is not Islam's teaching. Jihad is a spiritual fight against evil, Attorney poverty, sickness, and sin. Killing is only from the devil. General:

Sheikh From where does the attorney general come up with this understanding? Are there verses Rahman: in the Quran that I don't know about that say jihad is a spiritual fight against evil, poverty, sickness, and sin? Perhaps there is new inspiration from Allah that our attorney general received recently and the rest of the Muslims do not yet know.

Declaring that our Islamic society is heathen, infidels, or apostates is an insult on our Attorney merciful Allah, his commands, and his law.

General:

Sheikh Which commands and laws are you talking about? The ones that compromised adultery, Rahman: gambling, and alcohol? Is this not our merciful Allah's command? Mr. Attorney General, your commands and laws are from the devil.

If any Muslim society confesses that Allah is the only God and Muhammad is his Attorney prophet, no one has the right to accuse them of being infidels.

General:

Sheikh What you say is not the real truth. Someone can confess that Allah is God and Rahman: Muhammad is his prophet, but he can do something against his confession, and this takes him outside of Islam.

President Al-Sadat was a great man who sacrificed his life for the love of Allah and the Attorney love of his country.

General:

Sheikh Do you know how this man sacrificed his life for the love of his country? He is the same Rahman: man who declared that all religions are equal. He made the infidels and the grandchildren of "monkeys and pigs" [monkeys and pigs is the description the Quran uses for the Jewish people] equal to the Muslims. He made the world's greatest criminal murderer his dear friend [referring to Begin, Israel's prime minister]. The same man who sacrificed his life for Allah broke all of Allah's laws in this country. The same man who worshiped Allah sarcastically described the Muslim women's veil as a tent. This man loved Allah? He also insulted Allah when he danced with and hugged women publicly before the international media and before the whole world. [In celebration of the peace agreement, Sadat and his wife danced with Carter and his wife on national television.] This contradicts what Sadat always preached about village behavior. This man led our country to free enterprise and nearly destroyed our economy. He led our country to a moral and social disaster, and it will take our country many years to recover from him.

You, dear reader, have seen how Sheikh Omar Abdel Rahman beat not only the attorney general but also the Egyptian legal system.

Yes, war means killing all of Allah's and Islam's enemies. Yes, Muslims think that they should break the law and kill Allah's enemies, as if Allah couldn't take care of them himself. Yes, the Quran is more important than the rules of the land. Yes, the person who planned to kill the president could use the Quran to explain what he did and be found not guilty by Egypt's top court. That's too bad.

Sheikh Abdel Rahman was officially set free because there was no proof that he was the one who told al-Jihad to kill Sadat because he was an infidel. I thought that the blind sheikh's own words were more than enough proof to put him behind bars.

But the person who did wrong didn't get away with it. Five men were killed by the military. Among them were the sharpshooter Khaled al-Islambouli and the author of The Missing Commitments, Mohammed Abed al-Salem. When the author was caught by the cops, they took all of his books and burned them. Now, the only place to get it is on the black market.

Even though the Egyptian government fought hard against al-Jihad, it lived, grew, and never stopped. Many of the leaders of the al-Jihad movement were able to escape to other countries, such as Sudan, Yemen, Pakistan, and Czechoslovakia. A lot of people joined the al-Jihad movement in Afghanistan by going there.

Later, they joined forces with Osama bin Laden, whose movement was based on the same ideas and views. The leaders of al-Jihad who had fled Egypt helped bin Laden start a new movement. It was called al Qaeda. One of the Egyptian al-Jihad leaders, Dr. Ayman al-Zawahiri, became bin Laden's right-hand man and then became the boss of al Qaeda. People who were being hurt by the Egyptian government went to Afghanistan to get away from it.

Later, the Taliban, an Islamic fundamentalist group in Afghanistan, accepted all of these men and helped them as partners in the same call to jihad. They were ready to die together, but they hoped to win when Allah's people ruled the world.

Chapter 21
The Exodus of Jihad from Egypt

When you throw a stone into the sea, the waves go in all directions. This is what happens when a group of people is very strict and violent. When something big happens in one country, it affects a lot of other places.

Egypt is like the stone that was thrown into the water. It is the heart of terrorism today. This is because Egypt is the most important place in the world for Islamic schooling. Al-Azhar University sends out preachers to spread Islam all over the world.

If a Muslim country anywhere in the world has a moral question, they ask Al-Azhar. When I was in South Africa, Muslims wrote to Al-Azhar if they had a question they couldn't solve. For example, they needed a decision on when Ramadan should start, which relies on when the new moon is seen. Al-Azhar said that Ramadan would start when people in Cairo could see the moon.

I was very involved in Al-Azhar University at the same time that the Muslim Brotherhood, IGM, al-Jihad, and other groups were growing. I went there for eleven years and got a bachelor's, a master's, and a doctorate. Also, after I got my bachelor's degree, the university sent me to teach at Islamic universities in Tunisia, Libya, Iraq, and Morocco as a visiting professor. From this place, I could see what was going on.

We have looked at the uprisings in Egypt and Iran in great depth. Now, let's look at what happened in North Africa after Sadat was killed. From Egypt, the movement went to Libya, Tunisia, and Algeria, which are all to the west. Things were felt in Sudan, which is in the south.

Libya

Sadat's death moved a lot of Muslim men in Libya, which is next door to Egypt. They were also ready to die in the name of Allah and for war.

The Libyan Muslims set up many groups to try to kill Muammar Qaddafi and get rid of his government. Qaddafi was finally taken out of power and killed on October 20, 2011, after a short civil war.

Even though Qaddafi was a Muslim, many people in the West might not realize that his views were very different from those of Islamic extremism. After he took power in 1969, the country was run by a constitution instead of Islamic law. The first thing he wanted to do was make a democracy.

Qaddafi liked how tough Gamal Abdel Nasser was with the Muslim Brotherhood Movement when he was president of Egypt. (President Nasser was known for not putting up with rebels in any way. He got them all together and killed them twice, in 1954 and 1965.) Qaddafi called radical Muslims "the street dogs" on Libyan state TV every chance he got. He did what Nasser did: he killed a lot of rebels to get rid of their power in his country.

The main reasons why the Libyan members of these extreme Islamic groups fought against Qaddafi were 1) his anti-Islamic political ideas and 2) his dictatorship and corruption.

Eventually, during the Arab Spring, they were able to end his rule with the help of the West, especially France and the United States. They were able to capture Qaddafi and kill him in public.

During the Libyan revolution, the vast majority of Libyans supported these groups. They hoped that once Qaddafi and his government were gone, these groups would work together to start over, form an Islamic government, and lead Libya to justice, freedom, and wealth.

But after Qaddafi was killed, people in his country saw nothing but division, chaos, bloodshed, killing, and destruction. This made a large number of Libyans wish they hadn't gotten rid of Qaddafi's government. This situation shows the real problem not just in Libya but also in Egypt, Yemen, Iraq, and Syria, among other places in the Middle East.

Tunisia

The Egyptian al-Jihad was felt in Tunisia, which is near Libya. Rashid al-Ghannoushi, the leader of Tunisia's Islamic resistance group al-Nahda who is now living in exile, was one of the people there. The former president, Habib ibn Ali Bourguiba, and the current president, Zine El Abidine Ben Ali, were always in their way.

I went to Tunisia in the early 1990s. Because I was from the country of Islamic heroes, the Muslims there treated me with a lot of respect. They said that Khaled al-Islambouli, who killed Sadat, was an Islamic hero of the modern era. They told me, "Our Islamic Arab countries need people like that to overthrow all the governments of infidels and set up an Islamic dynasty, just like in Muhammad's time."

Algeria

To understand the full effect in Algeria, we need to look at the country's unique past. It was one of the first places that Islam took over.

Ten years after Muhammad died, the Islamic troops moved into Algeria. Algeria stayed an Islamic state under the Islamic rule until 1830, when the French took it over. Algeria was ruled by the French until 1962. The French had such a big impact on Algerian society that even after the country was freed, French was still the main language and Arabic was almost forgotten in most of the country.

Algeria was run by a national government that was not based on Islam after the Algerian Revolution, which was led by Ahmed Ben Bella. Algeria got rid of the French and established Islam and the Arabic language with the help of many Arab Muslim countries. My uncle was one of the top preachers that Al-Azhar University sent to Algeria to teach Arabic and spread Islam again.

Algeria slowly but surely turned back into an Arab country. During this time, Algeria was affected by the educational purpose of Al-Azhar University and the Muslim Brotherhood Organization.

Between 1954 and 1960, when Nasser, the president of Egypt, was very harsh on the Muslim Brotherhood Organization, many of its members moved to Algeria. They taught Algeria's young people what they thought was right.

Ali Belhadj and Dr. Abbas al-Madani, both teachers at the University of Algiers, started a new Islamic movement called al-Gabha al- Aslamia Lilncaz, which means the Islamic Salvation Front. The Muslim Brotherhood of Egypt just changed its name. This group worked closely with other Islamic groups all over the Arab world, especially in Egypt.

At the time, the leaders of the Algerian and Egyptian movements worked together closely to lead all Islamic organizations around the world. These two groups worked hard to get into Morocco, Tunisia, and Libya so that the Islamic country could take over all of North Africa. They planned to join forces with the groups in Sudan and Iran so that the world could see the Islamic government return to the whole Arabic region.

Muammar Qaddafi knew right away that his government in Libya was in danger. From the east, the Egyptians put on him, and from the west, the Algerians did the same. Qaddafi offered to help the Algerian government fight the extreme groups and their leaders, al-Madani and Belhadj.

Seizing Control of the Election

At the beginning of the 1990s, the leaders of the Islamic Salvation Front put on one of the biggest gatherings of Islamic fundamentalists ever. They filled up the national sports stadium to the brim. The crowd's cheers of "Allah is great!" will always be remembered in the Algerian city. "Hold on, hold on, all you Jews! Muhammad's army is coming."

All of these cheers against Jews came from the guest speaker, who was Khaled al-Islambouli's mother. Yes, the mother of the man who killed President Sadat and was killed by the Egyptian government talked to the top leaders of jihad in Algeria.

During her speech, she moved the crowd to give their money and their hearts to make jihad happen in their country and around the world. She said she sacrificed one son for jihad and was ready to sacrifice her other son, Mohammed, who was standing next to her on stage, for the same cause: to see the flag of Islam take over the world. She said that she was ready to die to help Islam win against the enemy.

When she said, "Nothing made me prouder as a mother than when the enemy of Islam sentenced my son Khaled to death," the crowds cheered loudly. When she talked about how many streets and roads in Islamic countries around the world were already named after her son, she got everyone excited about war and dying for a cause. She also said, "Even the people who hate Islam think my son is a hero for dying for what he believes in." She used a hadith saying by the prophet Muhammad: "Any nation that gives up jihad will be conquered and put down."

Don't get it twisted; this woman made the crowd really hate their country. She told the Algerian movement what they could expect during their fight to get rid of the government. This gathering had a very powerful effect. It gave the Algerian Muslims the strength to do what they had to do.

A new election was held in 1991, not long after this gathering. The Islamic Salvation Front took advantage of this chance to use the election for their own benefit and try to take over. The movement won the election because it scared away all the other candidates, but it wasn't going to take over the country that quickly.

Algeria's upper class, elites, and most educated people spoke up right away to warn and protest against the current government giving power to these rebels. Many Arab countries, like Egypt, Libya, Tunisia, and Morocco, knew how dangerous these groups could be. They also told the government what would happen if extremists took over. Algeria had no choice but to tell the troops to keep the country safe and call off the election. This was the start of the long fight between the troops and the Islamic movement, which is still going on today.

More than 150,000 people were killed in the 1990s to stop radical Islam from taking over their country. The Algerian government arrested the leaders of the Islamic Salvation Front, but it could not stop the violence. Afghanistan sent a lot of fighters with a lot of experience to try to overthrow the government.

And the bloody fight goes on.

Sudan

After he got out of jail, Sheikh Omar Abdel Rahman went south to Sudan. He was there with Dr. Hasan al-Turabi, the leader of the Sudanese group al-Islamia, for a few months. With the help of one of the Sudanese military's generals, Al-Turabi was able to overthrow the government and take control of the country.

Except for the small number of Christians in south Sudan, Al-Turabi's movement was founded. Al-Turabi is getting rid of them, though. Al-Turabi killed Christians by cutting off their arms and legs and giving them HIV, just like Islam told him to do. He showed the world what Islam will do to Christians if it can.

The Christians in Sudan don't want to become Muslims. They are also poor and can't pay the high taxes that come with being a Christian. Because of this, thousands of them are dying under al-Turabi's rule. The Islamic government run by Al-Turabi has killed Christian men, rounded up Christian women and children, and sold them into slavery. Many groups that care about helping people have rushed to buy these Christian slaves and set them free.

Conclusion

In short, the well-organized conservative group in Egypt did not manage to get rid of its own government. However, its members went to Libya, Tunisia, Algeria, and Sudan to try to change the minds of radical groups there.

These groups are slowly making their way into our world, and their goal is to take over. They are always on the lookout for the right situation or a fight to start.

Chapter 22
Revised Tactics: Targeting the West

Since the early 1970s, terrorism has changed in two ways: first, in terms of who it is aimed at, and second, in terms of how it is done. At the beginning of the 1970s, the targets of terrorists began to change in a big way. Terrorists used to go after specific people, like diplomats, top military leaders, and politicians. Terrorism no longer threatens specific people; instead, it is now aimed at the public as a whole.

Attacking people at random is more successful because it scares more people and spreads fear in a bigger way. They help attackers get what they want quickly and give them more power to get what they want. Terrorism has become a way for politicians to talk and talk about politics.

Sheikh Abdel Rahman's Global Jihad Shift

Sheikh Abdel Rahman was set free after he won his case in front of the highest court in Egypt. He went to Sudan, where his fellow war leader, Dr. Hasan al-Turabi, was happy to see him. Sheikh Abdel Rahman went there and stayed there for a few months to help him.

Then, Sheikh Abdel Rahman chose to try something new to bring Islam's glory back. This time, he didn't want to fight a single country. Instead, he wanted to start a global war. Remember that Sayyid Qutb and other writers stressed how important it was to bring jihad to the whole world and create an Islamic country that covers the whole world.

Sheikh Abdel Rahman was now going after America and Europe, which Muslims say are the source of sin and evil. Sheikh Abdel Rahman chose to use the freedom and democracy that are only found in the West to help him reach this goal. He went to the U.S.

When Sheikh Abdel Rahman got to New Jersey, the Muslim leaders of the United States gave him a warm welcome. He moved to New Jersey and started meeting people at the al-Salaam Mosque in Jersey City right away. Muslims from all over the US asked him to come teach them as well. In many big towns, he held seminars and training sessions.

Do you think he was trying to teach them something? Is Islam about love, peace, and forgiving? In no way! He showed the American Muslims what war was really about. He told all American Muslims to come together and work for the call of Islam, which is for Islam to rule the world again.

First World Trade Center Bombing: 1993

The only goal of Sheikh Abdel Rahman's residency in the United States was to lead jihad from within. The following are his objectives:

- To base the Islamic jihad movement in nations of the infidels— these are his own words—in preparation for the worldwide revolution
- To pressure the US government by threatening America's security from within
- To use this pressure to change US policies in the Islamic world — particularly to break down support for Israel and to resolve the Palestinian dilemma

Muslim fundamentalists don't like the fact that America backs Israel and other Middle Eastern countries that aren't religious. Sheikh Abdel Rahman thinks that the sword of Islam should be used to overthrow all of these countries. Since America helps them, it is the biggest threat to the Islamic terror movement in the world.

Sheikh Abdel Rahman's first job was to shake up the United States by attacking the twin towers of the World Trade Center in New York City, which stood for success, freedom, and wealth. In 1993, the jihad movement set off a big blast in one of the towers that killed six people. This was news to the whole world. Sheikh Abdel Rahman will spend the rest of his life in a US federal jail because he planned and led this attack. Yes, he is still alive, and we are eating and taking care of him with money from taxpayers while he keeps inspiring the jihad movement from prison.

Obstacles to Worldwide Revolution

The Islamic movement believes there are three main ideologies that stand in the way of worldwide Islamic revolution.

1. Judaism, as manifested in Israel
2. Christianity, as manifested in the United States and the West
3. Communism, as manifested in the former Soviet Union and China

They also believe these obstacles must be destroyed before the revolution will take place.

U.S. in the Crosshairs

There are five clear reasons why America is a special target of Islamic fundamentalists:

1. America represents those whom the Quran calls "People of the Book"—Jews and Christians.
2. America supports Israel.
3. America is the source of all that Muslims consider to be evil —pornography, alcohol, homosexual rights, evil music, evil fashion, and evil culture.
4. America supports Christianity all over the world. More Christian missionaries come from the United States than any other country.
5. America is a government "of the people, by the people, and for the people," which makes it a heathen government in Muslim thinking because Allah is to be the head of all government.

America and the West are seen as Allah and Islam's real enemies. The West is always there to help Arab countries kill Muslim extremists and destroy their groups. Also, the West helps Israel kill Arabs when it fights them.

The Emergence of Al-Qaeda's Saudi Leader

The Islamic organization had a new leader. He was a Saudi millionaire whose life was a lot like that of Sheikh Abdel Rahman. He left his home country because the government was after him. Like Abdel Rahman, he went to Sudan for a short time. In 1996, he left to go to Afghanistan to join Dr. Ayman al-Zawahiri and other original members of the Egyptian al-Jihad to start the al Qaeda group. This is an international group that has many countries that are not Arab as members. These countries include Chechnya, Kashmir, Uzbekistan, Pakistan, Kenya, and many others. Even though the people are different, the goal is the same: to go to war with the West, the U.S., and Israel. Israel is bad because it stands for Judaism, and the U.S. is bad because it stands for Christianity. On May 2, 2011, US troops killed him.

The Evolution of Al-Qaeda: Key Differences

Bin Laden did not start out with nothing. Al Qaeda is the result of the Egyptian al-Jihad group being repackaged, regrouped, and reorganized. But there are three ways in which al Qaeda is different:

Tactic: Assailing the West

Previous Islamic groups thought they should start close to home. They thought they should first take over their own country, build a country where Islamic law was the only law, and then take over the rest of the world. After trying and failing to take over Egypt in the 1980s, Dr. Zawahiri and Sheikh Abdel Rahman decided that it would be better to go for a worldwide war. They chose to go for the "head" instead of the "hands."

The political views of the head helped to identify it. America and Europe helped Egypt get rid of the Islamic sects. America helped Iraq fight the fanatics of the Iranian revolution, and America is still helping Israel fight Palestine. Al Qaeda decided that the United States is the head and that the secular Arab countries are the hands. (Don't forget that militant fundamentalists think that almost all Muslim states are too secular.)

They think that if we cut off the head, the hands won't work anymore. In other words, we can do whatever we want to the little boys if we kill the big brother.

So, al Qaeda's leaders agreed that the West should be their main goal. Bin Laden agreed with Sheikh Abdel Rahman's new idea that war, the fight against Islam's enemies, should take place on the enemy's territory.

Preparation: A Broad Global Network

The police, the army, or the government are no longer the goal. Now, the goal is civilization, the economy, and the safety of the world's source of power, which are the United States and European countries. The Islamic movement's new theory is to kill civilians and destroy economies, but this is still in line with the Quran.

Since the goal has changed, so has the way to get ready for it. Al Qaeda wants people from all over the world to join, which gives the group a lot of different kinds of experience. Osama bin Laden was worth a lot of money, and he used all of it to help his cause. He also got a lot of help from the Taliban government, which took a lot of weapons from the Russians after their war, and from the United States, which helped the Afghans fight communism.

Most of al Qaeda's members have been in war before, which may be the most important thing they can do to get ready. Many of bin Laden's people lived through the Egyptian jihad movement, the war in Afghanistan, the war in Kashmir, the war with Israel, and many other wars. These guys have been trained to be terrorists, but their own governments don't want them.

Execution: Targeting Smaller Objectives First

The plan was put into action by first looking at what Sheikh Abdel Rahman did. In 1993, he tried to bomb the World Trade Center but failed. Al-Qaeda learned from its mistakes and came up with better plans. At first, it went after smaller US targets. They bombed the US offices in Kenya and Tanzania on August 7, 1998, killing more than 200 people. The US reaction was weak: on August 20, 1998, President Bill Clinton fired two cruise missiles at sites in Sudan that were thought to be used by terrorists. Al-Qaeda laughed at the Clinton government because it used missiles that cost millions of dollars to blow up tents that only cost ten dollars.

Later on October 12, 2000, al Qaeda tried to sink the USS Cole while it was in the harbor at Aden, Yemen. The USS Cole was one of the biggest ships in the American Navy. The bomb killed 17 soldiers and hurt a lot of others. It also made a huge hole in the middle of America's big ship and sent it back to port. This time, the government did not strike back. Like nothing had happened. Now, al-Qaeda thought the US was sending a message of tolerance, and bin Laden thought he had the go-ahead to do bigger and worse things, like attack US land for the first time since the World Trade Center bombing in 1993. On September 11, 2001, four planes were taken over and used to carry out his plan. This act caused the World Trade Center to fall down and caused damage to the Pentagon. Everyone on board the planes also died.

Al Qaeda's goal was to spread fear and shake the national security of the West, especially the United States. The worldwide media played a big role in helping al Qaeda reach its goal.

Sayyid Qutb wrote about this in his books—Muslims are moving the fight to the home country of the infidel and using fear to rule the world. Sheikh Abdel Rahman started this, and Osama bin Laden kept going with it.

Osama bin Laden learned a lot from the Egyptians in al Qaeda, especially his right-hand man Ayman al-Zawahiri and others. There are a lot of similarities between how the Egyptian al-Jihad tried to take over the country and how al Qaeda attacked the United States. The Egyptian al-Jihad stole from Christians and tried to kill President Sadat with a soldier who had been taught by the government how to use a military weapon. Al-Qaeda stole four airplanes from the United States and used them to hit its targets.

The cheap sacrifices for the Islamic terrorists' game were the harmless Christians in Nagh Hamadi, Abo Karacas, Al Minya, Dyroot, Malawi, and Asyut, as well as the Americans in New York and Washington, DC, and the passengers and flight crews on the planes.

In the name of Allah, Muslims all over the world often kill innocent people. It is happening to millions of Christians in the south Sudan, Egypt, Nigeria, and other places.

What happened in January 2000 in the Egyptian town of Al-Kosheh is a good example. During an attack on their town, 21 men, women, and children were set on fire with torches and burned to death. Their bodies were cut open vertically from the throat down so their attackers could see their innards beating. Others were set on fire while they were still alive. The people who did it cut off the opposite arms and legs and sent them back to their village to make people afraid.

Where do militant Muslims get the ideas for their cruelty? From the Quran.

> *The recompense of those who wage war against Allah and His Messenger and do mischief in the land is only that they shall be killed or crucified or their hands and their feet be cut off from opposite sides, or be exiled from the land.*

Even though this English translation says "cut off hands and feet," I think the Arabic phrase means "cut off the whole arm and leg," which is what they did to the Egyptian people.

Yes, this is going on in the 21st century. The Egyptian government did a good job of hiding what had happened, of course.

Chapter 23
Strategies for Dealing with Radicalism in Islam

Radical Islamic groups are a big problem in the world right now. They are driven by the teachings of Islam, want to spend all of eternity in paradise, and are determined to take over the world for Islam. They work for Allah until Islamic power is the only form of government in the world.

Now, you might be wondering: How can we deal with this threat? What should we do? Is there any chance that Islamic terrorism can be stopped and peace can come to the Middle East? People have said that we are in a "war on terrorism." I would rather say that ideas are at war.

The Paradox of Violence: Can It End Itself?

Dealing with Islamic terrorism in the Muslim world is very complicated and hard, and using violence to get rid of a radical group is not a good idea because violence leads to more violence. Violence isn't a good way to fight radicalism. It's like trying to treat a major illness with a painkiller. It might stop the pain for a while, but it doesn't solve the problem. It is better to look for the problem's roots and deal with them so that we can find a real answer that will last.

Under President Abdul-Fattah al-Sisi, the Egyptian government chose to use the military to stop Islamic extremism, just like Nasser had done in the past. This kind of strategy might only work for a short time within the borders of one country. But this method will never be able to stop all radical Islamic movements around the world because it can't get rid of their ideas. Radical Islamists will never be stopped by armed force, no matter where they are in the world.

When I saw the military take over Egypt's government, which had been chosen by the people, I was shocked. I have nothing good to say about the Muslim Brotherhood as a group, and I don't even like them. But I am for a fair process that gives everyone the chance to take part in the political process of their country and use the rights they have. I also think that the peaceful approach to politics that the Muslim Brotherhood has taken is much better than the violent approach that ISIS and other extreme groups, like al Qaeda, have taken.

If someone disagrees with me and says that the Muslim Brotherhood is a radical group with its own goals, I will say that I agree with that, but it is better to sit down and talk about these goals in a peaceful and democratic way than to kill people with guns, grenades, or missiles. It is better for a country to go back to democracy so that people can hold politicians responsible than to go back to dictatorship.

Foreign Policy Reconsidered

If we want to know if and how the problems in the Middle East can be fixed at their roots, we need to look at the things that started the war and keep it going. At the start of the Arab Spring, when young people took to the streets to protest, they talked about their hunger for food, freedom, and social justice. This was the first thing that people talked about. Another factor is corrupt dictatorships, which extreme Muslims see as one of the biggest threats to Islam because they break Islamic law. When Western countries work with or back these evil regimes, they are seen as just as bad.

I think Western countries could help solve the problem if they took on a fair and helpful role and really tried to help the people. So far, though, Western countries haven't done much to help the Middle Eastern countries, like Egypt, grow and improve. Instead of trying to find the best way to spread democracy in the Middle East, they often work with cruel, corrupt dictatorships to protect their own interests in the area.

When the Arab Spring began with calm protests by young people, the Western countries didn't say a word. They did not help this new generation start a new birth of democracy and freedom in their region, nor did they back them. So, the first try at real democracy didn't work. After the Muslim Brotherhood and Salafists used democratic means to gain power, the rich and corrupt Arab Gulf regimes felt very threatened and used their oil money to kill this new birth of democracy. They worked with the Egyptian military to get rid of the first government in Egyptian history that was chosen freely and democratically. And in countries like Libya, Tunisia, and Yemen, they put the new hopes for democracy in danger by supporting the old governments and political systems.

It is common for crooked governments to stick up for each other. After the Tunisian dictator ran away from his country, Saudi Arabia gave him political refuge. This gave him a safe place to stay. United Arab Emirates gave refuge to the relatives and family members of both the tyrant of Tunisia and the dictator of Egypt (the Mubarak family). And Muammar Qaddafi's family and kids were safe in Oman.

But Western countries, including the United States, didn't care about these facts and kept helping these corrupt governments. This fact alone hurts the image of the West in this part of the world, and it gives the angry and upset young Muslim youth another reason to think that the West is lying when it talks about democracy. Muslims say that the West only cares about itself and will work with their abusers and back dictatorships to get what it wants.

So, my advice to the U.S. and the other Western countries is that they should rethink their foreign policies. They shouldn't have different rules for different people. Instead, they should be honest. They shouldn't be friends with dictator regimes. Instead, they should work to help the general interest of regular people by standing with them and helping them fight their cruel dictators. The best way to protect Western interests and improve the image of the United States and other Western countries in Muslim countries is to support the people, not these bad ruling families. This could be a great step toward finding a way to deal with the problem of extreme Islam.

Chapter 24
Al Qaeda: Background, Current Status, and U.S. Policy

Al Qaeda (AQ, also written as Al Qaida or Al Qa'eda) is a Sunni Islamist terrorist group that operates across borders and has a large network of branches. The group became famous around the world after the attacks in the United States on September 11, 2001 (9/11). Since then, the US and its allies have been working hard to stop terrorism, which has made the group weaker, especially in Afghanistan, where it has a history of being strong. For many years, U.S. officials and international observers have said that the major threat from AQ comes from the group's affiliates in Yemen and Africa. The U.S. Intelligence Community's 2024 Annual Threat Assessment (ATA) called Africa the "centre of gravity in the Sunni global jihad." However, it did not say that members of these groups were directly dangerous to the U.S. country. As directed and overseen by Congress, the U.S. has used military action, partnerships with other countries, sanctions, and law enforcement actions to fight Al-Qaeda.

Background

In 1988, Osama bin Laden formed Al Qaeda from a group of Arab and other foreign veterans of the U.S.-backed insurgency in Afghanistan against the Soviet Union. His goal was to support Islamist causes in wars all over the world. After the 1991 Gulf War, the group's main goal was to attack the United States because they didn't agree with Saudi Arabia's choice to house U.S. troops and for other reasons. That year, Bin Laden left his home country of Saudi Arabia for Sudan. He stayed there until the Taliban took over Afghanistan in 1996 and gave AQ members and other armed Islamists a safe place to live.

Before 9/11, Al Qaeda carried out terrorist attacks on U.S. and allied targets, such as the attacks on the USS Cole in Yemen in 2000 and the bombings of U.S. embassies in Kenya and Tanzania in 1998. After those attacks, the US began airstrikes against targets in Afghanistan and Sudan. Al Qaeda was named a Foreign Terrorist Organisation (FTO) by the US in 1999. After 9/11, the US used military action to remove the Taliban government from power in Afghanistan and grew its efforts to stop terrorism around the world. Some chiefs of AQ ran away to Pakistan, where Bin Laden was killed by US troops in 2011. In the years after 9/11, AQ continued to attack U.S. and Western targets around the world, but the group has not been able to pull off a big attack in the US since then.

Leadership

When Bin Laden died, Ayman al Zawahiri took over as head of AQ. He had been Bin Laden's deputy for more than ten years. As compared to Bin Laden's charisma, some onlookers said Zawahiri's quiet leadership was to blame for AQ's problems, such as its failure to launch an attack inside the United States. Others said that Zawahiri's more moderate approach was a good thing because it let AQ groups use methods that worked in their area and get involved in local communities. Zawahiri was killed by a U.S. drone strike in Kabul, Afghanistan, on July 31, 2022, but neither al-Qaeda nor the Taliban officially confirmed his death. Al-Qaeda hasn't said who will take over for Zawahiri either, but Sayf al Adl is seen as the group's real boss by the UN sanctions monitors and others. Reports say that Al Adl lives in Iran. Some AQ members are working in Iran, even though Sunni Al Qaeda and Iran's Shia Islamic Republic have a history of fighting. Leaders of AQ may think that Iran is not too vulnerable to U.S. counterterrorism efforts. On the other hand, leaders of Iran may see AQ's presence as a way to gain power over the U.S. and a chance to back another U.S. enemy.

Structure

Al-Qaeda used to be organised in a hierarchy, and its members were mostly small groups that lived in the same areas. The group has changed because the core leadership of AQ has weakened, regional allies have grown, and the Islamic State (IS) rose in 2014, putting AQ's claims to being the world leader in Islamist terrorism to the test.

Analysts have long argued over how to describe the changing ties between AQ leadership and groups that have sworn allegiance to it, as well as the links between these groups that say they are affiliated with AQ. The 2022 ATA says that AQ seems to have "shifted away from centrally directed plotting and given operational responsibility to regional affiliates." The traditional balance of power may have even been turned around, with the affiliates now giving the group's core leadership resources and legitimacy. The 2024 ATA said that AQ affiliates "on the African continent and Yemen will sustain the global network as the group maintains its strategic intent to target the United States and U.S. citizens." Al-Qaeda may continue to be a group that supports terrorist attacks around the world that are driven by ideology and takes advantage of local conflicts to get people to join or support them. If the balance of these parts of the group's character and structure changes, it may cause the U.S. to shift its focus on fighting terrorism over time.

Status in Afghanistan

Many things have changed for Al Qaeda since the Taliban took back power in Afghanistan in 2021. They have been friends for a long time, and in early 2024, U.N. sanctions monitors said that their "relationship remains strong," even though the Taliban were trying to "constrain some [AQ] activities." Regional governments told U.N. sanctions monitors that Al Qaeda "continues to pose a threat in the region and potentially beyond," but they also said that "the group cannot at present project sophisticated attacks at long range." This second opinion is mostly in line with what the U.S. government says, which is that Al Qaeda is at a "operational nadir" and is keeping a "low profile" in Afghanistan because the Taliban have told them not to do any "external operations and recruitment."

Select Global Affiliates

Events in the region, like the U.S. invasion of Iraq in 2003 and the chaos that hit some states after the Arab Spring protests in 2011, made it easier for AQ members to do business in the Middle East and North Africa. In Somalia and the Sahel area, affiliates have also taken advantage of civil wars and political crises.

- Abu Musab al Zarqawi, a Jordanian living in Iraq, started the first branch of al-Qaeda in 2004. It was called Al Qaeda in Iraq (AQI). AQI changed its name to the Islamic State of Iraq (ISI) in 2006. As things got less safe in Syria in 2011, AQI/ISI started working there as the Nusra Front. The Nusra Front quickly grew into one of Syria's most powerful armed forces. Abu Bakr al Baghdadi, head of AQI/ISI, tried to include the Nusra Front as part of the Islamic State of Iraq and Syria in 2013 (see CRS In Focus IF10328, The Islamic State: Background, Current Status, and U.S. Policy). Nusra and Al Qaeda did not agree with this plan. The Nusra Front joined with other groups in Syria in 2017 to form Hayat Tahrir al Sham (HTS). Idlib is in the northeastern part of Syria. The leaders of HTS have reportedly tried to separate themselves from AQ and have been attacking some Islamic State members in areas they control. Hurras al Din, a rival group that grew out of HTS, is seen as more like AQ and less strong than HTS.

- With help from the United States, Saudi Arabia was able to break up an AQ branch in the country by 2005, leaving only a few scattered groups. These groups joined with AQ members from Yemen in 2009 to form Al Qaeda in the Arabia Peninsula (AQAP), which was named an FTO that same year. Because of Yemen's turmoil and civil war after 2011, AQAP grew very quickly. It's possible that AQAP has tried more than any other AQ group to carry out and plan strikes in the US and Europe. The group is "in decline" because of ongoing pressure from the CT and problems within the group, but it "remains the most effective terrorist group in Yemen" and plans to carry out operations in the region and beyond. It is said that Sayf al-Adl's son lives in Yemen and "is close to AQAP leadership."
- As Al Qaeda's foreign reach grew with groups like AQAP joining, other groups with similar goals became interested in it. An FTO was named to the Somali group Al Shabaab in 2008. Its founders had ties to Al Qaeda, and in 2012, the group officially pledged its loyalty to AQ. In the middle of the 2000s, al Shabaab took over land in central and southern Somalia. Since then, they have attacked both domestic and foreign targets in Somalia and neighbouring countries. Officials in the U.S. have called the group the biggest and richest branch of Al Qaeda. With between 7,000 and 12,000 fighters, it allegedly brings in "over $100 million" a year. In August 2023, the Somali government began an offensive against Al Shabaab. This assault has "stalled" since then.
- Al Qaeda in the Islamic Maghreb (AQIM) began as a group during the civil war in Algeria in the 1990s. It swore loyalty to Al Qaeda and changed its name to AQIM in 2006 and 2007. After 2011, AQIM's centre of gravity went to the south and east, giving rise to a number of split groups and local affiliates. Even though AQIM has been less active in North Africa, some of its branches have grown stronger. JNIM, which stands for "Group for Supporting Islam and Muslims," is the most well-known. It was created in 2017 when AQIM's Sahel branch, a spinoff called Al Murabitoun, and two Mali-based groups came together. JNIM has been an FTO since 2018 and does most of its work in Mali and Burkina Faso, where military juntas have taken over, kicked out French counterterrorism troops, and made security ties with Russia stronger. JNIM has gone back and forth between a "localised detente" and direct fighting with the IS affiliate in the area. JNIM has also grown into some coastal countries in West Africa.

U.S. Policy Responses

The U.S. war against Al-Qaeda has been going on for ten years and covers a lot of different policy areas. Since 2012, the US has attacked AQ targets from the air in at least seven countries. The United States pulled its troops out of Afghanistan in 2021 and started Operation Enduring Sentinel, which is the goal of the U.S. to fight threats from inside Afghanistan "over the horizon" from outside of Afghanistan. In the beginning of that year, President Trump told U.S. troops to leave Somalia. In 2022, President Biden told them to be sent somewhere else. Before the coup in 2023, more than 1,000 U.S. troops were stationed in Niger to help with security, data gathering, surveillance, and reconnaissance. In April 2024, U.S. officials said they would be pulling their troops out because the ruling junta had broken the U.S. status of forces agreement.

The US wants to fight Al-Qaeda and other terrorist threats "by, with, and through" local partners. One way they do this is by helping with security and sometimes by providing logistical, information, and/or advice support. Some people have said that these kinds of efforts can't work without the U.S. troops being there. The United States also tries to improve the governance and civilian law enforcement of its partner states.

U.S. policymakers also try to fight Al Qaeda and other terrorist groups by focussing on the things that lead people to become extremists, by using sanctions and other tools to stop Al Qaeda and its affiliates from getting money, and by going after people in the US who help the group and its affiliates. Congress has dealt with the problem of AQ members staying around by keeping an eye on the executive branch's counterterrorism policies and procedures and by giving the president the power to authorise and spend U.S. money on counterterrorism activities. Congress talks about getting rid of or changing the 2001 Authorisation for the Use of Military Force (AUMF, P.L. 107-40) from time to time, which could affect U.S. efforts to fight Al Qaeda and its allies.

Chapter 25
Islamic Perspective: Terrorism and Human Rights

Introduction

The monk who used the word for the first time in French in 1355 brought it from Latin, where it originally meant fear and danger in a wide sense. By the French Revolution in the 1800s, the word "terror" had a more specific meaning. Back in the day, it meant that the government was oppressing the people. But as terrorism against the state has grown over the last thirty years, it has come to mean only actions against the state. At this point, terrorism is known to be any act of violence against harmless people that is done for political reasons and includes threats, intimidation, and coercion. There are two main reasons why this is done: to fight the government or to control the people by making them afraid. Exactly the opposite of what terrorism is supposed to do, the world has come together to create the idea of human rights to protect each person from these kinds of actions. These are the rights that everyone is born with and must have, no matter what race, religion, or disability they have. They are based on respect, dignity, fairness, equality, and freedom. To Muslims, terrorism is a very bad thing that goes against basic human rights. Human rights are protected by Islamic law, and they are given a lot of importance. Many people in the modern world doubt that Islam is a faith that supports terrorism because of the many theories and beliefs that surround it. There is a lot of truth to these untrue beliefs, but they come from extremists misinterpreting Islamic teachings and global agencies only looking out for their own interests.

In the next part, we'll talk about these false beliefs by looking at what Islam says about terrorism and how important human rights are. Additionally, the impacts of terrorism on basic human rights and the ways that Islamic laws and other laws can help get rid of terrorism will be talked about. Before getting to the main point of the talk, it's important to take a look at the main types of terrorism that are in use around the world right now.

Types of Terrorism

Here are some of the most common types of terrorism in the world today.

State Sponsored Terrorism

Terrorist attacks like these are carried out by one country against another for political reasons. Taking a close look at what's going on in Kashmir and Palestine shows that these situations are definitely state-sponsored terrorism. It also makes sense that behind most big crimes, there is a bigger hand running the show. Those hands are usually states supporting and helping these kinds of activities through organisations in exchange for political gain, and Iran is the worst at this.

Dissent Terrorism

This kind of terrorism is caused by terrorist groups that have broken away from their government. There is a lot of dissent terrorism in Yemen, and there has been for a year in Afghanistan as well. But there are also groups in Pakistan that don't support the country. This is especially true in Balochistan, where there have been rebel movements in the past.

Religious Terrorism

This is done by terrorist groups that are very religious and don't like people of other religions. Indian Hindu extremists have used this kind of terrorism many times, like in the Hashimpura slaughter, in which 42 Muslims were killed.

Criminal Terrorism

Acts like these are terrorism because they are used to help crime and make money for criminals. One example would be using violence to put pressure on the government to free prisoners who have been guilty.

Islamic Perspective on Terrorism

At first, there was no word for "terrorism" in Arabic dictionaries. Because of this, we can't find clear proof of terrorism. Instead, we have to use interpretation. In the same way, there was an idea called Hirabah, which means illegal war against innocent people. Terrorism is called Hirabah by Muslim lawyers because it is against the law in Islam.

Law of Hirabah (Terrorism)

A category called "Hirabah" is used to describe horrible acts that are done for political reasons. These are the worst kinds of crimes because they put people's lives, property, and honour at risk. Hiraba is based on a verse in the Quran that says:

> *"Those who fight against Allah and His Messenger and try to cause trouble in the land will be put to death, nailed to a cross, have their hands and feet cut off from opposite sides, or be sent away from the land."*

Crimes that fall under Hirabah are seen as war against Allah, so they are punished harshly according to the Quran. At first, it only applied to highway robbery, but later, Muslim jurists added modern terrorists to the list of crimes covered by Hirabah. An act of terrorising people is what Hirabah is all about, and highway robbery is a type of terrorism.

Evidences against violence and terror

This is the name of a faith that teaches people to be good and kind, and its main goal is to spread peace throughout society. It tightly forbids unprovoked violence because the Quran says that starting a fight, violating other people's rights, or hurting innocent people is wrong. For the sake of progress, Islamic law also forbids damaging or cutting down animals or trees. There are many verses in the Quran and sayings of Prophet Muhammad (S.A.W.) that condemn all kinds of bloodshed, which is what terrorism is all about. In the Quran, Allah says that killing someone is illegal unless there is a good reason. And to protect life, Islam has the law of revenge, which says that one life for another life. A huge number of innocent people are killed by terrorism. As a Muslim, if someone they kill is harmless, they have broken the law, but they can't blame Islam for what they did. Shariah's second goal is to protect and preserve life for the safety of all living things. Also, the Holy Prophet said:

> *"Those who torture others in real life will be tortured by God on the day of judgement." Islam is very against any kind of harm to people, and it has very harsh sentences for people who do this. These are some of the rules and conditions: First, Muslims can't start a war before it happens. War can only be used to protect yourself. Allah only lets Muslims fight back when they are being mistreated and forced to leave their homes. If these kinds of wars are necessary, the Quran also sets limits on them. These are the duty of the state, not the citizens.*

Terrorism and Islamophobia

People who are not Muslim and hate Islam are said to have "Islamophobia." This is a form of discrimination that made people angry in the United States after the 9/11 terrorist attacks. It is not Muslims who cause Islamophobia; it is the world media and extremist Muslims who do the misrepresenting. 9/11 made people more hostile towards Muslims, and Muslims had to suffer all over the world. In the United States, this hate was called love for their country. The start of this was when radical groups called what they did "jihad," which is a subject in Islam. To explain their actions, they took the wrong meanings from texts in the Quran that talk about Jihad. They were seen as part of Islam by most people because of how they behaved. People who aren't Muslim started to think that this was normal in Islam and began to hate it as a cruel religion. In Islam, jihad is a way for the people to protect themselves from the abuse of the ruling class. Terrorism, on the other hand, is when someone or a group uses violent methods to scare and terrorise a large group of people. Extremists have linked attacks to Jihad. Due to false information like this, Jihad and terrorists need to be set apart.

Jihad and Terrorism

"To strive" is where the word "Jihad" comes from. It is a fight to protect one's faith, country, family, or a human life. It can come in many forms, including a battle against bad habits that you have to beat in order to get better. It has nothing to do with or support the killing of innocent people and sending them away. This idea is wrong because terrorism always targets harmless people and causes them pain. It is the illegal use of violence or force for political or moral reasons. Jihad does not allow the killing of civilians, children, adults, and women who are not fighting, which is what terrorism does. A well-known supporter of Shariah, Dr. Aslam Khaki, says that jihad is "defence of state by state for state." Based on this description, it is clear that terrorism does not belong to Jihad. Terrorists who fight wars in the name of Jihad today are not really practicing jihad; they are breaking the law of Hirabah.

Anti-extremism efforts are needed to teach people the right way to follow Islam instead of the radical ideas that terrorists believe in.

Human Rights in Islam

From an Islamic point of view, human rights are rights that God has given us. They were not made by the legislative body or any king. Since these rights come straight from God, they can't be taken away by any government or legislative body. No one has the power to terminate or withdraw these rights.

Islamic law doesn't make any distinctions between races, groups of people, or colours. It treats all people with care. On his last trip to Makkah, Prophet Muhammad (S.A.W.) set this rule by telling the people, "Your God is one and your father is one. Because of this, do not favour an Arab over a non-Arab or a non-Arab over an Arab, or red over black or black over red, except for the most righteous." God sees all men as equal, even if they have different skills, potentials, goals, wealth, and other things. These differences cannot, by themselves, make one man better than another. God only looks at how good and spiritually excellent someone is as a measure of their superiority. Based on equality, this means that all guys have the same human rights. Here are some of the most important human rights, along with Islamic law's ways of protecting and keeping these rights.

Right to Life

Man has the right to honour and respect because everyone is equal. Every effort must be made to protect human life because it is holy and cannot be taken away. In the Quran, Allah says not to kill the soul, which is against His will. People who break this rule will be punished severely in Islam. In the Quran, Allah Almighty says that anyone who kills a Muslim on purpose will go to Hell and stay there forever. When Allah sees him, he gets mad, curses him, and plans a very bad sentence for him.

In addition, many true hadiths say that killing is one of the worst sins. Holy Prophet said that killing a follower without a good reason would be more important to Allah than the end of the world. In another hadith, the Prophet says that Allah would punish everyone who helped kill a Muslim by sending them to the Fire. All of these things show that the right to life is completely protected in Islam.

Right to Freedom

Because Allah Almighty made man free at birth, no one should be able to take away his right to freedom without a good reason. Islam says that everyone has the right to be free in all ways, including politically, economically, culturally, and physically. The right to freedom of religion, freedom of thought and speech, and freedom to move around are all included in this broad term. While talking about religion, the Holy Quran says that there is no such thing as force in religion. A lot of texts in the Quran show that people are free and don't have to follow anyone else's will but Allah's. In everything, man is free to do what he wants, and Islam has only told him what is good for him.

Right to Protection against torture

Torture is when someone is hurt physically or mentally, usually by someone in power trying to get them to confess. In Islam, torture is not allowed, and the Holy Prophet said that those who beat others will be tortured by God in the next life. No person shall be tortured in any way, not just mentally. The Quran makes it clear that arresting or detaining people without a reason is torture, and if a criminal process breaks this rule, it is no longer legal. Islam says that anyone who is charged has the right to a quick and fair trial by a judge who can protect them from being tortured or detained illegally. As Allah orders, the accused can defend himself for justice. This is because Allah wants justice, doing good, and being kind to family and friends. He says that all dishonourable actions, injustice, and defiance are wrong.

Right of Social Security

From the beginning, Islam has been about meeting the basic social needs of everyone, especially those who can't meet their own. In Islam, zakat was the first thing that was set up to help people in need. In Islam, it was the State's job to collect zakat and make sure it got to the people who deserved it. People who believe in this system say that not paying zakat is the same as going to war with the State. In Islam, both wealthy people in the community and the government are expected to help poor people. For example, the Prophet said that if someone in a community goes to sleep hungry and wakes up hungry the next morning, Allah will take away His protection from that community. Additionally, Islam says that it is the state's job to protect society from anything that could be harmful and to meet people's basic wants.

The Islamic view of human rights is broad and clear, and it strikes the perfect balance between rights and responsibilities. In Islam, each person has a unique set of responsibilities. It also sets up a full legal system for protecting and preserving basic human rights.

Effects of Terrorism on Human Rights

When you look at both terrorism and human rights from an Islamic point of view, it's clear that they are connected. The harm that terrorism does to human rights is also proof that it is illegal in Islam and other religions. On the list below are some of the ways that terrorism violates human rights. There are effects that happen directly because of a terrorist act and effects that happen because of efforts and systems set up to fight terrorism.

Direct influence

Terrorism spreads fear and terror and goes against human rights that protect peace and safety. These things have forced the State to spend money to fight terrorism, which hurts the State's budget. This effect lowers the standards of social, economic, and artistic life, all of which are human rights. Kidnapping and holding people hostage are acts of terrorism that violate the human right to safe personal freedom and the freedom to move around. People have the natural right to life, which is attacked by murder. Life is the source of all other rights. A lot of people's rights are taken away by a single evil act. Unfortunately, terrorism doesn't follow the rules, so it gives people who aren't involved in the fight the right to vote. Terrorists attack harmless people to scare people in power into changing their policies so that terrorists can achieve their goals. An rising number of innocent people are being killed in terrorist attacks that spread violence and fear, which can never be justified, according to the United Nations and other international groups. It's clear that these actions violate human rights and hurt the health of civil society.

Counter Terrorism and Human Rights

In order to fight terrorism, states are forced to do things that violate basic human rights, like the right to move around freely and not be detained without a warrant. Because terrorist acts are so serious, people are forced to go through processes that would normally be against their human rights in order to fight terrorism. Government officials sometimes use these steps in a bad way to help themselves. To protect basic human rights, the European Convention on Human Rights set up the Human Rights European Committee and the European Court of Human Rights. These bodies set up borders and limits on the powers of states in the fight against terrorism. It says that states must defend the basic rights of their citizens by not torturing or otherwise injuring them, and it requires them to do so.

In some parts of the world, rules against terrorism make people angry and encourage extremism and bias against certain religious groups. This led to violations of the human rights of minorities, like the rise of Islamophobia in the US after 9/11. The United States used the idea of secret proof to deport immigrants as a way to fight terrorism. The government has a lot of power to call any group terrorist. They added the idea of "guilt by participation," which meant that anyone with even a small link to terrorist groups would be punished, even if they were working with the groups without knowing why or for good reasons. In the name of national security, these kinds of rules and laws take away people's freedoms.

The idea behind it is that the government shouldn't hurt democracy, not even when it's trying to protect it. To fight terrorists, we need to find a balance between protecting individual rights and a democratic society. In 1987, a report on the case of Teren Ce Broyan and others showed that in order to protect society as a whole, the fight against terrorism sometimes needs sacrifices from every individual. It raised the amount of time someone could be detained before their hearing for terrorism from four days to five days. The 1996 Convention on Extradition between the States of the European Union does not allow extradition if the request is made so that a person can be tried or punished because of their race, religion, nationality, political views, or legal status.

In order to fight terrorism, European conventions said what had to be done. They also said that if a threat came from another state that was a party to the convention, that state had to take extra steps that weren't in the convention and sometimes went against other international law obligations. Governments are supposed to keep their people safe from attacks by extremists, but they need to make sure that all methods they use to fight terrorism don't violate human rights. International Organisations for Human Rights keeps an eye on what governments do to fight violent terrorism to make sure they don't violate people's rights to life and to be free from torture and other bad treatment.

Eradicating Terrorism

To get rid of terrorism, both international and state systems have been used, but there needs to be a balance between the counter-terrorism act and violating human rights. The steps that states usually agree on to get rid of terrorism from the world are listed below. Sites and news sources that spread hate speech, call for violence, or discrimination should be taken down after a proper check. The Counterterrorism Alert System was created so that the government would know about terrorist dangers quickly and be able to stop them before any damage is done. People who might be terrorist threats are watched by many groups around the world, including the cops in your own country. To stop terrorists from getting money, proper tracking of financial transactions has been put in place. With the help of new technology, states are always working to make their intelligence and security services better. The national and foreign terrorism list is used to keep track of people and groups that are involved in terrorist activities. Terrorist acts are also crimes that carry harsh punishments for those who commit them. To show how serious this crime is, the sentence for a crime that is similar to terrorism is tougher than the sentences for other crimes. Pakistan and the UN Office on Drugs and Crime have worked together to make Pakistan's Action to Counter Terrorism with a Special Reference to Khyber

Pakhtunkhwa official. The major goal is to improve the steps used in terrorism cases, including pre-investigations, investigations, prosecutions, and decisions. It is the goal of the project to improve the skills and understanding of police officers, prosecutors, and judges. It is also trying to make it easier for provincial and federal governments to work together. This has led to the creation of the National Counter Terrorism Authority (NACTA), the Counter Terrorism Department (CTD) of the Khyber Pakhtunkhwa Police, and the Islamabad Capital Territory (ICT) Police, among others.

Conclusion

After reading the chapter, it is clear that Islam is a faith that values peace and does not allow acts of terrorism. Terrorism is the worst kind of violence, and even small acts of violence that hurt one person are against Islam. It's not terrorism at all; jihad is a way to fight terrorism, which is the job of the government, not the people who live in it. Also, it's clear that Islam protects human rights completely, while terrorism directly threatens life, physical purity, and safety, taking away those rights. The least likely outcomes are states being attacked by terrorists, which limits people's basic rights like freedom of speech, freedom of movement, freedom of thought, and so on. There have been countless acts of terrorism throughout history. Many people have worked hard to get rid of it, but more needs to be done. Instead of pointing fingers, everyone needs to work together to protect human rights completely.

Chapter 26
Islamic State-Khorasan: global jihad's new front

139 people were killed in an attack on the Crocus City Hall in Krasnogorsk on March 22, which was another dramatic terrorist attack by Islamic State-Khorasan (ISIS-K) in the past few months. Attacks have already happened in Iran, Turkey, and other places. Attacks that were planned in Germany, Sweden, and other places were stopped. These events show that the group has changed its plan, which was mainly focused on Afghanistan until recently. They also say that ISIS-K has a lot of ability to make threats. One unique thing about the current situation is how quickly more people from post-Soviet Central Asian states (especially Tajikistan) are joining. But this is mostly because of things that happen in Russia itself that make people more extreme. There is a high chance that new acts will be planned or inspired by ISIS-K.

A historical perspective

Islamic State-Khorasan is a terrorist group with extreme Islamic beliefs. It was officially formed in January 2015 as one of the regional branches of Islamic State that worked in Syria and Iraq. At first, its main goal was to organise the sending of troops to Syria, where they would later set up independent groups in Afghanistan. ISIS-K was started by radicals in Pakistan and Afghanistan, including members of the Taliban and other terrorist groups. People from outside of Afghanistan who fought, like Uzbeks from the Islamic Movement of Uzbekistan and the Islamic Jihad Union, Uyghurs, and volunteers from South Asia, and people from other Afghan ethnic groups, like Tajiks, Uzbeks, and Balochis, have been important parts of the organization's membership since the beginning. ISIS-K, like other Islamic terrorist groups like al-Qaeda, was made up of smaller, independent groups and branches of other radical groups that worked together and fought to take control of them permanently.

When it came to philosophy, ISIS-K stuck to the rules set by Islamic State's main office in Syria. It backs the establishment and growth of a global state that would follow strict (Salafi) rules and wage a worldwide war against those who are against "pure Islam." In a real sense, this group includes all states, but mostly

Western ones, like the US. ISIS-K mostly went after the Afghan government, the coalition troops in Afghanistan, and places that got money from them, like schools for girls. People with different ideas, especially Shia Muslims, have also been attacked by the group a lot. It was not easy for ISIS-K to get along with groups connected to al-Qaeda (IS formed after a split in al-Qaeda's organisation) and the Taliban at first, and things got even worse over time. When it came to the Taliban, the fighting was caused by both their desire for power in Afghanistan and disagreements over strategy. It was and still is important to the Taliban to create a state that is accepted by other countries. They have had political talks with the US and other countries.

Insurgency groups called ISIS-K spent most of their time fighting in Afghanistan and Pakistan. Its main bases were in the eastern and north-eastern parts of Afghanistan. As time went on, this area grew to include the northern provinces, where Tajiks and Uzbeks mostly lived, as well as the provinces that bordered Central Asia after the fall of the Soviet Union. These areas gave people land, a way to find work, and money. The group got money from a variety of sources, such as funding from the Syrian HQ, foreign sponsors, and illegal activities. Its main sources of funding were "taxes" from the local people and taking control of mines and roads. Several thousand fighters and their families were thought to be part of ISIS-K in 2018, its busiest year. While the group was still active, its main activities included attacks on Afghan and coalition forces, like the huge attack on Kabul airport in August 2021, and bombings in Afghanistan and Pakistan that targeted schools, Shia mosques, and other places, often by suicide bombers. ISIS-K was the most violent and radical group working in Afghanistan, but its activities outside of Afghanistan and Pakistan, such as in Central Asia, Russia (among migrants), Western Europe, and Turkey, were not widely known. This mostly meant getting new members, raising small amounts of money, and keeping lines of contact open with Syria (through Turkey).

The government of the Islamic Republic of Afghanistan, which was backed by the West, fell apart in 2021. ISIS-K continued to attack Shia Hazaras, schools, and other places. It also attacked international targets, like the Russian consulate in Kabul, the Pakistani charge d'affaires, and a hotel where Chinese businessmen were staying. In 2022, it launched several rocket attacks on Uzbekistan and Tajikistan. However, the most important thing was that it kept fighting the Taliban, which made it much less likely to do other things. According to estimates, the organisation probably has a few hundred fighters right now. Including the fighters' families, this group may have a total of about 4000 people. A lot of its power has been lost in the eastern part of the country, but it hasn't changed where it stands in the north. It has also tried to strengthen its place in cities. A rising trend of Tajiks, Uzbeks, and people from other countries joining the group has been seen. But its leader, Sanaullah Ghafari, is an Afghan with Indian roots and is the emir. Its leaders are Afghan and Pakistani Pashtuns. It's hard to say how much cooperation there is with the IS headquarters in Syria, but it does happen and is important. There is no question, though, that it has gone down a lot since IS was defeated in Syria around 2019.

Islamic State-Khorasan: a new incarnation

After the Taliban took back power in Afghanistan in 2021, ISIS-K's potential dropped significantly. This is likely the main reason why the group is changing the way it operates now. After the war in the Gaza Strip started in October 2023, things became less stable in the Middle East, which seems to have pushed this change even further. Because of the first event, ISIS-K has had to look for help and strengthen its position outside of Afghanistan. This has made it possible for Islamic terrorists, their supporters, and those who fund them to work together. Because of this, there has been a return of IS abroad in the form of terrorist acts. This may help its reputation and get the attention of donors and volunteers.

According to what ISIS-K has said and what its leaders have said, the group has carried out several large-scale attacks in the past few months. On January 3, 94 people were killed in an attack in Kerman, Iran, marking the anniversary of Qasem Soleimani's death, and on January 28, one person was killed in an attack on a Catholic church in Istanbul. It also said it was behind the attack on Krasnogorsk's Crocus City Hall on March 22, in which at least 139 people were killed. Every single one of these acts shows what the group believes in: Iran is a Shia state, and all of the countries that were hit were fighting IS in Syria, Afghanistan, or their own countries. All of these countries are seen as heretics or pagan enemies of the caliphate.

The number of people arrested on suspicion of having ties to ISIS-K can be seen as a secondary sign of how active this group is. Iranians (several times in the summer of 2023), Germans (in July and August 2023, later in December 2023 in connection with a planned attack in Cologne, and in March 2024 for a planned attack on the Swedish parliament), Russians (including the killing of two Kazakhs accused of planning an attack on a Moscow synagogue the day before the 22 March attack), and especially Turks (692 people suspected of having ties to IS and ISIS-K have been arrested since June 2023, including 40 people after the Krasnogorsk attack).

Doubts surrounding Islamic State-Khorasan

Some people aren't sure if ISIS-K really carried out the killings that were reported. The official stories from both Iran and Russia say that the group's actions may have been influenced by the US and Israel (the attack in Kerman) and the US and Ukraine (the attack in Krasnogorsk). In a different situation, Russia's police should be blamed for the second attack; this is said to be a sign of greater competition among the country's elite. Concerning the most recent attack in Russia, there are a lot of things that make me very sceptical. These include how easily it was carried out, how professional the attackers were during the attack but how awkward they were while trying to escape, how unclear the circumstances of their capture were, how much evidence was used to show that people who were presented as terrorists were involved in the attack, and how reliable the testimony they gave after being tortured (which was filmed). There are many different ideas about what happened. Some are very political and sound like propaganda. Others are based on guesses that are hard or impossible to prove for sure. There are no strong arguments in any of these ideas that ISIS-K wasn't involved in the attacks in Kerman, Istanbul, and most importantly, Krasnogorsk, even if their role was small. The specifics of these events are still unknown, though. There is still a chance that the organization's activities were managed or filtered by the secret services of outside players. But it's hard to deny that ISIS-K's goals and power have grown, or that it has "succeeded" politically and in the eyes of extreme Islamic groups.

The group's actions over the past few months show that it has moved some of its activities to places other than Afghanistan. It did this because it lost the war with the Taliban and because it wants to hire more people and get more money. ISIS-K has also shown that it can work in a wide range of situations, from Iran to Turkey and Russia to Western Europe. It has also created a good way to reach and interact with Central Asian migrant groups. In light of how IS has been working so far, the "lack of professionalism" of the attackers (the rifles used by the attackers in Istanbul were said to have jammed; both these attackers and those at Krasnogorsk were successfully detained) and the fact that suicide attacks have stopped happening (in both Istanbul and Krasnogorsk) are interesting. What this means is that the attackers may have come from groups that were not part of the main groups of these organisations. This could mean that they were less prepared and didn't have as strong of an ideology. They may have also been motivated by money, which was a big issue in the Krasnogorsk attack. This probably has to do with the fact that ISIS-K is short-staffed and wants to improve its security by doing things like lowering the risk of maintaining large structures and setting up long training and indoctrination times for new members. This might also be important for growing the pool of people who can be hired. ISIS-K seems to have grown and strengthened its position with the help of all of these factors.

The problem of terrorists hailing from Central Asia

One thing that makes this case unique is that a lot of the ISIS-K attackers are Tajiks. Other people from Uzbekistan, Kazakhstan, Kyrgyzstan, and Turkmenistan have also been arrested. Extremist groups have had people from this area involved for a long time. Islamic radicalism has shown up in Central Asia on a small scale before. For example, during the civil war in Tajikistan (1992–1977), the Islamic Movement of Uzbekistan and the Islamic Jihad Union were active, and there were also a few terrorist attacks in this part of the world, the most recent of which happened in 2016. Two thousand to five thousand people from this area were involved with Islamic State and other similar groups in Syria and Iraq from 2011 to 2009. Terrorist attacks were carried out by people from Central Asia in the US (2013), Turkey (2015, 2016, 2017), Sweden (2017), and both Russia and Sweden (2018). They were also involved in planning several attacks that did not happen in Germany. The culture and political conditions in Central Asia were good for radical Islam, which helped it grow. People joined the movement because it looked like a way to fix the bad economies and dictatorial governments in those countries. It never really took off, though, and most people in the area didn't back it. Central Asia's strong social conservatism and the fact that the local governments' large security forces paid a lot of attention to this problem also slowed its growth.

The uniqueness of this problem, which ISIS-K has cleverly used to its benefit, seems to be the large-scale economic migration from this area, mostly to Russia. In a strange way, that's where Tajiks and people from other countries are becoming more radicalised. In Russia, it's easier to find radical material, and there isn't as much social control as there is in Central Asian countries. Extremism is fed by anger caused by feeling alone and having a hard time adjusting to a new environment. Being discriminated against by the Russian government, police, and people who live there is another very big problem. After Russia invaded Ukraine, all of these things got worse. People who have fled their homes are being sent to the occupied areas or forced to join the Russian military. So far, almost all of the attackers from Central Asia became more extreme while they were in Russia. A smaller version of the same problem has happened in Turkey, which is another popular place for people to move for work, though most of these people are from Turkic countries in the region. At the same time, Turkey has been getting a lot of radicals from Western Europe, Syria, and Iraq. It looks like ISIS-K has specifically targeted Tajiks and people from their neighborsing countries in Central Asia. This is because this group is lonely, angry, and open to both a radical form of Islam and the chance to make quick money. It is also culturally and linguistically available to the organization's Tajik and Uzbek recruiters who work in Afghanistan.

Outlook

The current rise in activity by ISIS-K (and IS as a whole) is likely the result of both a deliberate change in the group's strategy and a response to events happening around the world, such as the worsening of the crisis in the Middle East, and issues happening in society, such as the difficulties Central Asian migrants face in Russia. People should think that there is a high chance that the group will launch more strikes. Even though there are questions about the attack in Krasnogorsk, this is especially true in Russia, where the current situation is very good for making things worse and could help ISIS-K expand its operating space. And finally, Turkey is another country that IS can directly attack. Getting rid of ISIS-K from Afghanistan (which is theoretically possible but unlikely because it would require determination from the Taliban and unofficial support from outside actors) along with dismantling all of its foreign structures would only seem like a temporary fix because the problem is systemic and groups like ISIS-K can change. The activities of ISIS-K and other radical and terrorist groups in general are making it easier for the secret services of many countries, especially Russia, to control and work with these groups for their own domestic and international political goals. This makes the problems that the radicals cause much worse.

The latest actions of terrorists from Central Asia, especially Tajikistan, are something that could make things less stable in the post-Soviet states. In Central Asia, people can expect more control and repression because of the danger of radicalism. The Russian Federation will also try to put pressure on these countries to let it get more involved in their security issues. But the fact that more and more Russians are publicly hostile towards economic migrants from Central Asia could be a bigger problem. This is because it could lead to tensions, pogroms, and more stress for the refugees who are already under a lot of it. It's possible that this will make them feel even more alone and angry, and it could hurt Russia and the Russian people in Central Asian states even more.

Chapter 27

More than to the West, Islamic Terrorism and Islamism is of immense threat to Africa

Abstract

There are already a lot of academic studies that talk about terrorism in Africa, how it works, and how it has changed the political and economic systems of African countries. So, the point of this review is to look at the terror threats from Islamism and Islamic extremism through the lens of their actions and ideas that are against the West and the United States. Because western cultures, beliefs, and ways of life have a big impact on Africa, it will always be a place where international terrorist groups want to live and work. These terrorist groups are especially interested in west Africa and the Sahel region of Africa right now, and the fact that they are doing more and more in these areas is scary. It will become a hard monster to stop if it isn't checked and dealt with right away. So, the researcher will look at how their operations work, from their ideas and beliefs to the ways they attack, from Al-Qaeda's political and ideological legacy to radicalisation, and show how each of these things is related to how Islamic terrorism works in African cultures. After that, suggestions will be made, such as using data mining in the fight against terrorism to find strange trends, dishonest actions, and common traits among radicals, as this chapter shows. To build and develop diverse but thriving African communities and avoid divisions, sectionalism, and the dangers of extremism that usually lead to terrorism, it is also important to have strategies for "whistleblowing" and "integration."

Introduction

Today, people in Africa still have to deal with horrible crimes against humanity. African communities and states are being destroyed by crimes like genocide, ethnic cleansing, mass rapes, and more. These crimes are planned and carried out by both state and non-state players. At the same time, Islamist-inspired international terrorism has spread to and across the continent. Saudi Arabia's support for the construction of Islamic worship places in African nations like Niger, Nigeria, Mali, and others creates chances for the Salafi branch of Islam to spread its ideas. The Salafi branch is a very small part of Islam as shown in Figure 1.

Figure 1: The Salafi Component of the Sunni Faction of Islam

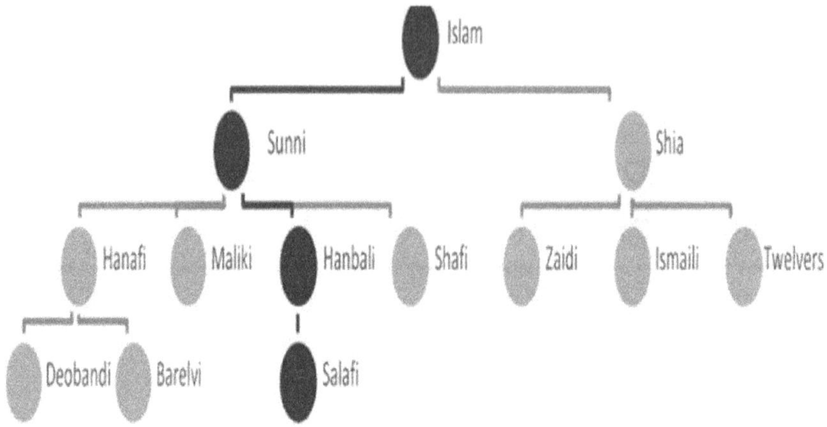

Photo Credit:protectuk.police.uk/threat-risk/threat-analysis/threat-islamist-terrorism

Over the years, this act has been closely linked to radicalisation and wars in Africa because so many young people are unemployed and the government isn't running things well. Because of these two things, there is a big hole for Salafist groups to fill and offer social services, which is why they have gained the support and love of upset groups. When Salafist ideas are used to define an enemy of Islam and explain why violence against them is necessary, anti-Christian violence is made holy and okay. Because of this, Boko Haram has killed about 50,000 people and forced more than 2.5 million to leave their homes in Nigeria from the group's start in 2002 to 2022.

Al-Shabaab has killed at least 4,000 citizens in Somalia from 2010 to 2019. From 2018 to 2021, Islamist rebels in Northern Mozambique killed at least 2,600 people. Several groups with ties to Al-Qaeda and the Islamic State have claimed responsibility for tens of thousands of other deaths in Africa. There is also a lot of evidence that terrorism makes it much harder for people in places like Nigeria to deal with their mental health. It's a shame that these Islamist groups are continuing to grow and spread, gain power, and have more freedom to operate on the continent. Like, the number of attacks by Islamist terrorists on African people has gone from 17% in 2017 to about 47% in June 2020. So, it's high time that jihadist terror groups spread across the continent and their actions are tracked so that possible anti-terror operations can be planned across the continent. If not, this monster will grow and become impossible to stop or reverse.

This review is not meant to argue against Islam. Instead, it is meant to show that Islamic violence and, by extension, terrorism are still very dangerous, not just to the west but also to Africa. The political and ideological factors, the legacy of Al-Qaeda that has been taken up by new terror groups around the world, the ease with which terrorists can join, and the radicalisation of citizens in western states will be talked about in more detail. These factors, which are still at play, either keep the potential for terror alive or keep terrorism alive, which makes it a threat to western societies and influences. There will also be suggestions for strategies like data mining, blowing the whistle, and integration that can help stop the trend towards segregation, sectionalization, and division that can lead to extreme views and, finally, terrorist activities.

Methods and Data

We looked for the words "Islamic terror threat," "Islamic terrorism," and "radicalisation" in eight academic databases that have a lot of works on the same topic, as well as in two "grey literature" databases. Some of these sites are Oxford University Press, Proquest, Research Gate, SAGE Publications, Springer, Taylor and Francis, Wiley Online Library, and Grey Literature: Google and Google Scholar. Based on titles that were similar, 299 papers were looked up. There were 299 articles in this collection. A quick look at the summary, introduction, and conclusion of these articles showed that 88 were duplicates and 103 had nothing to do with the theme of the chapter. Out of the last 112 articles, 17 were not released in English, so only 91 were included in this chapter.

Discussion

Origin of Islamic Terror in Africa

Some people think that Islamic terrorism began in Africa after the Soviet-Afghan war from 1979 to 1989. Algeria, Egypt, and Sudan were among the North African countries that sent soldiers to fight with the Afghan Mujahideen against the USSR in this war. When they got back to their home countries after the war, they brought violent fundamentalist ideas with them. The first was the Pro-Palestine Liberation Organization's bombing of the Jewish-owned Norfolk Hotel in Nairobi, Kenya, in 1980. The second was the civil war in Algeria between Islamists and the government that lasted from 1991 to 2002. Islamic terrorism kept spreading into Africa, but it wasn't until the 21st century that it really made a difference. That's when well-known global terror groups like Al-Qaeda and ISIS became very interested in the continent, moving their operations from the Middle East, South Central Asia, and even the North Caucasus of Africa to the Sahel and Lake Chad Basin regions.

The Ideological Factor

Huntington wrote in 1998 that the biggest threat to world peace is the fight between Islam and the West that is caused by a global "Islamic Resurgence," or a fundamental change of Islam in a more militant, sectarian, and anti-Western direction. Modern Imams have made this clash of civilisations worse by calling for a strong fight against all kinds of American and western impact, whether it's social, political, or moral. The idea that these extremists talk about—that westernisation causes anxiety, chaos, and, in turn, the loss of Muslim identity—has been a useful tool for most Muslim worshippers.

Figure 2: The Salafi Run Jihadi Groups as Extremist Islamic groups

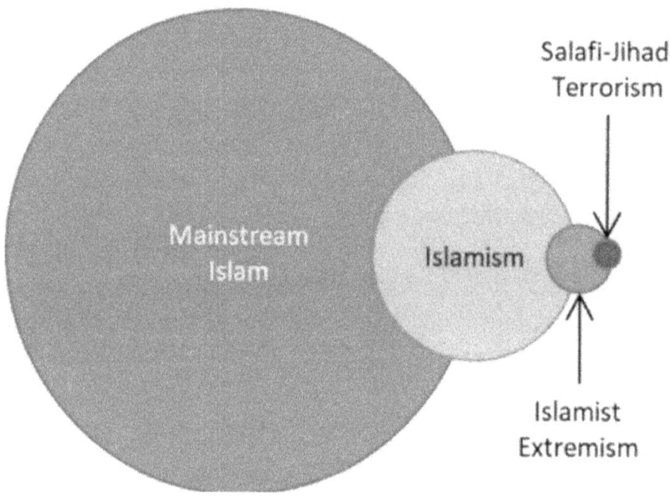

Photo Credit:protectuk.police.uk/threat-risk/threat-analysis/threat-islamist-terrorism

As you can see in Figure 1 and Figure 2, Islam is not a "single-unique entity." There is no separate faith or political group that speaks for all Muslims around the world. But because a lot of Muslims, whether they are radical or moderate, think that Western culture is immoral, materialistic, decadent, and seductive, militant Islamic fundamentalists take advantage of this to make people hate and anger the west because they see it as anti-Islam. This means they fight against human rights and democracy because they think they are in conflict with how the Qur'an is interpreted.

Because extremists say that Islam is spiritually revealed and not a law, it can never be democratic, pluralistic, egalitarian, or pro-Western. The Universal Declaration of Human Rights and any other policy or deal that lets people choose their own way of life must be very different from Islam. Making Islam any of these things only means stretching, reforming, changing, or getting rid of it. Because of this, liberal democracy needs to be strongly rejected. In this way, the Islamic state is basically one that is run by God, which is different from, say, Christianity, where the church and clergy run the holy state. Anything that goes against the autocratic and theocratic spirit of Islam is totally against it, and going against Islam is the same as going against God. When you disobey God, bad things happen.

These things work together to make a harmful ideology that is easy for even moderate Imams to teach and spread. This makes it easier for regular Muslims to support and agree with Islamic militancy and extremism. But because of this, it is very hard for the majority of Muslims to effectively fight extremists on their own cultural, religious, and intellectual ground. This makes the connection between religion, politics, and the Muslim state stronger instead of weaker. As time goes on, a long-lasting "reluctance" to fight extremists grows. It's hard to keep terrorists and extremists in one place so that you can closely watch them or bring them to justice when there is real fear.

Sir Mark Rowley, who used to be the Metropolitan Police Commissioner in the UK, agreed. He said that it was like trying to find "a needle in a haystack" when trying to find an Islamic terrorist, even though the UK already has a very well developed system and network for fighting terrorism. He said that thousands are being investigated in less important ways, and tens of thousands are not being investigated at all but have shown some kind of support for terrorists. As more people become sympathetic to radical Islam, it will become harder to tell who is truly extreme. This is something that the west should be very worried about.

The Sahel area of Africa is where Al-Qaeda and the Islamic State especially like to fight. Armed fights between these two terror groups have caused five times as many deaths in Burkina Faso, Mali, and Niger between 2016 and 2020, which is a record number of deaths. Most of these fights are between the Islamic State in the Greater Sahara (ISGS) and the Jamaat Nasr al-Islam wal Muslimi (JNIM), which is linked to Al-Qaeda. They are competing for resources, to recruit locals, and to control areas where they can operate. There have been civilian deaths in the open fighting between the two groups, but many people in the area still support one or the other. This backing for competition will only lead to worse things happening in the future.

Political Factor

The political drive behind Islamic terrorists is anger, which pushes them to take on the duty of vengeance. Terrorists from the Middle East began to hate America because of politics. This is a real threat that has spread to African cultures. Anti-

Americanism may have its roots in the unfair effects of U.S. foreign policy and the desire of Islamists to establish an Islamic political power around the world. People think that America wants to destroy Islam and Muslims because of its actions, such as its support for Israel, its support for authoritarian regimes in Egypt and Saudi Arabia, its opposition to Islamic governments in Afghanistan, Sudan, Iran, and Algeria, and its war against Iraq. Extreme religious beliefs and politics combine to make people feel angry and want to get back at America and the west, whom they see as godless, evil, and immoral and who must be destroyed so that the moral and godly Islamic civilisation can grow. Many speakers use Islam as a way to get people to do what they want in politics. It has to be hostile, fight-like, and spread hate in many places, leading to the coming together of different cultures. Some Islamic followers are unwilling to give in, which means that you either have to do what they say or keep fighting with them, even if they live in your area. To get young people interested, they show Islam as a language of resistance, which makes it sound harsh and militant. Because of this, radical leaders keep spreading grievance propaganda to make it seem real, terrible, and in urgent need of repatriation that someone is ready to kill innocent people for, and this is a threat.

One good example is Osama Bin Laden's August 1996 Fatwa, which is a seminar called "The Declaration of War Against the Americans Occupying the Land of the Two Holy Places." It says that the US and UK's "Crusader Military forces" are planning to bring about a new wave of imperialism in the Middle East in order to control the oil wealth of the area. People who passively support Islamist terrorists are tempted to join the huge number of active backers and loyal followers of these terrorists when they hear these kinds of views and compare them to interactions between the "west" and "others."

Interestingly, this has turned into the "Jihad-collective revenge" propaganda, which tells all Muslims that it is their duty to revenge America for everything it has done to the Muslim world. This point has already been made. Bin Laden held not one but several of these types of lectures in which he declared war on the United States. The message was clear: Muslims all over the world should see it as their duty to fight Jihad and get rid of anti-Islamic forces. They should use the bloodless takeover of Baghdad, the killing of Muslim children in Iraq and Palestine, and the fact that they think the west has historically defeated Muslim countries to make their case for revenge. For other terrorist groups to follow, this choice of messaging and the way it was spread stands out.

"Western education is an abomination" is what Boko Haram, which was founded in Nigeria's northeastern state of Borno, means. Their only goal is to create an extreme, fundamentalist Islamic state based on Islamic law (Sharia).

It is to use the strict Salafi understanding and application of Sharia to reach their goal. The group turned into a terrorist organisation by attacking markets, destroying churches, stealing from people, killing civilians, and regularly abducting women and girls. The 276 "chibok girls" were one of the most well-known and widespread cases of this. Other factors included long-standing religious tensions in the area, political corruption, growing economic inequality, and the federal government's harsh police and counter-terrorism tactics.

In Africa, these complaints might not just be standard anti-Western or anti-American ones. They might also be local complaints that are linked to anti-Islam or pro-Western ideas that could be turned into good reasons to hurt others. As one way that terrorism spread through African societies, it used local issues and reasons like social anger and complaints, especially against things or actions that are seen as counter to Islam, western, or "unclean." For example, Nigeria's election of President Goodluck Jonathan in 2011 led to a lot of religious violence in the north of the country, killing many and destroying property. This was because Muhammadu Buhari, a Muslim from the north, was not elected. These kinds of complaints can be used to get young, ignorant boys to join the fight against "infidels." It's not just religious people who have these complaints. They could be political, economic, or social, and some have been going on for hundreds of years and have caused many wars. The "territorial capture" of Northern Mozambique by Islamist terrorists was clearly caused by local grievances, illegal income opportunities, and international ties to the formation of terror groups. This has made it impossible for the country's economy to grow and thrive, even though the country has a lot of money invested in large-scale gas exploration.

The Al-Qaeda legacy

Al-Qaeda has a bad name around the world for being a terrorist group that is very hostile to America and the west. It is a really extreme sunni pan-Islamist group that supports the idea of a global Islamist movement to bring all Muslims together under an Islamic state called the Caliphate, which would be run by Salafi Jihadists. It is behind attacks on both citizens and military personnel all over the world. The September 11 attacks in 2001 and the Bali Bombings in 2002 are two well-known examples. From operating without a face, spreading lies, and attacking, they left huge marks that other terror groups can learn from and maybe even copy. Here are three ways that Al-Qaeda has perfected tactics that will put the west on high alert if they are used by other terror groups, both inside and outside of western countries. Following in the lines of Al-Qaeda is Boko Haram, a terrorist group in Nigeria. Now, they are split into several groups.

One is Al-Qaeda in the Islamic Maghreb (AQIM), which is connected to Al-Qaeda Central. The other is the Islamic State's West Africa Province, which calls itself a "caliphate" in northeastern Nigeria. Not only has this group caused trouble for Nigeria, but also for Chad, Niger, and Cameroon. So, here are some of the traits that Islamic terrorism groups around the world, especially in Africa, have taken on from Al-Qaeda.

Vague Identity

The question is "What is Al-Qaeda really?" Even though this terrorist group destroyed the World Trade Centre and the Pentagon, people still don't know who Al-Qaeda really is or what it stands for. Is it one big international group with a clear chain of command and control that spreads fear, or is it a bigger, less organised movement that is held together by a loosely connected transnational authority? Does it work like a franchise, with local reps who are independent but work for the same parent organisation and promote their goals? Does it work like a central power with representatives all over the world? Is it an idea or a virus? Is it a philosophy or an army? Is it a transnational populist group or an international militant or criminal group? Everything? Not any of these? Some of these? It's interesting that these questions cause more disagreement than agreement between governments, intelligence organisations, and academics.

One good example is the capture of Khalid Sheikh Mohammed, also known as KSM, the leader of the Pakistani Islamist Militant group that is said to have planned the September 11 strikes. Many people were happy that he was caught, but it didn't reveal much because he hadn't talked to bin Laden in more than a year and didn't know anything about future threats by Al-Qaeda or how they worked. Also, when Hambali, the former head of the Indonesian terrorist group Jamaah Islamiyah, was captured in August 2003, the people in charge of the capture couldn't tell the difference between Al-Qaeda and Jemaah Islamiyah.

Even though almost half of Al-Qaeda's top leaders were killed or captured in 2003, which should have made the terrorist group much weaker and limited in its ability to carry out operations, the group still has a large, highly functional leadership group that has not been found. This is the main thing that makes the organisation last and be able to grow again. Attacks and abuse of the Al-Qaeda organisation never stopped after September 11, 2001. However, the group seemed to stand strong and continue to work. Its ability to make new levels of leaders to replace mid-level operational commanders who were killed or taken helped them keep their size.

A German intelligence agency said that 70,000 people around the world have been trained by Al-Qaeda camps in Afghanistan, Sudan, and Yemen.

President Bush had said that tens of thousands of jihadists had been taught there. In the same way, its money is fine. It was said that funds linked to Al-Qaeda worth about $120 million were frozen or taken away. It was said that Osama Bin Laden had billions of dollars in assets because he owned or controlled about 80 businesses around the world. Peter Bergen wrote in 2001 that he owned all of Sudan's most profitable businesses. The well-run businesses helped local Al-Qaeda cells grow and become almost self-sufficient in the countries where they worked.

Al-Qaeda left behind the "cat-with-nine-lives" trait of Al-Shabaab, a terrorist group that has terrorised not only Somalia but also Kenya and Uganda. It's not a surprise that the group gets back up right away every time they lose or get trapped. As Al-Qaeda's agents in Africa, Al-Shabaab has become a dangerous, unexpected, and constant threat in the eastern part of Africa. These ways of doing things are used by terrorist groups like ISIS, Fatah al-Islam, and Tawhid al-Jihad. ISIS has gotten very good at hiding their faces and managing their own money. They make money by smuggling and producing oil, collecting and selling ransoms for people they kidnap, stealing and selling artefacts and antiquities, imposing "taxes" or extortion, stealing, harvesting and selling organs, controlling crops, and running a separate economy. The Muslim Brotherhood in Egypt and the Front Islamique du Salut (FIS), which is also known as the Islamic Salvation Front, are both strong radical Islamic groups with a large network of charitable organisations, well-equipped health facilities, places of worship, and schools. As long as they stick to this policy of sustainability and do well, it will only encourage more terror groups, which will cause more problems for the west.

Africa's economy is growing to the point where it is important on the world stage. Africa is likely to become a new hub for global growth, even with the COVID-19 pandemic. Terrorist groups around the world are also interested in this. Therefore, it is not a surprise that Osama Bin Laden chose to use Africa as a target for Al-Qaeda's global network and reach.

Dangerous Propaganda, disseminated in Sophistication

Islamist terrorists have a strong and well-connected way to spread their propaganda, which is full of hate speech against the West, twisted stories about real historical events, and wrong interpretations of Qur'an verses to make people feel like they need to defend Islam as a major way of being Muslim. To reiterate what we've already talked about, their propaganda includes spreading harmful ideas that make Islam look very anti-Western and the West very anti-Islam. They also use political manipulation of America's relationships with Muslim countries, based on those countries' foreign policies, to show that America is against Muslims. However, they spread this lies in a very smart way. They are very smart because they use a lot of different tools, like pre-recorded audio and video tapes, CD-ROMs, DVDs, and the internet; they also plan and stage ways to spread information, like the Al Neda website, which is known as "Al-Qaeda's Phantom." Most of the posts are meant to spread hate and get people to join the group.

Hate speech from Islamic leaders is accepted and not taken seriously in some African countries, such as Nigeria. People who follow Islam are deeply affected by these hate messages, which makes them easy targets for radicalism and extremism. For example, in 2024, an Islamic preacher from Northern Nigeria named Idris Tenshi said that the President's wife was an unfaithful woman who should be killed. "Tinubu's (the president) wife is an unbeliever, and even among the unbelievers, she is a leader (being a pastor herself)," he said in Hausa, calling for violence against the first lady of the country. People from all over the country wanted to arrest him, but he wasn't caught. He only said sorry, and that was it. Extremism and fundamentalism grow stronger in African cultures when things like this happen, and these preachers should never be spared if Islamic terrorism is to be stopped.

Figure 3: The top locations claimed by IS supporting Twitter users

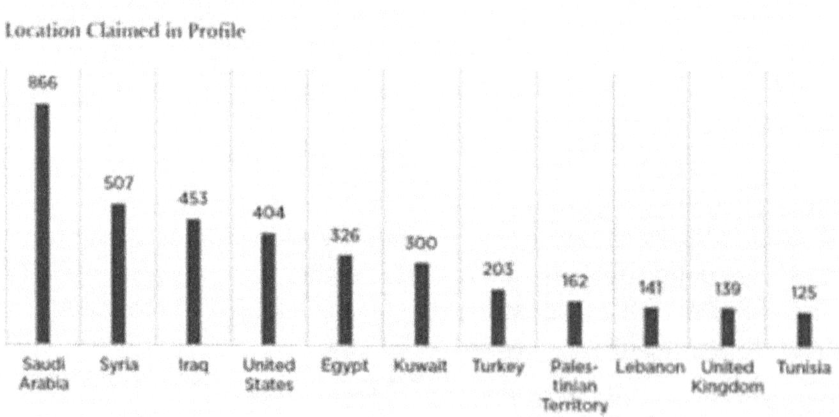

Brookings Institute

They have not only kept up the tradition of using sophisticated methods to spread their harmful propaganda, but they have also moved on to using social media to spread fear and support their propaganda. Almost all known terror groups that pose a threat to the west today spread their ideas through social media. The use of the internet by the Taliban in Pakistan has been said to make their organisation stronger than before. In a 2015 study from the Brookings Institute called The ISIS Twitter Census, Berger and Morgan say that social media metrics are used to map out where IS supporters live. It also shows trends of tweeting, the number of accounts followed, and the ratio of followers to accounts. It's interesting to see that the U.S. ranks fourth in the world for IS-supporting Twitter users who can be found, while the U.K. ranks tenth. Even though these numbers are small compared to the 46,000 Twitter accounts linked to ISIS, they still show that ISIS has a fairly strong online support base in these two countries, which are clearly high on ISIS's list of places to attack (see Figure 3).

Operational Tactics- Guerrilla Warfare

Bin Laden has talked a lot about how successful it is to use guerilla warfare to beat the Americans. In October 1993, Somalia fought American forces as an example. He said this because of the imbalance of power between them and the American troops. Heads of the terrorist group Suleiman Abu Ghaith and Saif al Adel, who used to be the most senior operational leader of Al-Qaeda and an officer in the Egyptian Army's Special Forces, carried on this tradition. After American troops invaded Baghdad in 2003, Al Neda wrote on April 9, 2003, that guerrilla warfare was the best way to keep fighting the crusader enemy because it was "the most powerful weapon Muslims have." Jihadists are encouraged to fight again by bringing up important lessons from past.In Vietnam and Afghanistan, the Americans and the Soviets both lost. This is how direct Christian colonialism was pushed out of most Muslim lands, with Algeria being the most well-known example. We can still see how the method stopped Jews from moving to Palestine and made Jews move away from Palestine. There were many successful efforts to beat invaders with guerrilla warfare, but we won't go into detail on them here. These efforts, however, have shown that guerrilla warfare is the best way for weak people to fight strong people.

Almost all terrorist groups that are known to be able to attack the government use guerrilla methods. This is even true for Al-Shabaab and Boko Haram in Africa, where they operate. Because of this, Al-Qaeda set an example for other terror groups around the world to follow by working under a vague identity, spreading dangerous propaganda through sophisticated means, and attacking their enemies through guerrilla warfare. People who are able to attack the west today are influenced by this history in their operations and information gathering, so the west should be worried.

Easy Recruitment

There are a lot of reasons why young people join terrorist groups and other radical Islamic groups. The fact that they are easy to recruit is a problem because it helps Islamic terrorism last. A study of 35 terrorists in prison in the Middle East in the past strongly suggested that their decision to commit terrorism was based on more than one thing. Jessica Stern talked to religious terrorists in Pakistan, Indonesia, Palestine, and the United States. She found that a lot of suicide bombers are troubled teens who have lived in refugee camps or Israeli prisons, don't have jobs or girlfriends, or are just living desperately. Because of this, it is very easy to find, convince, and train them to be terrorists. Because of this, the Sri Lankan Liberation Tamil Tigers of Eelam (LTTE), a political terror group, chooses its suicide bombers from among the group's most experienced combatants. On the other hand, Hamas, Hizbollah, and the Palestinian Islamic Jihad (PIJ), Islamist terror groups, only need to find teenagers who have no official ties to them until months or weeks before an attack. People from low-income families are easy to find with these teens. This makes Islamic terror groups even deadlier than other terror groups and, by extension, a bigger threat to the world and the West in particular.

Middle East bombers are driven by a wide range of reasons, including personal, religious, political, economic, or social ones. But the most important reason is usually one of these: getting payback for the death of a loved one, getting a reward in the afterlife, becoming famous in the bomber's community, or giving in to peer pressure to avoid being shunned by their friends if they don't join a terrorist group. Ayman Mohammed Rabie Al-Zawahiri, who was Bin Laden's deputy and was known as the "brain" behind Osama's operations and Al-Qaeda's growth into a global network, had a lot of education and was a very good surgeon. His unwavering desire for revenge came from the fact that in November 2001, a U.S. air strike in Afghanistan killed his wife and only son.

It was said by a Muslim family to Jessica Stern, "Now that I have a martyred son, everyone treats me with more respect." When a kid dies in jihad, the community looks up to the family a lot more. I sent my son to fight in the jihad, and I would do the same with all seven of my boys. In Palestine, getting back your pride after being shamed is a big reason to join terrorist groups. Some terrorist groups help the families of kids who have been killed by giving them housing, money, or other financial aid. The main Islamic party in Pakistan set up a charity that helps more than 900 families of martyrs by giving them money. This is done to keep these families and others motivated so that there are still sources of recruits.

In Pakistan, there are two types of secondary schools: those that are run by the government and are free (often called "Madrasahs") and teach the Qur'an and Muslim complaints, and those that are run by private individuals and cost a lot of money. A huge chunk of Pakistani parents can't afford to send their kids to the second set of schools because they are so expensive. These schools are called Madrasahs, and they offer free books, housing, food, and medical care. Since most people in Pakistan are poor, a lot of young boys and girls are sent to Madrasahs, where they are taught religious beliefs for a long time. The same is true for Indonesia and Palestine. In fact, the Indonesian Islamist group "employs" college students and recent grads and pays their families "stipends" while they work for these groups.

This is a good summary of Osman Antwi-Boateng's (2017) academic paper, "The Rise of Pan-Islamic Terrorism in Africa: A Global Security Challenge." He said, "Although the vast majority of Africans are peaceful moderates, radical Islamic ideology that fuels pan-Islamic terrorism is on the rise in the continent because of factors that can be categorised under push and pull forces." The push forces are the things that make people want to follow the violent jihad philosophy. Some of these are local resistance to globalisation and Americanization, oppressive and authoritarian governments, a lack of basic human rights, a lot of young people and high unemployment, corruption and a lack of meritocracy, the fall of states, and porous borders. The pull factors are the good things about terrorist and jihadi groups that make people want to join their cause. Some of these are radical Islamic ideas, networks of helpers, media propaganda, giving people a "purpose and mission," the allure of martyrdom, and the impact of madrasas.

Radicalization

If radical Islamists want to fight the west directly, they need to be in western societies. The same is true for Africa and its societies. Radical Islam, also known as Islamism, doesn't have a central office. It has grown beyond ISIS and al-Qaeda to include smaller, more stable groups of Muslims all over the world. When a person or group adopts strong social, political, or religious beliefs, they reject modern ideas, the freedom of choice, and the violence that comes with them in order to make the change they want to see. This is called radicalisation. From Australia to Western Europe, the west is plagued by radicalisation right now. As an example, every day in 2015, more than one suspected Australian Islamic terrorist was caught on an overseas flight. Also, in 2016, about 850 Britons joined ISIS and other similar terrorist groups abroad. Since the September 11 attacks in 2001, there has been a rise in the number of young British Muslim men and boys becoming radicalised into terrorism. It has also messed up the patterns of integration in British society, which is multicultural. There are now and will continue to grow many groups that are very similar to each other in the UK. People in Britain who have become radicalised like the names Kadiza Sultana,

Mohammed Emwazi (also known as Jihadi John), Amira Abase, Shamima Begun, Aqsa Mamood, Salma and Zahra Halane, and Khadijah and her son Isa Dare. Some of them were top students in their class, but they were all born and raised in the UK and had never been to the terror-country before they went on the trip. One of them was even recorded swearing war on the West while travelling with the terrorist group. For the same reason, most of the Australian terrorists of 2015 were young, second-generation refugees who were born and raised in Australia and didn't know anything about the war-torn countries they went to. In the same year, Australia was found to be the country that sent the most Jihadists to other countries than the Middle East.

Fears were made about how the country's 4 million Muslim citizens were becoming more radicalised over time. This is also true in Germany. As a result, 300 Germans went to Syria to join the radical militant group Islamic State. The USA, Italy, Spain, and France are all the same. They are clearly a danger because they could use their passports to go back to western countries and spread hate against the places where they live, putting innocent people at risk of terrorism attacks of all levels. Because of this, Shamima Begum lost her case against the decision to take away her British citizenship after she went to Syria to join the terrorist group Islamic State, even though her lawyers presented strong evidence that she is a victim of sexual exploitation and trafficking. Some strong evidence suggests that the level of violence in terror strikes has been rising over the last five years. Western societies may still be able to live, but only if radicalisation is stopped.

Radicalisation is a problem in societies that are stable and well-developed, like those in the West. It must be even worse in societies that are poor, unstable, chaotic, and open to outsiders, like those in Africa. There are 830 million people in the world who don't have enough food to eat. Of these, 58% live in the 20 countries in Africa that are most hit by terrorism. This will make it easy for young Africans to become radicalised, especially if food and social rewards are used. Also, there are a lot of criminal groups that help smuggle illegal goods, people, and drugs, and these groups are easy for Islamist jihadists to join without much urging. The Liptako-Gourma border area, which is made up of the three countries of Mali, Niger, and Burkina Faso, is very far away and not connected to anything else. It has become a major hub for terrorism in the Sahel because it is a great place to plan strikes and find new members. As of 2022, Muslims make up 26% of Cameroon's population. However, they are growing and spreading faster than other groups because they have strategically put themselves in all parts of the country's population. It's a bad thing that this rise leads to more radicalisation. Sufi Islam is being spread in Cameroon by Wahhabism, which has been supported for years by Gulf monarchies. According to their plan, they will build Wahhabi schools that give free education and grow Wahhabi groups that help people in times of economic trouble. This will make Wahhabism more popular in Cameroon. When boko haram terror actions reached the border of Cameroon, the government arrested Wahhabi Imams and people who supported them in the country. This made Muslims all over the region very angry and upset. This made more Cameroonian Muslims more likely to become radicalised.

Conclusion

ISIS is still a threat to Africa, and this is talked about by looking at these risks through the lens of the west. The first factor is the clash of civilisations, with the west being in direct conflict with Islam. The west is seen as immoral, materialistic, and evil, while Islam is seen as pure and holy and must live alone by getting rid of the west. Radicals use this to spread lies against the United States and the West. Even normal, reasonable Muslims are exposed to the dangerous ideas, which means that many of them support them. This is a very big problem for the West if it gets to Muslim people as well.

The political reason is based on anger towards the United States and other Western countries for what are seen as anti-Islamic and Muslim policies in other countries. People use the bad past relationships between the United States and some Muslim countries as proof to accuse Muslims of being "anti-American." At the same time, they use these relationships to encourage Muslims to protect and act, which is required by Islam. The way Al-Qaeda works and its ability to stay alive are also very important. The organization's heritage is marked by its persistence and hard work. It thrived by keeping its identity secret, using sophisticated methods to spread harmful propaganda, and using guerrilla tactics in attacks. Its style has been copied by modern terror groups all over the world. They are still a threat to the west because this has made it hard to wipe them out. Then there are socio-economic, psychological, and personal factors like wanting to get revenge for the death of a loved one, social pride, and even nationalistic factors that make it easy for terrorists to join. The Islamic terror groups, especially Al-Qaeda, are stronger and more dangerous because they use high-tech tools like the internet and social media sites. Finally, one more thing that keeps the danger of Islamic terrorism to the west alive is the radicalisation of people who live in western countries. There is still a lot of Islamic terrorism that threatens the West, and there will always be a danger of terrorism until these things "go away." By putting all of these things into the context of Africa, I've shown how terror groups like Boko Haram, Al-Shabaab, and others from Al-Qaeda and the Islamic State Organisation have used these patterns to cause chaos in many African countries.

During the past few years, the west has used data mining to find threats and possible attackers. In recent years, real-time analysis has also been used to find tweets that support terrorists in real time. Both of these strategies should be used together to find terrorists more quickly and make integration into western societies more mandatory. This should be done mainly at the school level to lower the risk of indoctrination and raise the chances of children integrating into western societies. These plans will also need to be used by Africans. Finally, blowing the whistle is also a good idea, especially for Muslim people who live near places where terror actions or plans are carried out. However, the most important thing that needs to be done to stop the growth of Islamic terrorism is to make life better for Africans.

Chapter 28
Royal United Services Institute for Defence and Security Studies

Introduction

The part is mostly based on data gathered during RUSI's STRIVE Afghanistan project, which ran from 2019 to 24. A lot of the information comes from interviews with current and past IS-K members. The chapter isn't meant to be a complete study paper. Instead, it's meant to bring up questions and concerns based on the preliminary work that has been done so far.

In Afghanistan in the spring and winter of 2023 and 2024, a researcher talked to nine former members of IS-K. This part also uses information from other works that came out of STRIVE Afghanistan. There are clear problems with the way the study was done. Because of the way things were set up and the risks that were involved, research could only use oral sources and, more importantly, an ethnographic method was not possible at the time. Former IS-K members didn't always want to talk about their lives in more detail, and the analyst couldn't spend a lot of time with them. Even though getting entry wasn't a problem, there was a chance that interviewees would overstate some parts of their involvement because of a social desirability bias.

There are three parts to this chapter. The first part briefly talks about how IS-K propaganda compares to propaganda from other jihadist groups. The second part talks about the main recruiting pitches that are unique to IS-K propaganda. The third one looks at how cash resources help IS-K recruits reach their goals.

Narratives in common with previous 'Jihads'

When asked why they joined IS-K, people who had betrayed the group to the Taliban in 2021–22 usually gave one or both of the following reasons:

1. A religious or ideological duty to protect the whole Islamic community (umma) against what some interviewees called American "colonisation," which meant an effort to not only take over but also change the thoughts and ways of life of Afghans.

2. Protecting the village and its people from the direct threat of bombing is their job.

Most of the people we talked to mixed the two issues—the umma and the town. IS-K propaganda also stresses the group's view that men have special duties and responsibilities, such as fighting military jihad to protect the umma. This is a theme that can also be found in IS Central propaganda. As Elizabeth Pearson pointed out, men who fight for the cause are seen as "real men" and men in Western countries are seen as "emasculated." It is important to remember that Afghanistan is still a society dominated by men, and people who are interested in jihadism only saw a small change towards a less male-dominated society from 2001 to 2011. There are certain kinds of problems in Afghanistan that make potential IS-K members feel like patriarchal men. There is proof that anger, shame, and humiliation play a big role in pushing men towards violent extremism. In rural Afghanistan, house searches by US troops and CIA Afghan militias were very effective at promoting patriarchal masculinity. These searches broke both people's right to privacy and the common practice of keeping men and women separate. A common theme in jihadist propaganda is the need to protect the safety and respect of Muslim women. Women are often shown as victims of IS-K's enemies and as prisoners who need to be rescued, whether they are in jails in Afghanistan or camps in Syria. In IS Central propaganda, women are sometimes said to be fighting on the front lines, but this is probably more to make men feel bad than to try to attract women.

On these kinds of problems, there is a lot of common ground with jihadist groups in Afghanistan before IS-K. In Afghanistan, where patriarchy is very strong, interviewees talked about bravery, protecting the family and its respect and community values, and being the breadwinner as important parts of being a man. Protecting their families was a big reason for Taliban village recruits from 2003 to 2011. They didn't want to be moved to different places because it would mean being away from their families. A common story about how people join the Taliban is that their family homes and the respect of women are violated. A strong link was made between being a man and having a job to protect the community. People who used to be in the Taliban who were interviewed tended to downplay how important pressure from family members (fathers, moms, and wives) was in getting them to leave, likely because they felt ashamed. Several of the people interviewed didn't say that family pressure was the main reason they left, but when pushed, they did say that it was.

Both IS-K and the jihadist groups that came before it have used the way that decades of war have made killing look good. For many men, joining the jihad has become a rite of passage. In this way, moms and other female relatives even support the idea that good men are dominant and aggressive.

IS-K'S specificity

The most clear thing that sets IS-K apart since August 2021 is that it is dedicated to fighting the Taliban. Even the small chances that the (modest) attempts to promote women's freedom in Afghanistan from 2001 to 2011 gave IS-K to play on angry male traits were taken away when the Taliban took over. The Taliban used that campaign to get people who didn't like these ideas to support them. For example, in the Salafi villages of eastern Afghanistan, where the Taliban often bullied and acted aggressively towards the local youth, IS-K has still been able to use masculinities that are sparked by being put down.

The case of college students who joined IS-K is especially interesting from the point of view of fighting dangerous extremism. Recruits and recruiters who were interviewed both agreed that the most likely people to join were those who were made fun of by pro-Taliban students and teachers. In order to grow into a big insurgent group, IS had to recruit people from a wide range of backgrounds and often had to adapt to the needs of each area. One thing that all of the recruitment drives for IS had in common, though, was the desire to build a strong group of what you might call "professional revolutionaries" who would carry on IS's organisational, military, and ideological knowledge even when things went wrong. The pitch for joining this hardcore group was aimed at educated, urban youth. Cultural anthropologist Scott Atran says that these are the kinds of youth who are "not attracted to the lure of a consumerist society but instead seduced by the offer of a life of fight, risk, and adventure." IS wants to use young people's desire to rebel, their energy, their ideals, and their desire to make sacrifices. Atran's account makes me think of angry men.

In places like the cities of Afghanistan, where US involvement created a new order, "the traditional sources that defined (and also imposed) a monolithic lifestyle and system of customs and values lost their power and authority." This pitch hit home. Borhan Osman said that young people were "adrift in an urban space where values looked confusing and fluid." They were facing a "new market of identities" because it was easy to communicate with the rest of the Muslim world and elements of culture, religion, and politics were being swapped around. They were also trying to figure out "what it means to be Afghan and Muslim in the twenty-first century."

IS-K advertised itself as a complete package, especially to young, college-educated "middle-class" men who wanted to join. One story told of "jihadi solidarity among ISKP's urban members was further reinforced by tales of female members offering to marry male recruits and elder male members marrying off their daughters to young men joining the group." It broke "standard Afghan marriage customs" for these things to happen without consulting the girls' families. This showed that recruits were ready to "reject tradition in order to live the kind of life they want." It looks like these chances to get married worked best for Salafi fighters who were having a hard time finding a partner before they joined IS-K. They didn't work so well for the girls whose dads wanted to marry them, in part because there were so many fighters killed and it wasn't cool for widows to marry other IS-K members again. Some of the women left IS-K before they could get married again. One former member didn't mind talking about this:

> *People who were single and part of Daesh (IS) Khurasan were allowed to get married in the land of the Caliphate (IS-K-controlled area). This was called Jihad-ul-Nika. The women in the village were asked by Daesh leaders and the Islamic Commission of Daesh to give their girls to Jihad-ul-Nika.*

It's important to understand that these women were treated like things that could be traded in a society that values men highly and where forced weddings and arranged marriages are common. What's new is that IS-K is taking on a job that used to belong to the family. Part of IS-K's message was that it was bringing back the old Islamic order right now. One former member talked about how in some parts of Nangarhar province

> *Muslims followed Islamic rule to the letter, just like they did 1,400 years ago. It followed the same Sharia and caliphate system as it did during the time of the Caliphs of Rashidun. The thieves' hands were cut off, enemies and spies were beheaded, and all of Islam's sentences for crime were carried out... People had to pray five times a day, and they couldn't avoid it. If any member couldn't wake up in the morning to pray or fell asleep, our leader would punish them the next day by whipping them 50 times.*

IS-K propaganda on social media, like the "Star of the Night" audio recordings, often talks about how people can make money, find a wife, and start a family once they join IS-K totally. IS-K propaganda often goes against local customs, but it creates a space where traditional gender roles are praised. Joining the group becomes a way to hit the milestones of manhood in traditional Afghan society. At the same time, the group was trying to get women to join by promising them marriage to "adventurous, loyal, true believers."

The first two parts of this chapter only give a short outline of the different types of IS-K propaganda. They don't try to figure out how important each one is, but it's clear that a lot of IS-K's propaganda is about being a man. For recruits from the middle class, it effectively creates a dream path to social progress in a different social setting. But IS-K has had to spend a lot of money to make its promises even slightly believable. This has turned out to be a major weakness for the group, which we will talk about below.

The impact of financial incentives

IS-K'S years of financial plenty

It's hard to find a link between a person's socioeconomic position and their willingness to support violence against civilians, but a lot of people in Afghanistan think that the promise of money and salaries makes a lot of people join violent extremist groups. In the beginning, between 2014 and 2015, one of the main reasons why people joined the IS-K in Afghanistan was because of how much money they had. In Iraq at that time, the "Caliphate" was at the height of its wealth and could give a lot. The group was able to pay its members well (a simple fighter could make up to $800 a month during IS-K's golden age, when the Afghan army and the Taliban only paid around $200 a month) and give them a lot of chances to move up in society—after all, it had to start from scratch when it came to building its structure. People who had been on the outside of the Taliban and the Pakistani Taliban (mainly the Tehreek-e-Taliban Pakistan, or TTP) could now become officers and leaders. People who were promoted were often known for having strong opinions in both groups, but it's possible that a lot of people in this first wave were drawn in by the high pay and benefits.

Over time, though, IS-K started recruiting people who were thought to be more politically and religiously in line with the main IS message. By 2018, not many new people were leaving the Taliban or TTP. Instead, new members came from one of three groups:

- Salafi villagers in eastern Afghanistan.
- Salafi madrasa students.
- Middle-class urbanites, mostly Tajiks and often university students.

This is where the third group, which includes middle-class city dwellers and college students, really stands out. Their track record over the years shows that these people were not opportunists or hired guns who were drawn to the relatively high pay at the time. If there is any evidence of what drove them, it doesn't point to greed. Instead, it points to the fact that there weren't many other ways for them to get gendered status, like getting married, having community status, and being stable. This made a career as an IS-K cadre more appealing. Being a part of the IS-K gave people more money, control over weapons, power over other people, and maybe even a motorbike. People were drawn to the growing group of highly motivated IS-K members who were building a system that was a lot more like the original IS model than IS-K had been in its early years. They thought that the high pay made it easier for them to get to the perfect Islamic society that IS-K promised.

As we already talked about, one of the main parts of the IS-K recruitment pitch was the chance of getting married through the group or meeting a Salafi student who shared your beliefs and getting married to her through IS-K. But for this to really work, the new IS-K family needed to have a good middle-class salary and the perks that come with it. This would give them a way to succeed that wasn't tied to their family and went against what young people see as a morally corrupt society. During its peak in 2016–18, IS-K gave that.

The dream evaporates: IS-K'S financial crisis

After 2018, IS-K started having money problems. This was mostly because its parent body, IS Central, was losing money and becoming less able to make money. The losses that IS-K had in 2019–2020, which caused them to lose control of land in the relatively rich Nangarhar province, made things even worse financially. From 2020 to 2022, IS-K paid $300 to $500 a month instead of $400 to $600 a month in 2016. However, those who joined at this time still saw this as a package that would appeal to their manhood based on men. In 2024, a conversation with a former member showed that they stressed that "families were also treated well by the organisation, and the organisation was responsible for helping the families of its members in both practical and financial ways." He "joined Daesh [not for] money, but only to beat the Americans and set up the Islamic Caliphate in Afghanistan." He claimed that the money he was getting was for "supporting my family and children." But, as the same former member remembers, IS-K's dream of an Islamist paradise was no longer possible by 2020:

> *The Caliphate government fell apart after the Taliban attacked Nangarhar and Kunar in 2019 and 2020. When I got back from Pakistan and joined Daesh again, I didn't find the same Caliphate rule and system that was there before. That's why I chose to give up and surrender to the Taliban in 2022.*

Another former member thinks he joined by being tricked by false information from some friends:

> *Two of my peasant friends who joined Daesh a few months ago told me about how strong Daesh was and how much the members and leaders of Daesh loved each other. They also told me about the real Islam and Caliphate in Daesh Khorasan. What my friends told me about Daesh, though, wasn't true. Daesh didn't control much land; we spent most of our time hiding in caves and mountains. Daesh wasn't as powerful as my friends told me; they were still getting back on their feet after losing the war in Nangarhar and Kunar provinces in 2019 and 2020. Some people in Daesh were unhappy with their position, the way they were treated, or the conditions in which they were living.*

But the worst was yet to come. By 2023, things were even worse because IS's overall fall had sped up and Turkey had cracked down on IS and IS-K's financial hubs in Turkey. Sources in eastern Afghanistan said that IS-K fighters were not getting their pay. During a few months in the spring, IS-K wasn't even able to feed its members or help with logistics. It wasn't until later in the year that fighters got back their food and expense payments of about $100 a month. Also at this time, members of the IS-K were either hiding in cities, planning terrorist strikes, and always being afraid that the Taliban would catch them, or they were hiding in mountain caves, where they and their families didn't have much comfort. Members had to beg for food in the towns, which was something IS-K had never done before, or they had to get money from the people there. At the end of 2023, new members who had joined online started complaining in IS-K's secret chats that they had been left alone for months after joining and that no one had tried to take them to the Islamic utopia that IS-K says it has in the mountains of Afghanistan.

Conclusion and Recommendations

A lot of IS-K's efforts to recruit people have been focused on guys. Because of this work, IS-K has been able to, among other things, build a strong core of members who are in charge of its organisational and tactical know-how and who will keep the group going through the ups and downs of jihad. But the work did not just happen by itself. To get educated people to join, IS-K had to offer real chances for angry, eager, and educated young men to rise in society. It was necessary to make a place that looked like the alternative Islamic utopia that IS-K said they were making. If IS-K had a lot of money from IS Central, which it did from 2015 to 2017, this would have been possible. After that, it became harder and harder to get money.

But IS-K's real money problems started in 2023, when it couldn't pay its members' salaries or even feed them sometimes. Years ago, IS-K's small utopian towns could not be kept up because they had lost even the few small areas of territory they still controlled. As of early 2024, the IS-K's core was still surprisingly strong even though the utopia was falling apart. This was in part because its enemies, like the Taliban, weren't taking advantage of its money and morale problems in a big way. In fact, the Taliban even put off their plans to bring back disgruntled IS-K members.

Are these stories about manhood now able to be used to create messages that try to get hard-core IS-K members to leave the group? Because the organisation can't give the same package it did when it was at its best, the IS-K story seems open to being changed. It's been said that counter-narratives don't work very well, but instead of them, there could be campaigns that showed how an IS-K (or more generally an IS) career doesn't lead to a fulfilled masculine role as saviour of the community and protector of women, but instead to a path of self-destruction; how instead of creating an Islamic utopia, this organisation sent middle-class members and their families to live in remote mountain caves or cities where they were constantly at risk of being caught.

You could use the same set of reasons to support media resilience campaigns, which shows that you can't trust these stories because the scenarios they paint often turn out to be false. Long-term solutions are always harder to come up with and need more study. Establishing programs that offer people at risk of joining IS-K other (nonviolent) ways to show their masculinity could be possible if there was a framework for preventing violent extremism that directly addressed masculinities. They could find reasons that wouldn't hurt others to fight for, like business, community, or NGO work. To be more specific, you would need to look at the views and wants of the people who are at risk. Any method like this would probably work better when groups like IS-K are short on money (like they are right now) and there are lots of business and community-based options (which isn't the case in Afghanistan yet). This is why work needs to keep going in this area.

Chapter 29
Talking Up Terrorism in Central Asia

Two Americans, a Dutchman, and a Swiss rider were killed in southern Tajikistan on July 29, 2018. The Islamic State's news source, Amaq, released a video of the attackers two days later making a promise to follow the group's leader, Abu Bakr al-Baghdadi, and saying that they wanted to "establish the Almighty's rule on this land." That was the first attack in the area on Western tourists in almost 20 years, and it was also the first attack in the area that could be clearly linked to ISIS.

Central Asians have also been in the news for acts that happened outside of Central Asia. People from the area were involved in well-known terrorist acts in New York, Stockholm, Istanbul, and St. Petersburg in 2017. People who spoke Russian were thought to be the biggest group of foreign fighters in Syria and Iraq by 2017, with more than those from the rest of the Middle East. Some recruits have worked their way up to important roles in foreign terrorist groups. In May 2015, Colonel Gulmurod Halimov, who was in charge of Tajikistan's armed police (OMON), famously joined the Islamic State. He then became the group's Minister of War.

As in the past, these events have led news sites like the Wall Street Journal and Business Insider to speculate again that the area is becoming a "growing source of terrorism" and a "fertile ground" for recruiting. There has been a long-running story that the area is becoming a hub for terrorism, but the danger from terrorists within Central Asia is still low. Since 2008, there have been only 19 attacks in Central Asia that were started by non-state players and were called terrorist attacks by the governments. These attacks have killed 142 people. Only 0.005% of the people in the area have joined violent groups.

As analysts Anna Matveeva and Antonio Guistozzi recently said, the danger of terrorism in Central Asia is "a reality that cannot be ignored." However, we can't ignore how people have used the danger against us. Central Asian governments are torn between wanting to play down the threat to show they are in charge, like in Uzbekistan, or using it as an excuse to crack down on other opposition groups, like we saw in Tajikistan. Over the past ten years, the government's fights against terrorism and extremism have killed many more people than terrorism itself. Because terrorism is such a touchy issue, it is important to be aware of how little we really know about its causes and the size of the danger it poses to other countries.

The Threat within Central Asia: Local Politics More than International Terrorism

Many people who study the Soviet Union saw Central Asia as the USSR's weak spot because of its stubborn Muslim population. Alexandre Bennigsen, one of the most famous Soviet scholars who wrote about Central Asia, said that "the Muslim community is prepared for the inevitable showdown with its Russian rulers" after Russia invaded Afghanistan in 1979. People continued to think of the area as "potentially one of the most explosive" in the world after it got rid of the Soviet Union. They looked for ways to "calm" local emotions, especially the threat of religious extremism.

Even though none of the worst predictions came true, the Islamic Movement of Uzbekistan (IMU) and its branch, the Islamic Jihad Union (IJU), were the biggest terrorist threat to Central Asia in the first 15 years of its freedom. From its base in war-torn Tajikistan, the IMU led armed attacks into Kyrgyzstan and Uzbekistan between 1999 and 2000, taking prisoners along the way. After these failed, the IMU went back to Afghanistan, where the U.S.-led attack in 2001 caused a lot of damage, and moved to Waziristan. In 1999, bombings in Tashkent were blamed on the IMU by the Uzbek government. In 2004, strikes in Bukhara and Tashkent were blamed on the IJU. The IMU and IJU had about 3,000 members by 2013. Tajikistan is the only country in the area that has had a civil war. Across the border, the government was fighting former commanders who did not accept the peace deal from 1997, which said that the opposition would give up its weapons in exchange for 30% of government posts. These commanders led a series of attacks from 1997 to 2001. Because of this violence in the area, at least 145 people were killed.

Terrorists planned 19 deadly strikes in Central Asia between 2008 and 2018. This number includes acts that killed at least one person, including the terrorists, were called terrorism by the government, and were planned by a terrorist group or an individual rather than by the government as part of an operation to fight terrorism. Since 2008, 138 people have died in terrorist acts. Most of them were members of law enforcement (78) or terrorist groups (49), but 11 were civilians. Kazakhstan is the most prosperous country in the area, and half of these events have happened there. More than half of the deaths have happened in Tajikistan. For some perspective, 11,553 people were killed in car crashes in Kyrgyzstan alone during the same time period.

***Table 1**: Terrorist Attacks in Central Asia (2008-2018)*

Date	Country	Location	Type	Deaths
19 April 2009	Tajikistan	Isfara	Murder of police officers	1
26 May 2009	Uzbekistan	Khanabad/ Andijan	Armed attack/suicide bombing	2
3 September 2010	Tajikistan	Khujand	Suicide bombing	4
19 September 2010	Tajikistan	Kamarob	Armed attack	25
17 May 2011	Kazakhstan	Aktobe	Suicide bombing	1
23 May 2011	Kazakhstan	Astana	Bombing	1
1 July 2011	Kazakhstan	Aktobe	Armed attack	3
31 October 2011	Kazakhstan	Atyrau	Suicide bombing	1
8 November 2011	Kazakhstan	Almaty	Armed attack	1
12 November 2011	Kazakhstan	Taraz	Armed attack	7
21 July 2012	Tajikistan	Khorog	Assassination	1
30 July 2012	Kazakhstan	Almaty	Mass murder	14
23 May 2014	Tajikistan	Khorog	Armed attack	1
19 May 2015	Kyrgyzstan	Bishkek	Suicide bombing	1
4 September 2015	Tajikistan	Dushanbe/ Vahdat	Armed attack	39
5 June 2016	Kazakhstan	Aktobe	Armed attack	21
18 July 2016	Kazakhstan	Almaty	Armed attack	10
30 August 2016	Kyrgyzstan	Bishkek	Suicide bombing	1
29 July 2018	Tajikistan	Danghara	Attack with car/knives	4

All of the events shown in Figure 1 were deadly, started by a non-state group, and were called terrorism by the government. Some of these cases of terrorism are not as clear. For example, in July 2012, General Abdullo Nazarov, Chairman of the Directorate of Tajikistan's State Committee for National Security in Badakhshan Province, was killed. This led to an armed conflict between the government and former opposition commanders in Khorog. In August 2012, 12 people were killed in Kazakhstan's Ile-Alatau national park. The authorities blamed a "extremist religious group." But there are a few things that can be said about all of these cases.

This year, almost all of the attacks were aimed at security services, cops, and the army. There are several ways that terrorism in Central Asia is linked to the government. The area has been stable thanks to the strong presence of state security forces. In 2016, the governments of Kazakhstan, Kyrgyzstan, and Tajikistan say they stopped 61 plots. But some people in the public have also reacted violently to state control. Violence in Khorog, the Rasht Valley, and Dushanbe, Tajikistan, was caused by people who used to work for the government. As part of the peace deal that ended the country's civil war, former leaders of the resistance were brought into the government and given jobs that let them make money through drug trafficking, favours, and other activities. However, as Emomali Rahmon's government took over, it fired these leaders from their jobs within the state. This is what John Heathershaw and Parviz Mullojonov call "authoritarian conflict management." As an example, Deputy Defence Minister Abduhalim Nazarzoda attacked with guns in Dushanbe and Vahdat in September 2015, and the government tried to get rid of him, but he responded violently. The terrorist attacks in Tajikistan are easier to understand when you look at these local dynamics of authoritarian consolidation rather than the government's story about foreign terrorists.

Some of the violent events that have happened outside of Tajikistan also seem to have been caused by state violence. Ruslan Kulikbayev, who killed three police officers and a civilian in Almaty in July 2016, is said to have become radicalised while he was in jail for robbery. He said that the attack was a "act of revenge" against the police officers who had abused him and his "brothers."" In Aktobe, Kazakhstan, on May 17, 2011, convicted criminal Rakhimjan Makhatov blew himself up in the headquarters of the country's security services. He was apparently doing this to protest the government's strict religious laws and jail abuse.

Cities in the area, like Almaty, Bishkek, and Dushanbe, have been attacked. But most terrorist strikes have happened in places that aren't in the middle, like Aktobe in Kazakhstan or the Rasht Valley in Tajikistan. Some of these remote places, like the Ferghana Valley in Kyrgyzstan or the oil-rich town of Zhanoezen, have also seen acts of racial violence and protests that were violently put down. These are places where economic growth hasn't helped as much and where people have a lot of problems with the local government.

Central Asians have been a part of transnational jihadist movements, but most of the strikes that have happened in the region since 2008 don't seem to have had much to do with groups outside of Central Asia. Up until 2004, the IMU and IJU could plan attacks from sites outside of Uzbekistan. Since then, it seems that outside groups are less able to carry out attacks in the area. Jund al-Khalifah is a Kazakh jihadist group based in Afghanistan that claimed responsibility for two attacks in Kazakhstan in 2011. However, many experts in the country don't think the group really planned the attacks and were just trying to make money off of them. A few groups from outside the area have been able to attack. Police in Kyrgyzstan said that an attack on the Chinese mission in September 2016 was planned by the East Turkestan Islamic Movement, a Uyghur group. ISIS gave the young people who attacked tourists in Tajikistan the idea to go after tourists.

Lone wolf strikes by radicalised people, like the Almaty gunman Kulikbayev, are a bigger threat. In a similar case, Maksat Kariev killed seven people in a string of killings in December 2011 in the city of Taraz. Other attacks have been done by groups that were inspired by jihadist propaganda but did not have clear orders from a jihadist group. It is said that top ISIS member Abu Mohammad al-Adnani's call for jihad inspired the 16 men who carried out the June 2016 Aktobe attack, in which they robbed two gun shops and attacked an army base. Terrorist strikes in the area have mostly been random, short-lived, and poorly planned, just like the attack in Aktobe. Not many of the attacks have been clear about what they want or made clear demands. And when they have, like with the latest attack in Tajikistan, these goals have been hard to pin down.

The Flow of Returning Ex-Fighters and Recruits to Afghanistan: A Trickle not a Surge

Since 2011, between 2,000 and 4,000 people from Central Asia have moved to Syria and Iraq to join terrorist groups there. But the fall of ISIS and Jabhat Fateh in Syria and Iraq makes people wonder what will happen to the rebels in Central Asia if these groups lose all of their land.

***Table 2**: Estimates of Central Asians Participating in Conflicts Abroad*

Country	Upper Estimate	Lower Estimate
Tajikistan	1,899	1,141
Kyrgyzstan	863	500
Uzbekistan	1,500	200
Kazakhstan	350	300
Turkmenistan	360	360

Former boxers can do one of three things. They could move to a different country, join a terrorist group in another war zone, or go back to their own country. A lot of experts have said that militants coming back to Central Asia is dangerous, but the proof shows that a large group of militants is not likely to come back. For many, this was a one-way trip to find excitement, death, or a new start. A lot of fighters have moved with their families, which is another sign that they will stay there. Eight hundred of the people who went to the Middle East have died.

The governments of Tajikistan and Kazakhstan have changed the law so that people who are found to be members of terrorist groups can no longer be citizens. This means that the state can bar or remove them. Over 300 former rebels from Tajikistan, Kyrgyzstan, and Kazakhstan have come back, either to be charged or to be forgiven. In Tajikistan, the law was changed in 2015 to allow this to happen. It might be good for the regimes in Syria and Iraq to send radicalised citizens to fight because it helps them "avoid the problem of Islamic terrorism by transferring it outside of the region," as Jozef Lang writes. More than 30 of the people who were freed in Tajikistan have gone back to the Middle East. It is unknown how many people are in jail in Syria and Iraq. There are still about 1,000 to 3,000 terrorists from Central Asia in the Middle East.

The fighters are more likely to move on to another theatre or come to Europe as refugees instead of going back home. Afghanistan seems like a good place for former fighters and new recruits to go because it is close to Central Asia and has languages that are similar to those there. Jamaat Ansurallah, which is linked to Al-Qaeda, the Islamic Jihad Union, and the Islamic Movement of Uzbekistan, which pledged loyalty to the Islamic State in 2015, are all possible places for new members to join. Since these groups have been weakened by years of war, the Islamic State of Khurasan Province (ISKP) has been the busiest trying to get new members and former fighters to join. Like ISIS, the group has built up a sophisticated media footprint that makes it stronger than the Taliban. The group put out a video in March 2018 in which Uzbek soldiers asked militants in Syria and Iraq to join. Since January 2015, when it admitted to being a branch of ISIS, ISKP has grown beyond its original base in Nangarhar. It now has bases in Badakhshan and Jowzjan in northern Afghanistan, which are run by former IMU commander Moawiya after he split with the Nangarhar branch in the summer of 2017.

It's still hard to tell how strong the group really is. Afghanistan's government says that the ISKP has about 3,000 foreign soldiers. Pakistani and Uzbek terrorists who have been fighting in the area since the 1990s make up a big part of this group. There is evidence, though, that some Tajik citizens have joined the group more lately. In May 2018, Tajik President Emomali Rahmon said that dozens of his countrymen had joined the ISKP. Most of them come from Iran and end up in Afghanistan. As an example, Shodidjon Boev worked as a foreign worker in Russia before he tried to go to Syria through Turkey. He tried to get to Syria but failed, so he went to Iran and crossed into Afghanistan in December 2017. Since the middle of 2017, nine more cases of Tajiks entering Afghanistan through Iran have been mentioned in the news.

People may be more interested in joining the ISKP because it says it wants to expand into Central Asia than the Taliban, whose nationalist vision says they can't grow into the north. But for now, this threat doesn't seem very big. Antonio Guistozzi, a top expert on ISKP, said at the end of 2017 that the group had been hurt by internal fighting and setbacks in the Middle East. He said that the group "is past its peak in Afghanistan, if not in terms of military capabilities, certainly in terms of jihadist image." There aren't that many fighters going to Afghanistan compared to when ISIS was recruiting a lot of people from Central Asia in 2014 and 2015.

Increasing Spillovers from Afghanistan

Central Asia and Afghanistan are connected by a river that runs for 2,387 kilometres. Since their borders are long and not well protected, Tajikistan and Turkmenistan are the most likely to be affected by what's happening in Afghanistan. Most border crossings and violent events happen because of the opium and heroin that are brought in from Afghanistan, mostly through Tajikistan, and are worth about $2 billion. Even though the Taliban are involved in drug trade, they don't really want to make things worse between Afghanistan and its northern neighbours, despite what many officials say.

Occasionally, fighting in northern Afghanistan has spread to other parts of the country. In the eight Afghan provinces that border Central Asia, the number of armed incidents has gone up over the past few years, especially since 2014, when NATO activities were slowed down.

Figure 1: Violent Incidents on the Tajik-Afghan Border

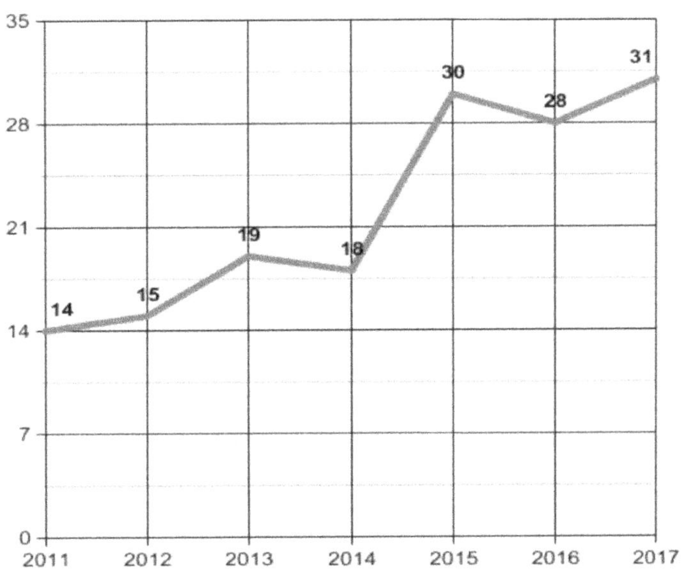

From 2011 to 2013, there were 38 armed events on the border between Tajikistan and Afghanistan. This number more than doubled, rising to 76 between 2014 and 2016. In 2017, another 29 cases were reported. There is now fighting between the Taliban and the Afghan forces all the way to the border with Turkmenistan. At least six Turkmen border guards were killed by Taliban militants in two separate events in 2014. But these kinds of things still don't happen very often. According to security expert George Gavrilis, being close to Afghanistan is more of a benefit than a threat for the Central Asian states because they could get help with their security from other countries and make a lot of money from drug trafficking.

Central Asia's Salient Security Issue: Clumsy Counter-extremism

Brian Jenkins, an expert on terrorism, has said that it is very hard to tell how the terrorist danger will change over the next few years. Analysts thought that events like NATO pulling out of Afghanistan in 2014 and the death of long-time Uzbek president Islam Karimov in August 2016 would make terrorism a bigger problem, but they didn't really make it worse. Events outside of the region, like the war in Afghanistan and the Islamic State's announcement of a "caliphate" in 2014, have had a bigger impact on the number of people joining. In August 2018, an attack on bikers in Tajikistan was different from other attacks in Central Asia because it was aimed at Western tourists. They did not use very sophisticated means or do a lot of planning, though, just like the attacks in Kazakhstan in 2011 and 2016. These kinds of things are hard to stop. Terrorist acts will probably keep happening from time to time by people and groups who are motivated by extremist propaganda or who have personal problems with the local government.

Terrorism is still a threat to security in Central Asia, and policymakers need to look at it critically and carefully. But what's more important in the region isn't how terrorist groups were able to recruit 0.005 percent of the people who live there, but how government attempts to fight extremism have affected the other 99.9955 percent. There is a lot of terrorism in the area, so governments have used it to keep their power, limit people's rights, and oppress them. Radio Free Europe recently held focus groups with people from Kyrgyzstan, Tajikistan, and Kazakhstan. The people who participated talked about how corrupt local officials and harsh law enforcement are making people angry, which has led to more people joining radical groups. Counter-extremism that isn't well thought out is making the problem it's supposed to solve worse.

Chapter 30
The Growing Threat of the Islamic State in Afghanistan and South Asia

Introduction

When the Taliban took over Afghanistan in 2021, concerns about future terrorism coming from the country shot to the top of the political list around the world. Even so, it wasn't the Taliban that were seen as the ones starting a new wave of terrorism. Rather, policymakers and counterterrorism experts in the West and the region were worried that the victory of the Taliban and the end of the Islamic Republic and the withdrawal of US and international troops could give rise to more militant Islamist groups in Afghanistan, such as al-Qaeda. The Islamic State Khorasan Province (ISKP), which is a regional branch of the Islamic State, is or should be the most important terrorist group for safety.

Since it began in early 2015, ISKP has spread its wings all over South Asia. It is now having a resurgence made possible by the Taliban's takeover, which could pose a threat to both South Asia and the West. There are many reasons why ISKP is such a serious danger, such as its strength, violence, and regional goals. Even though the group had to give up control of land it had held in northern and eastern Afghanistan in 2019, it chose to focus on urban warfare as a strategy. Since then, it has carried out many attacks, including one in August 2021 that killed 170 Afghans and 13 US soldiers. ISKP is now trying to expand its reach beyond its "core" area of Afghanistan and Pakistan to what you could call its "periphery" by connecting with extremist groups in India, Bangladesh, Myanmar, Sri Lanka, and the Maldives.

This chapter looks at the current situation and threat that ISKP and its networks face in South Asia. The chapter talks about the "Khorasan" area, which used to mean the central Asian countries like Afghanistan and Pakistan, as well as eastern Iran and western India. For the Islamic State and other groups like it, the region has always been at the centre of their world goals.

The chapter uses a variety of first-hand sources, such as official and unofficial publications, interviews, statements and speeches, and propaganda materials put out by the ISKP and other groups and people connected to it. This kind of first-hand information tells us a lot about the group's beliefs and identity, as well as its actions and attempts to show who they are. Since a lot of the main data is just propaganda, this chapter also looks at secondary literature to back up claims and give more information about the Islamic State's presence in South Asia.

The first part of the chapter talks about how the Islamic State got started in South Asia and how it is connected to the Levant. The next part of the chapter talks about ISKP's main areas of influence, which are Afghanistan and Pakistan. It looks at the group's history and current goals, its violent actions, attempts to recruit new members, and its use of the media. In the past few years, ISKP has tried to show that it is a power player in Afghanistan by fighting the Taliban and making more people afraid of their terror in the area. The next part looks at the affiliate's position in India and Kashmir, Bangladesh and Myanmar, the Maldives and Sri Lanka, which are all countries on the edges of ISKP's South Asian territory. This chapter looks at ISKP's network in all of these outlying areas as well as the actions of the local groups, which vary from country to country but have been under a lot of pressure to stop terrorism. In the last part, the likely future path of ISKP's activities in South Asia is talked about, along with a list of steps that can be taken to reduce a possible terrorist danger to the West and make the region more resistant to extremism.

The Islamic State's Origins in South Asia

ISKP was officially formed in January 2015, during the second wave of the Islamic State's expansion outside of the Levant. It quickly gained the support of well-known militant Islamist groups and people. In South Asia, the first public show of support for the Islamic State came earlier, when nine al-Qaeda commanders in Afghanistan and Pakistan swore allegiance to the group. This was months before the Islamic State announced that parts of Afghanistan and Pakistan would become part of its self-proclaimed caliphate, which it calls Wilayat Khorasan, or Khorasan Province. In the months that followed, more promises were made, including one by Hafiz Saeed Khan, who was the first leader (wali) of the ISKP and used to be the leader of the Tehrik-i-Taliban Pakistan (TTP, also known as the "Pakistani Taliban"). Abdul Rahim Muslim Dost and Abdul Qahir Khorasani, two other important Afghan extreme ideologues, would also say they were loyal to Abu Bakr al-Baghdadi, the leader of the Islamic State. Individual militants and splits from foreign militant groups, such as a big part of the Islamic Movement of Uzbekistan, which had been a major militant group in Afghanistan for years, joined Khan in supporting al-Baghdadi.

There are two main reasons why support for ISKP grew so quickly at first in Afghanistan and Pakistan. First, there were many different kinds of militants living in the two countries. Many of them were unhappy with the regional jihadist groups' nationalist goals and were ready to join a new, more extreme, and globalist group. In addition, some Muslim groups in the area have become more like Salafis over the past twenty years. The militant Salafi community in the region responded strongly to the Islamic State's message. Shaikh Jalaluddin, a young, powerful Salafi leader who became the ISKP's most senior ideologue and was a key figure in recruiting new members, is a good example of this.

In terms of reaching out to other groups, the "ISKP" label first covers activities of the Islamic State in Afghanistan and Pakistan. It started doing business in Bangladesh in 2016, and after the Islamic State lost control of land in Syria and Iraq in May 2019, there was a big reorganisation of the group. It included announcing that India and Pakistan would each have their own provinces and defining the ISKP as an Afghan group that included parts of northwest Pakistan.

The Islamic State has been building a more complex bureaucratic system since 2014 so that it can spread to places other than Iraq and Syria. The caliphate has tried to run ISKP and other regional groups through a central body known as the General Directorate of Provinces (Idarat al-'Ammat al-Wilayat, or GDP).6 The GDP has a special office for countries in South Asia. It is called the Maktab al-Saddiq and is in Afghanistan. Fighters and supporters from all over South and Central Asia work together through this office.

It looks like ISKP and the leadership in the Levant have a good bond. There are signs that ISKP has kept in touch with the leadership on a regular basis since it was founded, but that it has also been able to make important choices on its own. But when it comes to recent changes in leadership, the branch has listened to the Levant. The first wali of ISKP was chosen by the affiliate's own shura (consultative council). The present wali, Dr. Shahab al-Muhajir, was suggested by the leadership in the Levant in an official letter.

The ISKP Core: Afghanistan and Pakistan

As long as they stay in Afghanistan and Pakistan, ISKP has been able to change its goals, how it works, and its relationships with other terrorist groups. Because it is so adaptable, it has been able to bounce back from defeats in Afghanistan, Pakistan, and against the Islamic State as a whole. The Taliban took over in August 2021, but the ISKP is still a strong force, even though the Taliban have arrested or killed hundreds of its members. ISKP is working to keep the Taliban from keeping their promises to people who support Islamism, the people of Afghanistan, and the rest of the world. This part gives a full picture of ISKP's actions from the beginning to the present day, including how its structure has changed over time, its use of violence, its efforts to recruit new members, and its propaganda.

Figure 1. Iskp's and Ispp's Areas of operation within Afghanistan and Pakistan since july 2021

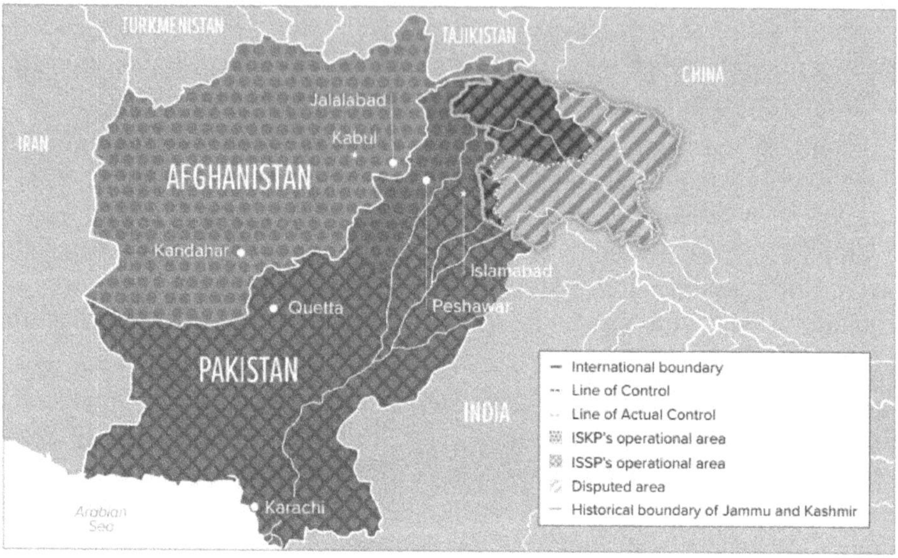

Goals and Evolution

ISKP has gone through two overlapping stages since it was founded, each with its own set of military strategies: from 2015 to late 2019, it focused on gaining territory and making its control stronger; starting in the summer of 2020, it switched its focus to urban warfare.

The original tamkeen (consolidation) strategy of controlling territory was meant to help the ISKP set up its own version of sharia law. In order to do this, the ISKP took over and ruled over areas in eastern, northeastern, and northern Afghanistan. By doing this, it set itself apart from other terrorist groups in the area and gained followers from South and Central Asia, the Middle East, and Europe. The ISKP saw the Taliban as a threat, in part because they had different ideas and in part because their goals in Afghanistan were competitive.

But taking control of the territory came at a high price. ISKP didn't have the money or people to police the people and make sure its rules were followed. ISKP's operational success also made it a major target for an air campaign led by the Afghan army and the US Air Force, as well as a strong Taliban attack to drive

ISKP out of its safe havens in Afghanistan. From 2018 to 2019, the group was under so much pressure that it had to leave the last areas it controlled.

ISKP suffered a huge defeat when their territory fell apart. Communication within the group shows that they were not sure how to hold on to territory as military pressure increased. An ISKP spokesperson, Sultan Aziz Azzam, even admitted that the group was about to break apart and that holding territory should not be their main goal right now. Starting in 2020, ISKP changed its goal from expanding its territory to fighting in cities. The idea behind the new strategy was that ISKP could go after its enemies, like the Taliban, in Afghanistan's cities and show how weak they are, which would make the local people less likely to support them. This change in tactical focus led to a series of attacks very quickly. These included a big, complicated attack on the Nangarhar prison, brutal suicide attacks on a funeral procession in Nangarhar, and attacks on the Shia community and Kabul University students. Pro-ISKP sources say that the new head of the affiliate, al-Muhajir, who is an expert in urban warfare, was the main force behind the change in strategy.

A Separate Wilayat for Pakistan

There are two main groups within the Islamic State's network in neighbouring Pakistan. The first group is made up of former TTP members, most of whom are Salafis from the northwest of Khyber Pakhtunkhwa (KPK) Province. The second is made up of groups that are against the Shia religion and work in the southern part of Balochistan Province. There were two different political groups in Pakistan, and their goals were different. At first, the Islamic State network in the country was split into two separate regional management units, one in Afghanistan and one in Pakistan.

It was officially split from ISKP in May 2019 when the Islamic State's central leadership announced the creation of a new administrative unit for Pakistan. It was called the Wilayat Pakistan, or ISPP. At a time when it was losing control of land in Syria and Iraq, the Islamic State probably set up ISPP to show that it was a strong force in the area. Thus far, however, ISPP has not significantly helped the Islamic State grow its operations in the country.

ISPP lost KPK in July 2021, just two years after it was founded. KPK then became part of the organisational network of ISKP. It looks like this reorganisation was part of ISKP's plan to use the chances in KPK to change how it fights the Pakistani government. This rearrangement is also caused by a number of other things. Most of ISKP's Afghan leaders came from Salafi schools in the province, and new members from KPK were very important to the group's early growth. The province also has a border with Afghanistan that is hard to control. Since the 1970s, this has made it a place where Afghan insurgencies can start.

Now, the ISKP is hoping that the large groups of fighters who live outside of Afghanistan and now live in KPK can help it win its war against the Afghan Taliban. The merger also lets the group do business in Pakistan, which the ISKP blames for the Taliban's fight against the ISKP in Afghanistan and for hurting the Islamist cause in Afghanistan. Since Afghan terrorists took over the ISKP affiliate, this story has become more common in ISKP propaganda.

ISKP-TTP Relations

After the ISKP lost territory in Afghanistan, its relationship with the TTP also changed. Tensions between the two groups have been present since the start of the ISKP because it has recruited a lot of TTP leaders and cadres, but they didn't become public until July 2020, when the two groups traded charges in the media. This happened at the same time that the TTP started to organise itself again. Several Pakistani terrorist groups, including former TTP splits, joined or returned to the TTP.

The TTP said in July 2020 that the ISKP was a front for regional intelligence agencies and was set up to hurt the terrorist movement in the area. After the Taliban took over Kabul in August 2021, these verbal fights got worse when the TTP openly pledged its allegiance to the Afghan Taliban. Soon after, ISKP said that the TTP was getting help from the Indian intelligence service and doing what it told them to do to carry out terrorist attacks in Pakistan. Following a year, these verbal fights turned violent and included murders and gun incidents.

The Use of Violence

ISKP and ISPP terrorist attacks have been very different in recent years in terms of how often they happen and how many people they kill. ISKP mainly does large-scale suicide attacks against strategic targets, while ISPP mostly does small-scale targeted killings of civilians and local security forces.

ISKP

ISKP said they would be stepping up their urban warfare plan with a big attack on the Nangarhar central prison in Jalalabad, the provincial capital, in August 2020 by an 11-person suicide squad. Because of the attack, about 1,000 prisoners were set free, including about 280 ISKP criminals. After this, the number of ISKP attacks in Afghanistan went from 83 in 2020 to 334 in 2021. In May 2021, less than a year after al-Muhajir took over as head, ISKP had the highest rate of violence among the Islamic State's global branches. Figure 2 shows that the number of attacks, which included suicide attacks, targeted killings, ambushes, beheadings, and the use of homemade bombs, went down to 170 in 2022, but it was still a lot more than the number of attacks in 2020.

ISKP doesn't control any land anymore, but the fact that strikes happen so often and so often show how strong the group is. This suggests that ISKP still has a large covert network in the country. Just two weeks after the Taliban took over, the group carried out a terrible bombing attack on Kabul's Hamid Karzai International Airport that killed 170 Afghans and 13 US soldiers. ISKP also said they were behind 119 attacks during an operation that began on September 18, 2021, and ended at the end of the year. The writers' research shows that more than 80% of these attacks were aimed at Taliban fighters. Before 2021, the ISKP was not as likely to kill Taliban members. It only attacked the Taliban 7% of the time in 2020, but that number went up to 33% in 2021 and 72% in 2022. This big change in targets is due to the fact that US and Islamic Republic of Afghanistan troops are no longer in the battle.

Figure 2. Attacks by ISKP in Afghanistan, 2020-22

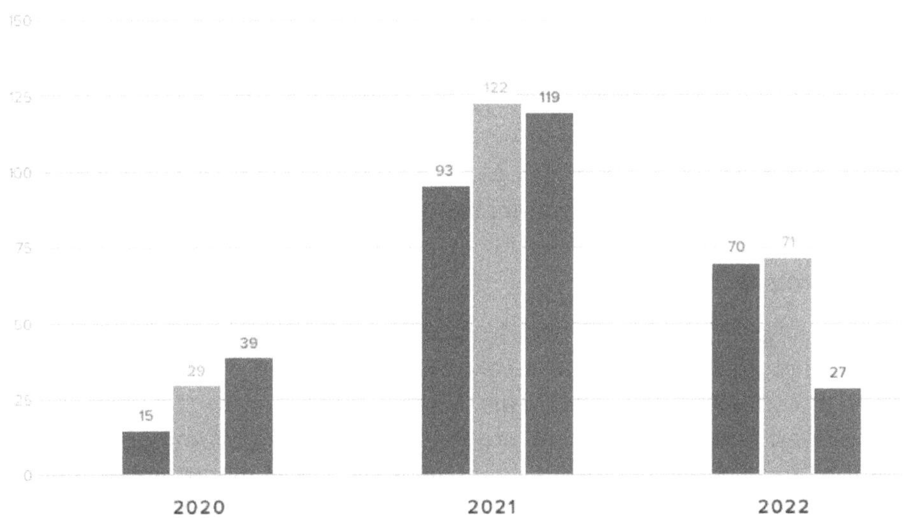

Source: Data reported in Islamic State weekly magazine al-Naba.

In KPK, the restructuring of the organisation has made strikes happen more often and with more force. There were only 25 small-scale killings by the Islamic State between May 2019 and June 2021, a period of 26 months. Nine people died in these attacks. But from July 2021 to December 2022, a huge jump in ISKP attacks in KPK led to 66 attacks that killed 117 people and hurt more than 200 others. There was an attack in March 2022 that killed 67 people at a Shia mosque in the middle of Peshawar, the government city.

ISPP

Even though the Islamic State hadn't killed many people in KPK until lately, it had attacked other parts of Pakistan in the same brutal way. The first one happened in August 2016 in the southern province of Balochistan in Pakistan. A suicide bomber attacked the Quetta hospital, killing 72 and hurting over 200 others. Over the next few years, the group's worst killings in Pakistan would happen in Balochistan and Sindh Provinces. ISPP only did one big attack outside of Balochistan and Sindh. It happened in KPK in November 2018 and was aimed at a market in the Kalaya Shia-populated area of the Orakzai tribal district. When the ISKP's war in Afghanistan hit its most important point in 2019, operations in Pakistan dropped off a lot.

Figure 3 shows the strikes that the Islamic State made in Pakistan's four areas from 2019 to 2022. According to the number, ISPP was not able to change how the Islamic State operated in the country. Militant actions didn't spread outside of KPK and Balochistan, which were controlled by ISPP. There were 68 acts that the group said they did between May 2019 and December 2022, but most of them were small and meant to be symbolic. ISPP said there were 15 killings in Balochistan in 2019, 2 in 2020, 4 in 2021, and 9 in 2022. In 2019, when KPK was under ISPP, there were seven attacks. That number rose to 28 in 2021 and 47 in 2022, when the province was under ISKP.

Recruitment

A huge influx of new members from Pakistan helped the Islamic State get established in Afghanistan and Pakistan in 2015 and 2016, but this source stopped coming in after two years. Several things led to this drop, but the two biggest ones were ISKP's failure to revive the anti-government uprising in Pakistan and fighting within the jihadi movement in Afghanistan between ISKP and the Taliban.

The main idea in the Islamic State's new propaganda since the group's comeback in 2020 is that the main people they want to recruit in Pakistan are still TTP troops from the Pashtun tribes in KPK Province and radical young people from the Salafi community in Afghanistan and KPK. The Islamic State in Pakistan also uses propaganda against anti-Shia fighters and the groups that help them. This group made it easier for ISKP to set up its network and do more in Pakistan.

In Afghanistan, the ISKP's recruitment goals have changed since the Taliban took over and lost most of their territory. Now, the ISKP wants Taliban troops and the Afghan Salafi community to join its fight against the Taliban, whom they say betrayed the jihadi cause through their leadership. In the same way, ISKP asks young Salafi Muslims to join their fight against the Taliban and get back at the Taliban for putting religious limits on the Salafists after they took over. It's hard to say how well this propaganda strategy is working, but the Taliban's efforts to repair relations with the Salafist community since 2022 show that the ISKP may be getting some young Salafis to join.

Media operations

Along with its operations and efforts to recruit new members, the Islamic State has put a lot of effort into spreading lies in Afghanistan and Pakistan. After the Taliban took over in August 2021, the ISKP put all of its marketing and media work under the al-Azaim Media Foundation, which is the group's main media arm. In a report made in September 2022, al-Azaim said that the group had put out 750 audio and 108 video products in the previous year, as well as 175 books, some of which were new and some of which were translations.

ISKP also published four new magazines in 2022. One was an English-language magazine called Voice of Khurasan, which was aimed at followers of Islamic State in South Asia other than Afghanistan. The other three were translations of Voice of Khurasan into Pashto, Persian, and Arabic. There are more and more of these magazines, and they have been very important in getting people to join terrorist groups in Afghanistan and Pakistan.

Figure 3. Attacks by Islamic State in Pakistan, 2019-22

Source: Data reported in Islamic State weekly magazine al-Naba.

When it comes to Pakistan, ISPP doesn't have a local media arm and doesn't seem to make any video or written materials on its own. Instead, its movies are released in Arabic by the Islamic State's main media office, called diwan al-'ilam. The only magazine that doesn't follow this rule is Yalghar (Invasion), which has put out three issues since April 2021.

The ISKP Periphery

ISKP's main areas of control are still Afghanistan and Pakistan, but the Islamic State has tried to expand its reach by joining radical networks and either calling them official provinces or working with them through unofficial networks. India (including Kashmir), Bangladesh, Myanmar, Sri Lanka, and the Maldives make up most of this peripheral region. All but India are administratively under ISKP. The Islamic State has also tried to spread its actions to Central Asian countries since the beginning of 2021.

This part talks about how the Islamic State is organised and what it does in these South Asian countries on the edges. It starts with India and Kashmir and then moves on to Bangladesh and Myanmar. Finally, it talks about Sri Lanka and the Maldives. In general, the group hasn't been able to make a name for itself in these areas yet, which can be explained by both strong anti-terrorism efforts and rivalry with other terrorist groups. Still, some of the countries on the edge are split along social, economic, and political lines that make it easy for terrorist groups like the Islamic State to operate. If these problems aren't fixed, radical groups will be able to grow and recruit in Muslim communities that don't feel like they have a voice.

Islamic State in India and Kashmir

India and the disputed region of Kashmir make up the Islamic State's most active border area in South Asia. It is also the only part of the region that is not Afghanistan or Pakistan that has been recognised as an independent province. But the Islamic State hasn't been able to get a lot of its followers in India to move to the Levant or do extremist things in their own country. The group first showed up in India when there were several pro-Islamic State groups working in Jammu and Kashmir, which is controlled by India. These followers changed their name to "Islamic State in Jammu and Kashmir" (ISJK) in July 2017. However, it wasn't until May 2019 that the Islamic State officially set up a separate province in India that included Kashmir. The creation of that province, Wilayat al-Hind (hereafter, ISHP), showed that there were Islamic State members in mainland India. However, the group mostly works in Kashmir and has a weak presence in other Indian states.

Origins and Status of the Local Network

As early as 2014, when Tanzim Ansar al-Tawhid fi Bilad al-Hind was formed, pro-Islamic State groups began to form in India. In October of that year, this network promised to support the Islamic State. However, the promise was never kept, just like it was for many other small networks in the Muslim world. Later, news of other networks with ties to the Islamic State came out. These networks were made up of small, separate groups that didn't have much of an effect on the ground.

Mohammad Eesa Fazili (also known as Abu Yahya al-Istashadi), working with Islamic State officials in Afghanistan, stated ISJK in the middle of 2017. This was the first step towards change. Even though the group's online identity looked amateurish and it didn't get official recognition right away, it was the first step for a large group of pro-Islamic State followers in mainland India and Kashmir to come together.

With the network's online presence growing and the start of small strikes in late 2017, the government put more pressure on it to stop terrorism. The government quickly responded by killing three important ISJK leaders in March 2018, including the emir, Fazili. Three months after Fazili's death, his replacement, Burhan Musab, was killed. He was replaced by Abu Anwar al-Kashmiri, who was killed in September 2018. The new pro-Islamic State network also had to deal with being attacked by both the government and rival militant groups in Kashmir, who were competing for support and new members. In June 2019, these problems got worse, and members of Adil Ahmad Dass's old group, Lashkar-e-Taiba, killed the important ISHP leader.

Supporters of the Islamic State and other militants have had less of a hard time getting along with each other in Kashmir than in other places where the Islamic State is directly fighting its terrorist rivals. Even though the jihadi movement had become very split up and divided, terrorists in Kashmir didn't seem to care much about these differences at first. But that changed in 2019.

While growing in India, the network of people who back the Islamic State also sent people to join jihadi insurgencies in other countries. Up to 200 people left India, most of them from the state of Kerala, and went to the Levant and Afghanistan to join the Islamic State. India has a big Muslim population, so that number is surprisingly low. However, the people who did participate had an effect on the domestic network and were an important way for the organisation to get advice and talk to people in Syria and Afghanistan.

Umar Nisar Bhat was one of the people who got something good from this link. Nisar has been a key member of the pro-Islamic State network in India since the start of ISJK. He was the wali of ISHP until he was arrested in July 2021 and played a big part in spreading the network's message. Nisar and his close friends were arrested, which was a huge blow to ISHP. However, the group has kept up its regular propaganda, and a video released in December 2022 suggests that it may be seen as a separate network within the Islamic State from ISKP.

Militant Activities, Propaganda, and Recruitment

Even though the Islamic State has been in India in the form of ISJK and then ISHP, it has never been able to launch a program of regular attacks there. The most well-known action by an Indian terrorist in support of the Islamic State was the attack on a Sikh temple in Kabul on March 25, 2020, by Abu Khalid al-Hindi, who was born in Kerala.

The group has said it was behind 23 strikes since November 2017, the first one being in Kashmir. All but one of those attacks happened in Kashmir. It said there were nine killings in 2021, eight of them in Srinagar. In 2020, there were only two. Abdur Rahman al-Logari, the suicide bomber who would later be responsible for the attack at Kabul Airport in 2022, was supposed to carry out an attack in New Delhi in 2017. However, he was caught by Indian police and sent back to Afghanistan before the attack could happen.

India has had fewer attacks than other countries in the region, even though it has a big Muslim population. This may be because India's counterterrorism efforts have gotten a lot better since the terrible Mumbai attack by Lashkar-e-Taiba in 2008. As an example of how hard the government's efforts to fight terrorism have made operations, the group didn't do anything for two and a half months after Nisar was arrested, and they only claimed two attacks in 2022. The National Investigation Agency (NIA), India's security agency, says that as of September 2021, 168 people had been accused of having ties to the Islamic State in 37 different cases.

So far, ISHP has only been able to carry out small-scale acts that have killed few people. Most of the attacks are either targeted killings that kill one person or petrol bombs that don't hurt anyone. There was only one time when an attack killed more than one person.

The NIA says that the main goal of ISHP members and supporters is not to carry out operations but to make and spread lies through different types of media. In contrast, the public media of the Islamic State rarely talk about India, which is an interesting contrast. As of early January 2019, the English-language Risalah (Message) magazine was released by ISJK. When it changed its name from ISJK to ISHP, the magazine was called Sawt al-Hind (Voice of Hind). Intelligence agencies' investigations have shown that the magazine is made by pro-Islamic State people in South Asia who are connected to groups around the world in complex ways. The people who gather material for the magazine are based in India and Afghanistan, but they work with supporters in the Maldives and Bangladesh to get stories from those places. In the end, Pakistan is where the magazine is written.

Figure 4

Sikh men mourn in Kabul, Afghanistan, on March 26, 2020, the day after Islamic State gunman Abu Khalid al-Hindi attacked a Sikh house of worship. (Photo by Tamana Sarwary/AP)

Voice of Hind, which was published by ISHP in Urdu and English starting in February 2020, mostly talked to Indian Muslims. Three issues that really bother the ISHP and people who support it are the destruction of the Babri mosque in Uttar Pradesh and the Supreme Court's decision to build a Hindu temple in its place, the 2019 law that gets rid of Article 370 of India's constitution and ends Kashmir's special status, and the changes that are being made to India's Citizenship Act. These problems are shown to be very clear examples of Hindu nationalist policies that are against the country's Muslim people.

In 2022, ISHP took steps to improve and focus its media output even more. It said on April 13, 2022, that its main news source would now be a new centre called Nashir al-Hind. It's possible that well-known media outlets like al-Tazkirah, al-Burhan, and al-Qitaal no longer exist as separate businesses. But on January 24, 2023, the first issue of Serat ul-Haq, an English-language ISHP magazine, came out from a new organisation called al-Jauhar Media Centre. It's still not clear if al-Jauhar is an official ISHP outlet or if it's run by sympathisers, but the news goes against the policy of centralisation.

The ISHP puts out a lot of lies to appeal to Muslims who feel left out of politics in a country run by a party that claims to be Hindu nationalist. There are times when the network tries to get people to help with activities, but their main goal is to spread propaganda. Recruiters talk to people on private media platforms and tell those who support the cause to help with translation, production, or spreading the word. But ISHP faces a problem in Kashmir: there are already a lot of militant groups there, and they are all fighting for new members.

Islamic State in Bangladesh and Myanmar

For at least 20 years, jihadist propaganda has made Bangladesh and Myanmar very important. In terms of propaganda, al-Qaeda has paid the most attention to these two countries. However, the Islamic State has been busier with actions. On the other hand, both groups see Bangladesh and Myanmar as linked, in part because of the one million Rohingya refugees in Bangladesh who are from Myanmar.

In Bangladesh, Islam is the official religion, and there are a lot of Muslims. In Myanmar, on the other hand, only a small portion of the population is Muslim, and most of those people are Rohingya, an ethnic group that the government has been targeting. Supporters of Islamic State have tried to use the fact that these countries have different religious groups to spread their networks and online talk that says Islam should be a system of government in Bangladesh but isn't and that Muslims are being oppressed in Myanmar.

Origins and Status of the Network

Extremists in Bangladesh were alarmed from the start when the Islamic State announced its kingdom in the Levant. Many people pledged their loyalty right away, but the Islamic State's representative in "Bengal" (Bangladesh) came from two extremist groups that were already there: Jund al-Tawheed al-Khilafah and Jamaatul Mujahidin Bangladesh (JMB). This group, JMB, has been around since 1998 and used to support al-Qaeda. After being dormant for a few years, a part of the group came back to life after the caliphate announcement. These two groups came together in 2015 to form the group Dawlatul Islam Bengal. But that group hasn't been officially recognised as a province by the Islamic State yet. Instead, fans of the group call them the "Soldiers of the Khilafah in Bengal" online.

Since its formation in 2015, the Islamic State's Bengal branch has suffered from the Bangladeshi government's crackdown on extremists. Even though the country doesn't have a lot of resources to fight terrorism, the group has had problems with operations and even getting the word out to the public. For example, when Islamic State members from around the kingdom renewed their loyalty to Abu al-Hassan al-Baghdadi in 2022, there was no pledge from Bengal. This was despite the fact that members of Islamic State Bengal had pledged their allegiance to two different caliphs in 2019.

Myanmar doesn't have a clear-cut network of people who support the Islamic State. However, on November 6, 2020, a group called Katibat al-Mahdi fi balad al-Arakan (KMBA) made a promise to support the Islamic State, but it hasn't been accepted yet. It's not clear if KMBA ever really put together a physical network of Islamic State members in Myanmar or if it was just a digital effort run from Bangladesh to find Rohingya people who had lost their citizenship.

Violence and Propaganda

In the 1980s, a lot of people from Bangladesh went to Afghanistan to join the war. Most of them joined groups that shared al-Qaeda's beliefs. There was already an al-Qaeda organisation in Bangladesh before the Islamic State's Bengal network was set up. Ansar al-Islam was the local chapter of al-Qaeda in the Indian subcontinent.

Al-Qaeda has been running a strong marketing campaign about Bangladesh and Myanmar, but it has been hard for the group to back up what it says with actions. It says that al-Qaeda has only claimed 10 strikes in Bangladesh, according to the Global Terrorism Database. The Islamic State, on the other hand, has claimed credit for 38 attacks.

The Islamic State network's attacks are different from al-Qaeda's in both the people they target and the way they do them. At first, in 2015 and 2016, the network killed a wide range of people it considered enemies, such as Western missionaries, Hindu and Buddhist speakers, and Shia holy places. The most well-known of these was the attack on the Holey Artisan Bakery in Dhaka in 2016. Five militants took prisoners and fought with police, killing 22 people in the process. The attack was the first time that more than one person was killed in an Islamic State operation in Bangladesh. More importantly, it showed that the group's network in Bangladesh could handle complex operations.

There wasn't much going on between March 2017 and April 2019, but since then there has been a big change in how things are done and who the goals are. Now, Islamic State members in Bangladesh mostly use homemade bombs to attack police. This is probably because of the harsh anti-terrorism campaign launched against Islamists after the Holey Artisan Bakery attack. Many people may be surprised to learn that the group's move to explosives has not led to more deaths. In fact, most of the attacks since 2019 have not killed anyone. The last attack that was said to have happened was on July 31, 2020. It looks like the network has been slowed down by the government's efforts to fight terrorism and can't do anything right now.

Along with its busy schedule of operations in 2015 and 2016, the Islamic State sent some propaganda to Bangladesh. In its Dabiq magazine, there were several articles about what one called the "Revival of Jihad in Bengal." In an interview for another piece, Abu Ibrahim al-Hanif, the leader of Islamic State members in Bangladesh, painted a positive picture of the group's rise and support in the country. One of the main ideas of the conversation is how the militant groups in Bangladesh and Myanmar are linked. Bangladesh is seen as the base that needs to be solidified before the jihad can successfully spread to Myanmar. According to Al-Hanif, the militants in Bangladesh play a bigger part in the region: "Bengal is on the eastern side of India, while Wilayat Khurasan is on the western side." So, having a strong jihad base in Bengal will make it easier for both sides to launch guerrilla attacks inside India at the same time. This will also make it easier to create a state of tawahhush (savagery) in India with the help of the local mujahidin.

In September 2016, the first public Islamic State video made in Bangladesh came out. The main point of the video was to show testimony from the people who did the Holey Artisan Bakery attack, but it also had a more general attack on the Bangladeshi government and the Islamic scholars who back it.

Figure 5

Clergymen visit St. Sebastian Church in Negombo, Sri Lanka, on April 22, 2019, the day after the church and other locations were attacked by a group thought to represent the Islamic State in Sri Lanka. (Photo by Gemunu Amarasinghe/AP)

The Islamic State has tried to get people to join them in Myanmar, mostly by using the Rohingya situation to its advantage. Myanmar's government propaganda, on the other hand, mostly shows it as linked to Bangladesh. Not one attack in Myanmar had been claimed by the Islamic State as of March 2023. Abu Dawud al-Arakan, the head of KMBA, said in the first issue of its magazine Arkan that the group's network is not strong enough yet to launch attacks in Myanmar. At the moment, the network is focussing on getting Rohingya people to join the group in Bangladesh or help spread its propaganda online.

The area between Bangladesh and Myanmar is the most appealing place for the Islamic State in South Asia, along with Kashmir. The Islamic State can tap into a long-standing extremist community in Bangladesh. Since things aren't likely to get better for the Rohingya in Myanmar, there is a huge chance for the group to find new followers and get them to work together.

Islamic State in the Maldives and Sri Lanka

Not long ago, neither the Maldives nor Sri Lanka were usually thought of as places where Islamic terrorism happened. This was different after the Islamic State came into power, but for two different reasons. A lot of Maldivians joining the wars in Syria and Iraq made people in the Maldives more aware of rising radicalisation in their own country. In Sri Lanka, the horrible Easter attack in 2019 made people more aware of the presence of militant Islamists.

Origins and Status of the Network

The Maldives have changed since the storm in 2004. After the disaster, foreign Islamic institutions began to work there and give money to Pakistani and Saudi Arabian schools to pay for religious education. People from the Maldives who had become radicalised quickly started moving to Afghanistan and Pakistan to join the Taliban and al-Qaeda. Thirteen radical Islamists set off a bomb in Male's Sultan Park in 2007 in what was the first known terrorist attack in the Maldives. As people became more radicalised, a local extreme network called "Dot" was formed onto an organisational level. At first, the network supported al-Qaeda. But in 2014, it split into two groups: those who still supported al-Qaeda and those who switched their support to the Islamic State.

2014 was a turning point for extremists in the Maldives. On August 8, al-Qaeda fans took journalist Ahmed Rilwan Abdulla hostage and killed him. A group called the "Islamic State of the Maldives" was formed the month before. Around the same time, the Haqqu Media Centre opened. It quickly became a major source of pro-Islamic State propaganda in Dhivehi, aimed at people in the area. A UN monitoring unit says that the Islamic State of the Maldives is not a formal Islamic State structure, but that the ISKP "works with networks of supporters in Maldives."

Sri Lanka is an even stranger place for radical Islam because of the mix of religions that live there. Even so, that's what the country became, if only for a short time, when terrorists attacked three high-end hotels and three churches in the city on April 21, 2019, which was Easter. The Islamic State claimed responsibility for the attack two days later. It was related to a local group called National Thowfeek Jamaath, which formed in 2009 in response to rising Buddhist nationalism and the government's harsh treatment of Muslims. Because of this mix of government oppression and Islamic extremism, Muslims and Buddhist separatists have attacked each other many times over the years. As war broke out in the Levant, Sri Lanka's government also started to pay attention to the rising number of Muslims (possibly as many as 50) who were going to Syria to fight with the Islamic State.

After the Easter Sunday attack, it wasn't clear at first if the cell was connected to the Islamic State. However, it turned out that Zahran Hashim, the leader of the attack, had talked to the Islamic State leadership in Syria and been accepted as the group's representative in Sri Lanka.

Militant Activities, Propaganda, and Recruitment

Even though they had been active since 2014, there weren't many signs that Maldivian Islamic State followers were planning to attack their home country of Maldives until 2020. A fair number of people from the Maldives joined the jihad in the Levant. In fact, about 300 people from the Maldives joined al-Qaeda or the Islamic State in the Levant, making it the country that sent the most terrorists per person in the world.

In 2017, police stopped an attack that the prosecutor said was linked to the Islamic State. This was the first sign that the pro-Islamic State network was working in the Maldives. Muhammad Ameen was caught by local police in October 2019 because they thought he was recruiting people for the Islamic State. In February 2020, someone stabbed three tourists. The attack was later claimed in an unconfirmed video made by people who support Islamic State. But it wasn't until April 15, 2020, that the first attack in the Maldives was claimed by Islamic State. Five boats docked at the port of Mahibadhoo were bombed, which was a big step up in the group's operations.

In January 2021, the Maldivian government said that eight members of the network had been caught two months before for planning an attack on a school. Ten people tried to kill Mohamed Nasheed, the former president of the Maldives and current Speaker of the parliament, on May 6, 2020, but their plan failed. The police say the people involved were supporters of Islamic State. It's possible that the network of followers hasn't been able to carry out more attacks because it is split up among itself. He says that the lack of a boss, bad manners, and information leaks are all bad for the network in the Maldives and were written about in Voice of Hind in August 2020.

Along with these increased operational actions, the Maldives have been featured more and more in Islamic State propaganda. In the May 2020 issue of Voice of Hind, there is an article called "A Letter to Mujahideen in Maldives" that says the Maldives is the newest country to pledge allegiance to the Islamic State. However, the Islamic State has never officially acknowledged that there is a group in the Maldives. Overall, lies about the Maldives is mostly about getting people to attack all non-Muslims in the country.

Three events in Sri Lanka can be linked to a group of people who support Islamic State. The first was the desecration of Buddhist statues in Mawanella in December 2018. The second was the coordinated bombings of three hotels and three churches on April 21, 2019, which killed almost 300 civilians. Five days later, police raided a safe house linked to the second attack, which led to a shootout between the police and the attackers. The Islamic State took responsibility for the last two events. Still, the Islamic State has not been able to set up a permanent presence in Sri Lanka since the group responsible for the Easter bombings was broken up. The harsh crackdown by the government seems to have stopped any further mobilisation.

Conclusion and Recommendations

As the Islamic State's reach grows in South Asia and the ISKP faces less pressure to fight terrorism since US troops left Afghanistan, it is important to know if Islamic State groups and allies in the area pose a threat to Western countries through terrorism. Some people in the West who work in intelligence think the answer is "qualified yes," at least when it comes to ISKP. General Kenneth F. McKenzie Jr., who used to be head of US Central Command, said in March 2022 that ISKP does not currently have the power to attack in the West, but that it can do so within 12 to 18 months, if not sooner. Although McKenzie didn't say it directly, it is likely that this danger comes mostly from the Islamic State's leaders in Afghanistan, if not only from them.

So far, terrorism in the West that has been linked to the Islamic State has either been carried out by people who support the group working alone or by people who were trained in Syria or Iraq or by virtual planners who are based in those places. Affiliates have usually only had a small part in planning or funding these kinds of operations. In this way, the Islamic State is like al-Qaeda has been for a long time: its members are mostly motivated by local political goals and having to deal with other terrorist groups that are competing with them. But by the middle of 2020, a virtual planner in Afghanistan was thought to be leading a group of four Tajiks who were part of the Islamic State and were planning to attack US and NATO sites in Germany. There was never any real attack, but this shows that ISKP can be used to plan or carry out strikes in the West. Two ISKP agents were arrested in Turkey in January 2023 as part of another plan that was said to have been linked to the group. And in February 2023, after secret Pentagon papers were leaked on the messaging app Discord, it was said that US intelligence had learnt of 15 terrorist plots against the West that were being planned by Islamic State members in Afghanistan.

Many people don't know much about the Islamic State's plans to attack the West from Afghanistan, but the way their local goals have changed since the Taliban took over show that they could become a bigger threat to the world from Afghanistan. The ISKP story is based on two main ideas: it says that it is the continuation of the global war that al-Qaeda gave up, and it shames the Taliban for being a nationalist group. So, planning a terrorist act in the West would be good for ISKP in many ways. An attack from Afghanistan that goes off successfully would raise the profile of the Islamic State around the world, show that Khorasan is an important part of the global Islamic State network, and show that the Taliban can't run Afghanistan. If it turns out that the Taliban can't stop Afghanistan from being used as a base for terrorist strikes outside of Afghanistan, they will face even more political pressure from around the world. In short, ISKP has a strong reason to plan an attack against its rival that will seriously hurt its reputation.

The Islamic State in South Asia is currently facing three problems that make it harder for them to attack other countries. First, ISKP and other networks in South Asia don't have a framework that is only for planning and carrying out attacks from outside the country. Second, ISKP is mostly limited to Afghanistan and is currently under a lot of security pressure from the Taliban, which makes it harder for it to plan and carry out complicated attacks against other countries. Third, some Western fighters have joined ISKP, but not many. This makes it less likely that the group can teach Westerners and then send them back to their home countries to carry out operations. It could be said that the biggest risk the West faces right now is that ISKP could use radical Afghan networks already in the West to get people to act and give them orders to attack. Even though the chance of this happening is small, it should still be taken seriously.

While ISKP may not pose a big threat to the West right now, the threat is likely to grow, maybe even a lot, in the next few years. This is because the withdrawal of Western troops has made it easier to fight terrorism and may have made it easier for ISKP to do its work. At the same time, there has been a lot more propaganda encouraging strikes from other countries. Threats to Western interests, ideals, and partners in South Asia, Pakistan, and Afghanistan are also part of the threat to the West. These include direct terrorist attacks on the West.

So, what can the West, especially the US, do to lessen, get rid of, or stop these threats? Since 2001, the US has been the world's leader in fighting terrorism in the area.

The US no longer has as many chances to fight extremists in Afghanistan and the surrounding area since it pulled out of the country. Still, there are some things that can be done to reduce the threat of terrorism to the West and make the area more resistant to extremism.

Look into the idea of working together with the Taliban on a small scale to fight terrorism. Because it would be politically sensitive, the US and other Western countries should look into the possibility of working together on counterterrorism problems on a small scale by taking advantage of the Taliban's lack of unity. Because it is hard to do business in Afghanistan, the West doesn't have many choices but to work with the Taliban to fight a shared enemy. The Taliban want to fight the Islamic State very much as a group. This kind of partnership should not go beyond gathering information about terrorist groups, and Western countries should be careful not to work together in a way that makes the Taliban stronger militarily or politically. As a first step towards cooperation, intelligence that will help US kinetic actions could be shared and checked.

Help the states on the edges of the world. With the possible exception of India, the peripheral states where Islamic State members or supporters live may not be able to handle the danger of domestic terrorism. The US should work with more countries to fight terrorism and violent extremism (PVE). It should also offer help, such as signal and human intelligence, as well as PVE expertise, to countries like Bangladesh, Myanmar, Sri Lanka, and the Maldives to deal with possible threats from networks linked to the Islamic State and to build up their ability to disarm domestic extremist groups, while not supporting Myanmar's military junta.

Help programs that demobilise and reintegrate people. People who want to leave violent groups and stop being extremists often face very tough problems. The US should look into ways to help South Asian governments and civil society groups create and grow demobilisation and reintegration programs, which could include amnesty, to make it easier for people to leave militant groups and become free from their control. These kinds of programs work best when they are run by and owned by the community themselves, but outside groups, like the US, can help with money and knowledge.

Stop the spread of lies online. Extremist networks and groups in South Asia spend a lot of time and effort making and spreading material that is meant to radicalise and mobilise people online. So, people should work to stop extremist material from being made and stop it from spreading on social media and encrypted platforms like Telegram and Facebook Messenger. This means going after both the networks that make the propaganda and the networks of people who back it and help spread it to a lot of people. Part of this effort to stop the spread of terrorism should be working together with established groups like the Global Internet Forum to Counter Terrorism (an initiative of the internet business) and Tech Against Terrorism (a UN-backed initiative) to stop the spread of content in regional languages.

Support different political views and treat minorities with care. South Asian countries have deep divisions between groups because of policies that discriminate against, marginalise, and even violently repress minorities. These policies have made groups so angry that some of their members are turning to the Islamic State to help them fight back. The US should push for political and religious diversity and expect all states to support all minorities in order to lower the risks of these kinds of policies. To begin, the US could look into the possibility of working with local partners to run targeted communication campaigns in Rohingya camps in Myanmar and Muslim communities in India. These campaigns would warn people about the Islamic State and promote stories of other possible futures.

Chapter 31
The History and Evolution of the Islamic State in Southeast Asia

While the Islamic State's East Asia Province (ISEAP) was thought to be dead until lately, it is just one of many groups that continue to be a threat to Southeast Asia. ISEAP formed in a very different way from its Middle Eastern ancestors. It was a loosely connected network that grew through factionalism, mergers, and taking advantage of opportunities. The ISEAP was a different kind of threat than other Islamic State groups because it wasn't centralised. However, after the group's spectacular siege of Marawi city in Mindanao, Philippines, in 2017, governments in the region worked together to make the group less of a threat. Southeast Asia is still at risk of violent extremism, even though ISEAP hasn't been very active lately. This is because of the fact that many of the groups that make up ISEAP are always changing, and there are also ongoing political problems in the region that keep people supporting these kinds of groups.

Origins of Contemporary Terrorism in Southeast Asia

Southeast Asia has had Islamic rebel groups for hundreds of years, and their activities have grown since the end of the colonial era. In 1981, an Indonesian group called Komando Jihad took over a Garuda Indonesia flight, which was the first big act of terrorism in the area. The hijackers wanted money, the release of hardliners who were in jail, and the removal of Israelis from Indonesia. At the time, this was in line with what other terror groups were doing and what they wanted. The CIA says that between 1968 and 1982, there were 108 hijackings.

It's possible that the hijacking of a Pakistani airline flight by extremists in 1981 sparked the Komando Jihad. The fact that this happened shows that Southeast Asian groups are likely to follow world trends. Also, Komando Jihad grew out of Darul Islam, a group that had fought an insurgency to set up an Islamic state in Indonesia after it became independent. This shows that dangerous splits often form from bigger groups in the region. Later, the same thing happened in the Philippines, where Moro fighters in the south formed the

Moro National Liberation Front (MNLF), which later split into the Moro Islamic Liberation Front (MILF) and other groups. On another occasion, in 1976, MNLF took over a plane and killed 10 people on board. The Moro people have been fighting back since the time when Spain and the United States ruled Mindanao, Sulu, and Palawan. The Moro are a group of 13 Muslim-majority ethnic groups. As long as the Moros (and their former Sultanates) fought against foreign rule, the war has had religious and racial overtones. In the 20th century, when the U.S. colonial government and then the Filipino government moved a lot of Christian Filipinos to the area, the religious and racial factor became more important.

MILF has had a peace deal with Manila since 2014, but in 2017, disgruntled former members of the group took part in ISEAP's siege of Marawi. This shows how unstable Southeast Asian militant groups are. These kinds of groups often work together on logistics and operations, with people moving from one group to another to help the most busy group or find safety. Lastly, these groups are often shaped by family and social bonds. This is especially true in the Philippines and Indonesia, where clan, social, and family relationships are important in driving people to join insurgent and terror groups. In this way, fighting terror groups in the region is especially hard because these ideas and people are so deeply ingrained in the social fabric of each area.

The 1990s and 2000s: The al-Qaeda Era

In the 1990s, the al-Qaeda movement and other remains of the Afghan mujahidin left a big mark on Southeast Asia. This is also the time when the groups that are now known as Southeast Asia's major terrorist organisations began to form. Extremists from Indonesia, the Philippines, and Malaysia who had been in Afghanistan during the war against the Soviet Union got in touch with al-Qaeda and the Taliban during this time. In the 2000s, Jemaah Islamiyah (JI) was the deadliest international terror group in Southeast Asia. Al-Qaeda helped make it possible for JI to form. Some groups in the Philippines were linked to this one. For example, the Abu Sayyaf Group (ASG) was formed by radical MNLF members and got help from al-Qaeda. The Kumpulan Mujahidin Malaysia (KMM) in Malaysia was also very close to JI. In this way, jihadist trends around the world had a big effect on networks of jihadists in this time frame.

At this time, the Bali Bombings in 2002 were Southeast Asia's most well-known terrorist act. These killings, which were carried out by JI, killed 202 people and hurt at least that many more. One of the attackers, Umar Patek, said that the attacks were caused by Israel's acts against Palestinians in Jenin earlier that year. However, another attacker, Ali Imron, said that they were caused by the U.S. invasion of Afghanistan in 2001. This lack of consistency shows that groups in the region are very aware of world trends, which they often use as an excuse for what they do. It also shows that some important people in groups have different ideas, which has led to leadership splits and breakoffs. Between 2002 and 2008, JI carried out several more bombings, mostly against Western targets, religious communities, and Indonesian security forces. They worked with ASG in the Philippines and planned to hit Malaysia, Thailand, and Singapore. During this time, ASG also became well-known for kidnappings for ransom, bombs, gunfights, murders, and beheadings. The group also bombed a ferry in Manila Bay in 2004, killing 116 people. This was the biggest terrorist attack in the Philippines before 2017. Umar Patek, a member of the JI, taught ASG how to make IEDs, showing how flexible these groups are within the area.

Because these groups are based on family and social links, they are very flexible. In the 2000s, foreign terrorist fighters (FTFs) also started to come to Southeast Asia. The Philippines had the most FTFs. At this time, FTFs came from other Southeast Asian countries, the Middle East, and other places, including at least one from Australia. By the late 2000s, counterterrorism measures and internal fighting had made JI much weaker, but the group still existed. Even though al-Qaeda had lost a lot of members in the Global War on Terror, they were still not providing any operational or other help to the southern Philippines. The violence there stayed very high. Long-standing historical grievances and ongoing racial and religious tensions led people in the area to back these groups. They got money from donations, business income, and crime.

The 2010s: New Groups Form from Old, the Islamic State Enters the Picture

Another movement like the Islamic State grew out of the rise of the group in the Middle East and Southeast Asia between Muslims. In the early and middle 2010s, a number of new terrorist groups formed in Indonesia and the Philippines. As in the past, these were mostly made up of the most extreme members of established groups. The Bangsamoro Islamic Freedom Fighters (BIFF) were created in the Philippines around 2010 when a MILF boss didn't agree with the group's choice to talk with Manila about getting more independence. The Comprehensive Agreement on Bangsamoro was signed by MILF and Manila in 2014. It was a big step forward for the Philippines and the Moro Groups after decades of talks. This made it possible for the Bangsamoro Autonomous Region of Muslim Mindanao (BARMM) to be made. Even though there is a deal, putting it into action has been slow and full of worries. The agreement also caused more disagreement within MILF, and the Maute Group, Ansar Khilafah Philippines (AKP), and other groups finally split off. These groups later made ties to other jihadist groups and individuals in Malaysia and Indonesia. After MILF was recognised and JI was broken, they became the leaders of jihadism in the area.

At the same time, splits within JI led to the formation of at least 18 new Islamist groups in Indonesia by the middle of the 2010s. One of these was Jamaah Ansharut Daulah (JAD), which is an umbrella group of pro-Islamic State groups run by the famous Islamist scholar Aman Abdurahman. Aman Abdurahman was one of many strict teachers who started to apply the Islamic State's ideas to Southeast Asia when the group became well-known in the middle of the 2010s. Around 1,000 fighters from the Philippines, Malaysia, Singapore, and Thailand went to the Middle East to join the Islamic State in Iraq and Syria (ISIS) and the al-Nusra Front, which is linked to al-Qaeda. This was because of these efforts and other things, like Abu Bakr al-Baghdadi's declaration of a caliphate.

While they were in the Middle East, these rebels formed Katibah Nusantara (KN), an ISIS group for all of Southeast Asia. Katibah Nusantara helped ISIS with its operations and fought against Kurdish forces. It also trained new members from Southeast Asia. One Indonesian person is also said to have been an executioner for ISIS. There were apparently some ideological disagreements among the Indonesian fighters, but they did not lead to violence between factions like it did among the Middle Eastern and other fighters at the time. This may show how Southeast Asian fighters are different from other fighters in terms of culture.

A lot of Southeast Asian terrorist groups and their leaders joined the Islamic State in 2014. Santoso of the East Indonesia Mujahideen (MIT), Aman Abdurahman of JAD, Esmail Abubakar of BIFF, and the Maute brothers of the Maute Group were some of these people. When Abu Sayyaf and some other groups made their promise, the Islamic State officially recognised it in early 2016. That's when they made Isnilon Hapilon of the Philippines their emir. In the middle of 2018, the Islamic State would officially recognise Wilayat Sharq Asiyya (East Asia region) as its Southeast Asian region. This led to the creation of ISEAP.

Around 2015, the groups that were part of ISEAP became busier and launched more strikes. Bahrun Naim was a key Indonesian leader in the Katibah Nusantara group. He planned attacks in Indonesia, such as the 2016 Jakarta bombings, which killed eight people, including four of the attackers, in a gunfight and multiple blasts. Then, on May 13, 2018, JAD carried out Indonesia's worst attack since the Bali bombings in 2002. Cells of terrorists killed 28 people and hurt 57 others by committing suicide attacks in several churches in the city of Surabaya. In October 2019, a member of JAD stabbed Wiranto, who was Indonesia's defence minister at the time, in a random act of violence. Wiranto survived his injuries.

From 2015 to 2022, JAD cells attacked different parts of Indonesia, mostly attacking police and religious minorities. Some of these were made easier by the fact that a member of the group called Bahrum Naim spread instructions on how to make bombs. Naim was also very good at using technology to help recruit Indonesians to fight in Iraq and Syria. The flammable triacetone triperoxide and other poisons and chemicals that were easy to get were used by JAD cells in experiments. One JAD group in Bekasi, which is in the Greater Jakarta metropolitan area, is said to have found a way to get around police signal jammers.

In the Philippines, there was also more ISEAP-related activity from Maute, BIFF, and ASG. ASG continued its strategy of kidnapping people across the Sulu Archipelago and holding them for ransom. Because of constant fears of kidnapping and smuggling from people in the Philippines and extremists, Kuala Lumpur made a special security zone in eastern Sabah in 2013. During this time, all of these groups attacked security troops with bombs, ambushes, killings, and gunfights.

ISEAP-aligned groups were mostly unsuccessful in Malaysia, unlike in Indonesia and the Philippines. In 2016, they only carried out one attack, which involved throwing a bomb into a pub in Movida, Puchong, which hurt eight people. Munira Mustaffa, head of the Chasseur Group and an expert on security in Southeast Asia, called it an act that showed "a lack of preparation and planning." The whole thing should have been seen as a sign of how weak, inexperienced, and immature the local group was, just like what happened with the people who did the 2004 Madrid Bombings. Similarly, pro-ISEAP groups tried many times to include southern Thailand in the story of global jihad by making false claims about loyalty vows and attack responsibility, linking local conflicts to ISEAP's goals. Unfortunately, these attempts mostly failed.

How ISEAP and Constituent Groups Functioned

ISEAP was more of an idea than a cohesive organisation. It never worked as a single, unified body, but rather as a roof over many different groups. Even though these groups believed in the same world ideology, they each had their own specific goals, problems, and ways of doing things. Some of these groups were not even working together. For example, JAD cells did not really work with each other, and the so-called ISEAP emirs in the Philippines did not have direct power over these fighters. Localised JAD cells in Indonesia had their own regional emirs. These emirs were not publicly recognised by the Islamic State, but they had more power over cadres than emirs appointed by the Islamic State, like Isnilon Hapilon. Also, no one knows if Abu Zacharia, who used to be the Emir of ISEAP Mindanao, had any effect on terrorist groups in the southern Philippines. Hatib Hajan Sawadjaan, a former Filipino emir, was the leader of the ASG but didn't really have any power over BIFF or the Maute Group. Broadly speaking, ISEAP wasn't really a single organisation. Instead, it was more like a collection of separate groups united by a shared philosophy. Also, the group's real leaders were killed: Swawidjaan in 2020 and Zacharia in June 2023.

In Indonesia, JAD groups and regional heads popped up all over the country. The public didn't know much about the leadership of these chapters, and cells worked separately from each other, even though there were some connections between regions. Though Islamic State ideas did spread online, JAD cells were mostly made up of family and social contacts; this was how most of their members were taught their beliefs. Indonesians mostly became radicalised in four different ways: radical study groups, local battles, family ties (including marriage), and pesantren (boarding schools, some of which were run or backed by terror groups or other hardline groups). One of Indonesia's top experts on terrorism, Alif Satria, says that 73% of all pro-IS supporters arrested in 2018 were connected to people who helped them become radicalised, while in 2021, only 13% of Indonesian terrorists were radicalised by internet propaganda alone.

JAD and other Indonesian groups got money for their operations and for paying the families of members who died or were taken in a number of ways, such as through donations, charities, and direct help from the Islamic State. JAD also became famous around the world as one of the first terrorist groups to use the nuclear family in an attack. For instance, in 2018, attacks in the city of Surabaya in East Java included a number of suicide bombs carried out by men, women, and children as young as nine. The Sulu Archipelago in the Philippines was also the site of suicide strikes by a family of JAD members. JAD also used marriage to connect its cells, which is similar to what happened in the Philippines when women remarried within jihadist groups. Even though JAD knew how to make bombs, not all of its groups had the same level of skill. So, different parts of Indonesia saw different types of attacks, such as suicide bombings, gunfights, stabbings, and attempts to break out of jail.

In the Philippines, groups with ties to the Islamic State also used common ways to get money, recruit new members, and do business. The most important things for recruiting were clan and family ties. There was even a group in the ASG called "ajang-ajang," which means rebels whose family members were killed by security forces. Smuggling, the drug trade, kidnapping for ransom, and other crimes also brought in money for ASG. In this way, the Maute group is unique. They mostly depend on the money and support of their brothers Omar and Abdullah Maute, who got it from their mother's real estate business, political ties, and private army. In fact, there has always been a link between crime and terrorism in the southern Philippines and throughout Southeast Asia. There are groups that commit bank robberies, cybercrime, kidnapping for ransom, trafficking, and extortion, and the government and security forces are very crooked.

The Siege of Marawi and ISEAP's Decline

ISEAP seemed to be one of the most powerful jihadist groups in the world for six months in 2017. However, its quick rise was just the start of its final fall. Over 1,000 terrorists from the Philippines and other countries took over the city of Marawi in the southern Philippines on May 23, 2017, as part of ISEAP's plan to set up a caliphate in Southeast Asia. The Maute brothers led the operation in their neighbourhood. The Islamic State planned it and helped pay for it in part. They also told foreign fighters to go to the Philippines if they couldn't get to the Middle East because ISIS's fortunes have been going downhill in Syria and Iraq. The Islamic State may have also helped the ISEAP groups with operations. This is shown by the fact that snipers were sent to high-rises, IEDs were put on buildings, and people were used as shields. These are all common methods of urban warfare in the Middle East, especially in Mosul at the time, but not so much in Southeast Asia.

The Armed troops of the Philippines (AFP) made slow progress against the rebel troops during the five-month siege. Islamic State and channels that back it were happy with what they saw as the success of the five-month operation against the AFP, who had little experience fighting in cities on such a large scale. Conservative figures say that when the AFP finally took back the city on October 23, 2017, it killed about 1,000 people, mostly terrorists, and forced hundreds of thousands more to leave their homes. Marawi is still mostly destroyed, and the fact that refugees from the area are still not being resettled is a big cause of tension in Mindanao. After ISEAP failed in Marawi, most of the Filipino terrorist groups went back to where they usually operate in rural Mindanao. People in these groups move around a lot, going from one group to another. And while groups like JAD and ASG worked together sometimes, they are not controlled from one place.

Because ISEAP wasn't united among its members, it was easy for governments in the region to work together to repress it. The siege of Marawi sparked widespread cooperation among governments in the region to do this. A pact called "Our Eyes" was made between the governments of Indonesia, Brunei, Malaysia, Singapore, Thailand, and the Philippines on January 25, 2018, just three months after the end of the Marawi Siege. This was done to share information about terrorist threats in the region. At its second working meeting on January 23, 2019, all ten ASEAN member states were added to the pact. In its first year, Our Eyes included a lot of cooperation between Indonesia, Malaysia, and the Philippines in areas like gathering information and patrolling the seas and skies between the three countries.

Along with better sharing of information, Indonesia and the Philippines changed their anti-terrorism laws in 2018 and 2020, respectively. These made preventative detention last longer and let people who were thought to have indirect ties to terror acts be arrested and detained. In 2018, Indonesian police arrested 396 people they thought were terrorists, which is 117% more than the previous year. In addition, the loss of Marawi and other Islamic State victories in the Middle East made members of ISEAP lose hope and become less united. Also, the government has tried "softer" ways to deal with complaints and deradicalisation, though the results have been mixed. In Indonesia, the government has used terrorists who have been restored to push stories about how to stop being radicalised.

But in the years that followed, there were still big attacks in Indonesia and the Philippines. In August 2020, ASG carried out a double-tap attack in Jolo, the capital of Sulu province in the Philippines. This attack killed about 15 people and wounded over 50 others. It used one IED and a female suicide bomber. A church in Makassar, Indonesia, was attacked by two JAD suicide bombs on Palm Sunday, 2021. The attack hurt more than 20 people.

Killing terrorist leaders like the Maute brothers, Hatib Sawadjaan, and Isnilon Hapilon in the Philippines and Bahrumsyah and Bahrum Naim in Indonesia has shown that cutting off the heads of terrorist leaders is an effective way to fight terrorism. Southeast Asian jihadists have lost leaders with ties to IS, which has led to division and factionalism among ISEAP's member groups. The Indonesian army killed Abu Wardah (also known as Santos) in 2016, which is another important killing. His funeral was held by thousands of people in Poso, a town in Central Sulawesi that was a key MIT support base. He was the former leader of East Indonesia Mujahedeen (MIT) and one of Indonesia's most well-known jihadists in the ISEAP bloc. Ali Kalora would next be in charge of MIT until he was killed by the Indonesian military in 2021.

As veteran investigative reporter Aisyah Llewellyn told the writers about cutting off the heads of leaders:

> *One of the biggest problems for terrorist groups is that people have different ideas and opinions all the time. This makes the groups unsteady and weaker in the long run. As with any group, it can be hard to get everyone on the same page and keep them there throughout the group's work. That's why there are so many split groups: people can't agree with each other.*

Leadership beheading has made it easier for terror groups in Southeast Asia to break up into smaller groups by getting rid of key ideologues and thought leaders.

The Philippines' Bangsamoro Autonomous Region in Muslim Mindanao (BARMM), which was made possible after years of talks between Manila and MILF, also helped to discredit IS views. As a result, the Moro people and Manila were able to get along again after decades of fighting. This proved that peaceful talks could lead to a certain amount of independence or autonomy instead of war. Because of this, there has been a steady trend of terrorists giving up in the Philippines, letting them return to normal life. Over 1,600 terrorists have turned themselves in between 2018 and 2023. Ex-combatants are given money and have to go through programs to help them become less extreme, learn how to get along with others, and get involved in their communities. But these programs haven't been very helpful so far. The strong crackdowns by security forces, who now have more experience fighting groups with ties to IS, may have played a bigger role in lowering the danger right now.

Current Threat Assessment and Conclusion

On a regional level, ISEAP is pretty much dead, but some of the groups that were part of it are still going strong, albeit in a very weak form. Because of this, the fact that these groups have worked together in the past could lead to a new, large regional movement in the future. Additionally, the unstable nature of these groups and the people who belong to them means that there will always be some kind of terrorist danger in the area, even after the time when these groups worked together within the area. There are still groups in the Philippines that support ISEAP. Most of their activity is in the south, where the Bangsamoro Independence Freedom Fighters, Maute Group remnants (also known as Dawlah Islamiyah, or Islamic State), and teams with ties to Abu Sayyaf are still active.

There is, however, a lot less action in these areas than there was in the past. The most recent major attack happened on December 3, 2023, when four people were killed and at least fifty were hurt in a bombing at a university in Marawi that was meant to target a Catholic mass. The Islamic State claimed credit for the attack. Given how violent things have been lately, this attack should be seen as an outlier, though it could also be a reason for worry because of how big it was and how important Marawi is as a place.

Since 2004, Brunei, Libya, and Malaysia formed the International Monitoring Team in Mindanao to keep an eye on things. Georgi Engelbrecht, a senior analyst with the International Crisis Group and a former member of that team, recently looked at the danger level after ISSEAP. What he said:

> *To most people in the Sulu Archipelago, the Abu Sayyaf are just ghosts from the past. This is especially true in Sulu, but not so much in Basilan. Some members of the Maute Group are still alive in Lanao, but they are thinking about how to stay alive as quiet watchers or hired guns instead of jihadists. It could be said that BIFF and its Dawlah Islamiyah (Islamic State)-influenced splinter groups are in the best place for militancy (Maguindanao), but their lack of leadership skills on the ground limits what they can do. Still, these groups could get going again if the right conditions were met.*

Most people say that the 2023 local elections in the Philippines were the bloodiest since 2010. Of the 96 violent election-related events that were reported, 55 happened in the BARMM area, which is home to the Moro people and is where most terrorist groups in the Philippines operate. Local political and clan rivalries, rising tensions over the delayed Bangsamoro peace process, and fights between the Philippine armed forces and MILF groups were some of the things that led to these events. In the past, these kinds of things helped people at first to back groups like Maute, BIFF, and Abu Sayyaf.

The Bangsamoro Autonomous Region of Muslim Mindanao will hold parliamentary elections in 2025. These elections will likely be the best way to see how long the ongoing Bangsamoro Peace Process will last. If there isn't any progress towards an agreement, frustrations are likely to rise, especially among the younger MILF fighters who are losing their support. About 65% of the 40,000 MILF fighters have reportedly given up their weapons and quit their jobs. The disarmament process has been delayed, but officials hope it will be finished by 2025. This is why the progress of the peace process is very important. If there is more fighting before the 2025 elections, and if MILF's political front loses, angry people in the area may be able to take their anger out on the government through armed groups that are already there. As long as the peace process isn't really put into action, there will probably be violence in the Bangsamoro for a long time to come.

From the point of view of other groups, ASG is now seen as its weakest, since there have been no kidnappings or other known incidents since January 2020. But the group's past criminal behaviour is still a threat. JAD has been severely weakened and doesn't seem to have any direct ties to the Islamic State anymore. However, Indonesian authorities recently foiled JAD plans to attack during the Christmas season and the 2024 Indonesian elections, showing that the group still wants to carry out attacks. (There were no attacks on the Indonesian presidential elections on February 14, 2024. However, terror groups and their followers tried to sabotage the process by spreading false information about the elections.)

Southeast Asian radical groups will probably keep using people who are left out of society's social, economic, and political life to attract new members. They are also likely to keep focussing their words and actions on the "near enemy," which in this case means their local and national governments. At the same time, they will use anger at "far enemies" like the West to gain followers and spread their ideas. These groups are also likely to keep taking advantage of the strong family and social ties in their communities. This is especially true in places where people are racially or sexually marginalised, like in the southern Philippines and Indonesia's Java, Sumatra, and Sulawesi.

Usually, Southeast Asian militant groups don't hold on to land for very long. However, the insurgencies they start are very dangerous for the states and communities where they work. Some might say that the governments of Southeast Asia have won their "war on terror," but this does not mean that terrorist activity in the area is completely over. Southeast Asian terrorist groups have also shown that they are very good at changing to new situations. Recently, JI's efforts to get into state institutions, start political parties, and spread its ideas among the general population show how it seems to have changed into a kind of political entity. JI used to be Southeast Asia's deadliest terrorist group, but it doesn't look like it wants to carry out terrorist acts to reach its goals anymore. JI even pays for its actions with money made from legal palm oil plantations, showing that it is still strong 30 years after it was founded. Members of the JI have also tried to start political parties and get into state institutions, security services, and large groups. There is still a chance that more violence will happen, even though this change in strategy shows that other groups may also be able to work within the rules of their own countries to achieve their moral goals. In this area, violent breakaway groups have often grown out of larger ones, and this could happen again if the groups that are now going the "political" route have trouble fitting in with political realities and state-sanctioned interpretations of Islam, for example. Even though there are specific goals, many people in Southeast Asia still like the idea of a larger "Islamic State" as an option to democracy and the economic, political, and social inequality that it may have caused in some areas.

Over time, Southeast Asia's terrorist groups have grown, shrunk, and gone back together again, with changes in their strengths and weaknesses. This means that even though these groups and their members seem to have lost faith in the Islamic State movement right now, a new wave of regional or global terrorism could start up in Southeast Asia again. The idea of a global holy war could become popular again, which could lead to more terrorist groups or attacks. This is especially true as the conflict between Israel and Hamas continues and tensions rise in the Middle East as a whole. As was already said in this chapter,

Southeast Asian terror groups are very flexible and can quickly change to fit new situations. They are also very open to global trends.

Extremist ethnonationalist groups in the region will probably also keep using the idea of a global war to shape their stories. Even though governments are trying to be less strict about fighting terrorism, the things that motivate terrorists and the fact that these people and groups are becoming more linked to each other around the world could lead to more violence. However, ISEAP is still not likely to be able to work as well as it did before if there is another big wave of terrorist activity in Southeast Asia. The bold attempt by ISEAP to take over Marawi was clearly unsuccessful, and the group is not likely to be able to pull off another successful operation like this one, given that regional governments are very good at fighting terrorism.

But ISEAP is still a danger, especially in the Philippines: One important event was the attack on a Catholic church in Marawi on December 3, 2023. It was claimed by the Islamic State. The attack also came before the Islamic State's new global campaign. In the first week of January 2024, the group claimed at least 30 attacks around the world, supposedly as payback for Israel's war in Gaza. Pawel Wójcik, an expert on Islamic State messaging, propaganda, and internet networks, says that since August 2023, there has been a big rise in ISEAP official propaganda. This is happening at the same time as the Gaza operation. Sayings and propaganda don't always mean that ISEAP will come back, but they do show how hard people are trying to get followers excited again during a rough time in the Middle East regionally.

Throughout the last 30 years, Southeast Asian terror groups' skills have gone up and down. However, many of them have stayed strong even as efforts to stop them have gotten better. In this way, there is still a fear of terrorism in Southeast Asia, even though it isn't very strong right now. In the future, many things could lead to a rise in Islamist terrorism in Southeast Asia, including not making progress in solving local grievances, the rise of charismatic terror leaders, and more divisions in the world.

Chapter 32
Debunking ISIS Beliefs

Terrorism from Islamic extreme groups like ISIS goes against the most basic rules of religion, society, and culture. ISIS says that it is the only real and faithful supporter of Islam and that it is doing Allah's work by defending Islam, the Quran, and the Prophet Muhammad. When ISIS leader Abu Bakr al-Baghdadi announced the restoration of the Islamic Caliphate, also known as ISIS (the Islamic state in Syria and Iraq), they used the Quran and Sunnah, the two main sources of Islamic law, to back up their plans and make their actions, like the different ways they punished Muslims and people who weren't Muslim, legal.

This brings us to the most important questions: How can we deal with this danger, and what can we do to stop or stop the spread of radical Islamic ideology? I think that the only way to stop this radical and harsh way of thinking is to look at the original sources in a different way. For Muslims to agree with this new understanding, it must be done by Islamic scholars. Most people, including radical Muslims, think that the Islamic law they follow is perfect, divine, and can't be changed. However, the truth is that the Islamic law they believe in and follow includes the interpretations and opinions of Islamic scholars, which can't be considered perfect and infallible because they are just human opinions. Also, many of the violent parts of Islamic teachings that are used by radical Islamic groups like ISIS today come from fatwas and interpretations that were added by Islamic experts but are not in the Quran. They can defend themselves by citing tales, which are not always thought to be true. This is why many centrist or liberal Muslims want the Sunnah to be filtered and the Quran to be reread with the 21st century in mind.

You might ask, "But what about all the violent verses in the Quran that call for jihad? Isn't that the first and most important source of Islam?" There are ways to deal with this problem, which is good news. One of the main points is that the call to war should be looked at from a totally different angle.

One could say that the verses about jihad need to be understood in the framework of Islamic history. As Muhammad's enemies tried to kill him with violence, he used violence and aggressiveness to protect himself and the Islamic community. Things are very different now than they were when Muhammad lived. Islam has been around for more than 1400 years, and 1.5 billion people around the world believe in it. So, Islam now has the chance to live happily with other religions. To keep the Muslim community safe, there is no need to turn non-Muslims or force them to follow Islamic law. So, one could say that the violent teachings of the Medina-Quran are no longer needed and that Muslims should go back to the peaceful teachings of the beginning of Islam, which talk about religious freedom.

Muslims can learn a lot from Muhammad's life, but one of the most important lessons is that he was always able to adapt to his surroundings. As we can see from the Quran and from what this book says, the rules about drinking have changed more than once. At first, it was okay. Later, it was limited, and then it was totally banned. Finally, Muslims were told that there would be a river of alcohol in paradise. When it comes to booze, the Islamic rules aren't really consistent. It seems like Allah might have changed his mind. This is only one case of many. I don't say this to make fun of Allah or the Quran, though. This is not what I want to do. This is an example of how Sharia can be "flexible," which is why I brought it up. I think it's important to point out that this is not my own idea or finding. Instead, it's something that Islamic scholars praise about Sharia: that it can be changed to fit different times.

In the 21st century, life is very different from when Muhammad lived. I'm sure that if Muhammad were living today, he wouldn't live the same way he did when he was in the Arabian Peninsula, but that's what most committed Muslims try to do. They try to live like Muhammad did back when he was alive. They wear clothes like the ones Muhammad wore and eat the way Muhammad ate. They try to be like him as much as possible. Also, they like to stick to what the first teachers of Islam said about things. If Muhammad were alive today, I think he would adapt to the way people live now, and I think he would want Muslims to reinterpret the Quran for themselves instead of just following the (violent) views of the early scholars.

Is this wishful thought on my part, or is there really a chance that Muslims will try to change Islamic law? The good news is that since ISIS came into being, more and more people in the Arab world have been calling for change. This makes me feel good. Faith, love, and hope are the things I hold on to in my life and don't ever want to lose.

Tackling National Security Risks

When I see terror attacks happen in our countries or hear about the terrible terror acts done by ISIS in the news, my heart breaks. We shouldn't give up, though. I hope that the shocking news will make some mainstream Muslims rethink what kind of God they believe in and make them make a clear break with radical Islam.

I'm sure that whining about all the bad things that are happening in the world won't help. "Lighting a candle is better than cursing the dark," is something I believe.

You might be wondering what type of candle you can light and what you can do to help. I am sure that having the right approach is very important and that each of us is important. How will you use the things you read in this book? Many people choose between two extremes. Some people stick their heads in the sand and don't want to hear any of this. Some people are afraid and angry. If you are scared or angry, I want to tell you that most Muslims don't believe in the radical Islamic ideas in this book. Most Muslims just want to live a good life that is peaceful.

My hope for our society is that hearing about the attacks by ISIS will make people think about what they believe in and what they stand for. How will you answer a committed Muslim who tells you on the street that Islam needs to come to the West to save the West from its moral decline? When Muslims see that adultery isn't seen as a big deal and that homosexuality is being allowed, they see this as proof that society's morals are getting worse, and they say it's their duty to bring people back to God. One reason Muslims are so good at getting young people to join Islam is that many young people don't have any morals anymore, and they know deep down that this is wrong. They think that God doesn't like them. If a Muslim tells them that reciting the Islamic faith statement is the easy way to get right with God, many young people will do it right away.

Young people are also drawn to Muslim groups because they feel like a family when they are there. Muslims stick together like brothers. So, if a young man or woman becomes a Muslim, he or she will join the larger Muslim family right away. Individualism in Western cultures and the high divorce rate, which causes families to break up, leave many people feeling very alone and hungry for close relationships. How can we deal with this problem? When was the last time you had someone over for coffee or a meal?

In today's Western societies, getting money is a big part of many people's lives, whether they need it to make a living or just to have fun. Many people only live for themselves and don't think their lives have any deeper value or purpose. How many people still make decisions based on whether they will spend all of existence in heaven or hell? Our society is set up in a way that makes it easy for Muslim groups to get new members by giving them a reason to live. Can we really wait for Muslim groups to tell our young people what life is all about?

So, to sum up, we can say that there are a few problems in Western countries that we need to solve ourselves if we don't want to wait for Muslim groups to do it their way.

I hope that this book will change your life for the better, dear reader. Remember that lighting a candle is better than cursing the dark.

Bibliography

Abbas, H. (2008). A profile of Tehrik-i-Taliban Pakistan. CTC sentinel, 1(2), 1-4. Abrar, M. F., Arefin, M. S., & Hossain, M. S. (2019, February). A framework for analyzing realtime tweets to detect terrorist activities. In 2019 International Conference on Electrical, Computer and Communication Engineering (ECCE) (pp. 1-6). IEEE. https:doi.org/10.1109/ECACE.2019.8679430

Adebayo, R. I. (2015). Islam in the Contemporary African Society. In Contemporary Perspectives on Religions in Africa and the African Diaspora (pp. 101-118). New York: Palgrave Macmillan US. https://doi.org/10.1057/9781137498052_9

Adesote, S. A., & Ajayi, A. I. (2021). Boko Haram Insurgency, Refugee crises, and Internally Displaced Persons in Nigeria, 2009-2017: A Preliminary Assessment of Governments' Response. African Journal of Terrorism & Insurgency Research (AJoTIR), 2(3). https://doi.org/10.31920/2732-5008/2021/v2n3a1

Ahmad Masood, Muslim pilgrims, The Globe and Mail, https://www.theglobeandmail.com/news/world/muslim-pilgrims-gather-at-mount-arafat-for- pinnacle-of-hajj/article26509778/.

Alexander, Y, & Swetnam, M. (2021). Usama Bin Laden's al-Qaida: Profile of a terrorist network. In Usama bin Laden's Al-Qaida: Profile of a Terrorist Network. Brill Nijhoff.

Aluede, J. A. (2018). Terrorism in the Lake Chad region: the Nexus between land borders and expansion of Islamic fundamentalism in Northeast Nigeria. Africa insight, 48(3), 105-118. https://doi.org/10.10520/EJC-1544c21039

Ani, K. J., & Uwizeyimana, D. E. (2022). Saudi Arabian-African Partnership. Journal of African Foreign Affairs, 9(2), 127-140. https://doi.org/10.31920/2056-5658/2022/v9n2a7

Antwi-Boateng, O. (2017). The rise of pan-Islamic terrorism in Africa: A global security challenge. Politics & Policy, 45(2), 253-284. https://doi.org/10.1111/polp.12195

Anzalone, C. (2016). The Resilience of al-Shabaab. CTCSentinel, 9(4), 13.

Babalola, T. O. (2022). International military cooperation in the Lake Chad basin region to fight terrorism: Roles and effects (Master's thesis, Istanbul Geli§im Universitesi Lisansustu Egitim Enstitusu).

Baldaro, E., & Diall, Y. S. (2020). The end of the Sahelian exception: Al-Qaeda and Islamic State clash in central Mali. The International Spectator, 55(4), 69-83.https://doi.org/10.1080/03932729.2020.1833566

Bazzichelli, T. (2021). Whistleblowing for Change: Exposing Systems of Power and Injustice (p. 376). transcript Verlag. https://doi.org/10.14361/9783839457931

Berger, J. M., & Morgan, J. (2015). The ISIS Twitter Census: Defining and describing the population of ISIS supporters on Twitter.

Bernard, L. (1998). License to kill. Foreign Affairs, 77, 14-19.

Bonner, R., and Johnston, D. (2003, August 15). Suspect in Indonesia Bombings is captured in Asia. New York Times, 19. August. 2003 Retrieved https://www.nytimes.com/2003/08/15/world/suspect-in-indonesia-bombings-is-captured-in- asia.html Accessed 11 April 2023.

Bowden, M. (2010). Black Hawk down: A story of modern war. Grove/Atlantic, Inc..

Brenner, Y. (2015, January 16). How Germany is attempting to De-radicalize Muslim Extremists. Retrieved: https://www.forward.com/news/212268/how-germany-is-attempting-to-de-radicalize-muslim/ Accessed: 29. March. 2023

Carter, D. B. (2016). Provocation and the strategy of terrorist and guerrilla attacks. International Organization, 70(1), 133-173. https://doi.org/10.1017/S0020818315000351

Casciani, D., and Seddon, S. (2023, February 22). Shamima Begun bid to regain UK citizenship rejected. BBC. https://www.bbc.co.uk/news/uk-64731007 Accessed 20 March, 2023. Cloud, D.S., and Lopez, L. (2003, August 15). U.S Captives Terror Suspect Tied to Indonesian Bombings. Retrieved: https://www.wsj.com/articles/sB106088718489158000 Accessed 17 March, 2023.

Coccia, M. (2018). The relation between terrorism and high population growth. Journal of Economics and Political Economy, 5(1), 84-104. https://doi.org/10.1453/jepe.v5i1.1575 Corfe, O. (2023, March 20). Met Police head says finding terrorists like 'needle in haystack' as attacks get deadlier. Retrieved: https://www.express.co.uk/news/uk/1748513/met-police- terrorist-attacks-uk-spt Accessed: 29 March, 2023.

D. Cole, Terrorizing the constitution, 1996 The Nation Company, 5.

David, D., (2023, December 17). Situation Report 2023 on the Growth of Islamic Terrorism in Africa. International Institute for Counter-terrorism (ICT). Retrieved: https://ict.org.il/situation-report-2023-on-the-growth-of-islamic-terrorism-in-africa/#: Accessed 04 April, 2024.

Denisova, T. S., & Kostelyanets, S. V. (2022). Terrorism in Africa: The Nexus of the Local and the Global. Journal of Globalization Studies, 13(2), 163-170. https://doi.org/10.30884/jogs/2022.02.11

Dictinary.com, Terrorism, https://www.dictionary.com/browse/terrorism.

DNI. (2022, October). Foreign Terrorist Organizations- Boko Haram. Counter Terrorism Guide [Online]. Available from: https://www.dni.goV/nctc/ftos/boko_haram_fto.html#: Aceessed: 03 April 2024.

Dowd, C. (2015). Grievances, governance and Islamist violence in sub-Saharan Africa. The Journal of Modern African Studies, 53(4), 505-531.

Dr. Abbass Khajeh Piri, Right to life in Islam, IMAM Reza, https://www.imamreza.net/old/eng/imamreza.php?id=12987.

Dr. Abroo Aman, Human Rights in Islamic Perspective, 2 International Journal of

Equality and Human Rights Commission, What are Human Rights? https://www.equalityhumanrights.com/en/human-rights/what-are-human-rights.

Esposito, J. L. (1999). The Islamic threat: Myth or reality?. Oxford University Press, USA. Faritz, A. (2015, February 19). How ISIS makes (and takes) money. CNN. 09. February. 2015. https://www.edition.cnn.com/2015/02/19/world/how-isis-makes-money/index.htmls

FAS. (1998, August 23). Jihad Against Jews and Crusaders. Federation of American Scientiests. Retrieved https://www.irp.fas.org/world/para/docs/980223-fatwa.htm. Accessed: 17. March. 2023

Foroughi, P., Peshkova, S., Abdullaev, K., Zartman, J. K., Thibault, H., & Roche, S. (2020). Book review roundtable: Book review roundtable of The faceless terrorist: a study of critical events in Tajikistan, by Sophie Roche, 2019, 377 pp., Cham, Switzerland, Springer,£ 46.99 (UK), ISBN9783030038427. https://doi.org/10.1080/17539153.2020.1737411

Gade, T. (2007). Fatah al-Islam in Lebanon: Between global and local jihad.

Global Terrorism Index. (2023, March). https://www.economicsandpeace.org/wp- content/uploads/ 2023/03/GTI-2023-web-1-1.PDF Accessed 23 April, 2023.

Goodman, A. E. J. (2018). When you give a terrorist a twitter: holding social media companies liable for their support of terrorism. Pepp. L. Rev., 46, 147.

Gordon, M.R. (2003, August 10) After the war: The Military, Terror Group seen as back inside Iraq. Retrieved: https://www.nytimes.com/2003/08/10/world/after-the-war-the-military-terror-group-seen-as-back-inside-iraq-html Accessed: 17 March, 2023.

Government of Netherlands, Counter Terrorism and National Security, https://www.government.nl/topics/counterterrorism-and-national-security/counterterrorism.

Gupta, D. K. (2020). Understanding terrorism and political violence: The life cycle of birth, growth, transformation, and demise. Routledge. https://doi.org/10.4324/9780429297427 Gvilia, T. (2021). Boko Haram-African Islamic State (Doctoral dissertation).

Haddad, S. (2010). Fatah al-Islam in Lebanon: Anatomy of a terrorist organization. Studies in Conflict & Terrorism, 33(6), 548-569. https://doi.org/10.1080/10576101003754677

Halliday, F. (1996). Islam and the myth of confrontation: Religion and politics in the Middle East. Tauris.

Hoffman, B. (2002) Underground Voices: Insurgent and Terrorist Communication. https://doi.org/10.13140/RG. 2.2.18816.92164

Hoffman, B. (2006) Inside Terrorism Columbia University Press: https://www.jstor.org/stable/10.7312/hoff12698

HRW.org, Terrorism/Counter Terrorism, https://www.hrw.org/topic/terrorism- counterterrorism.

Humanities and Social Science Research (2016), 21.

Hunter, R., & Heinke, D. (2011). Radicalization of Islamic terrorists in the western world. FBI L. Enforcement Bull., 80, 25.

Huntington, S. P. (1998). The Clash of Civilizations and the remaking of the World Order. London: Touchstone, Simon & Schuster, 1998. ISBN-13: 9780743231497, ISBN-10: 074323149X. https://doi.org/10.4324/9781003060963-50

Ibrahim, A., and Venzke, B. (2003). The Al-Qaeda Threat: An Analytical Guide to Al-Qaeda's Tactics & Targets. Alexandria, VA: Tempest Publishing. ISBN-10: 0966543734; ISBN-13: 978-0966543735

Imam Ahmad, 4 Musnad Imam Ahmad Ibn Hanbal, 443.

International The NEWS, Jihad and Terrorism (Dec 24, 2013), https://www.thenews.com.pk/archive/print/474711-jihad-and-terrorism-striking-a- difference.

IslamWeb.net, Equality in Islam, https://www.islamweb.net/en/article/109364/equality-in- islam.

IslamWeb.NET, Islam does not tolerate killing innocent, https://www.islamweb.net/en/article/113432/islam-does-not-tolerate-the-killing-of- innocents.

Jain, P N., & Vaidya, A. S. (2021). Analysis of social media based on terrorism—a review. Vietnam Journal of Computer Science, $(01), 1-21. https://doi.org/10.1142/S2196888821300015 Jenkins, B. M., & Kamien, D. G. (2006). The McGraw-Hill Homeland Security Handbook. Kamara, S. (2020). Threats of Terrorism in the Sahel Region of West Africa (Doctoral dissertation, Monterey, CA; Naval Postgraduate School).

John Philip Jenkins, Terrorism, Encyclopedia Britannica, https://www.britannica.com/topic/terrorism.

Khan, M. M. (2003). Radical Islam, Liberal Islam. Current History, 102(668), 417-421. Khan, M. M. (2016). Is a Clash between Islam and the West inevitable. Strategic Studies, 36(2), 1-23.

Klausen, J. (2021). Western Jihadism: A Thirty Year History. Oxford University Press.

Kumar, M., & Santoro, D. (2017). A justification of whistleblowing. Philosophy & Social Criticism, 43(7), 669-684. https://doi.org/10.1177/0191453717708469

Lieberman, A. V. (2017). Terrorism, the internet, and propaganda: A deadly combination. J. Nat'l Sec. L. & Pol'y, 9, 95.

Lynch, O. (2013). British Muslim youth: Radicalisation, terrorism and the construction of the "other". Critical Studies on Terrorism, 6(2), 241-261.

MacAskill, E. (2016, August 11). Tally of Britons joining ISIS and similar groups abroad grown to 850. https://www.theguardian.com/world/2016/aug/11/britons-joining-isis-grown-to-850-100-killed-syria-khadiza-sultana. Accessed: 29. March. 2023

Majekodunmi, A. (2015). Terrorism and counter-terrorism in contemporary Nigeria: Understanding the emerging trends. Journal of Policy and Development Studies, 289(2379'), 1-18.

Marmion, D. (2003). Fundamentalism and the 'Clash of Civilizations' The Furrow, Jan. 2003, Vol. 54, No.1, pp. 23-28. https://www.jstor.org/stable/27664667

Marshall, S., and Spitaletta, J. (2012). "19- Al-Qaeda: 1988-2001" Casebook on Insurgency and Revolutionary Warfare Volume II: 1962-2009. Fort Bragg, North Carolina, USA. United States Army Special Operations Command, pp. 533-544

Maszka, J. (2017). Al-Shabaab and Boko Haram: guerrilla insurgency or strategic terrorism?. World Scientific.

McNeill, W. H. (1995). Epilogue: Fundamentalism and the world of the 1990s in Marty, M. E., and Appleby, R. S. (eds.). Fundamentalisms and Society: Reclaiming the Sciences, the Family, and Education Chicago: University of Chicago Press, 1991-1995.

MEMRI. (2003, April 11). MEMRI Special Dispatch-Jihad and Terrorism Studies. Retrieved: https://www.memri.org/jttm/ Accessed 17. March. 2023

Merriam Webster, Jihad, https://www.merriam-webster.com/dictionary/jihad. MUSLIMS4LIBERTY, The Concept of freedom in Islam, https://muslims4liberty.org/the- concept-of-freedom-in-islam/.

Miller, J. (1993). The challenge of radical Islam. Foreign affairs, 43-56.

Mintz, J. (2003, August 12). Saudi Says Iran Drags Feet Returning Al Qaeda Leaders. Retrieved: https://www.washingtonpost.com/archive/politics/2003/08/12/saudi-says-iran-drags-feet-returning-al-qaeda-leaders/1d708930-7ac7-494b-9323-fed50e1e167d/ Accessed: 19 May 2024.

Moghadam, A. (2003). Palestinian suicide terrorism in the second intifada: Motivations and organizational aspects. Studies in conflict and terrorism, 26(2), 65-92.

Morier-Genoud, E. (2024). Towards Jihad?: Muslims and Politics in Postcolonial Mozambique. Oxford University Press.

Mroszczyk, J., & Abrahms, M. (2021). Terrorism in Africa: explaining the rise of extremist violence against civilians. E-International Relations.

Muhammad Safeer Awan, Global Terror and the Rise of Islamophobia, 49 Islamic Studies, 521.

Mustapha, A. D-A., Makama, F. T., and Ologun, V. E. (2024). Determinants of Mental Health in Nigeria. International journal of current science research and review. 7(4): 2046-2055. https://doi.org/10.47191/ijcsrr/v7-i4-07

Nakashima, E., and Sipress, A. (2003, August 15). Al-Qaeda Figure seized in Thailand. Washington Post. 15. August. 2003. https://www.washingtonpost.com/archive/politics/2003/08/15/al-qaeda-figure-seized-in- thailand/d7fb2fb2-0999-47d0-ba95-8f4556a7b082/ Accessed 17. March. 2023

News Corp Australia. (2015, November 15). Why young Australians Choose to fight with ISIS in Syria and Iraq. https://www.news.com.au/national/why-so-many-australians-are-choosing-to-fight-in-syria-and-iraq/news-story/8d1cad31f43108fec58ebf26ed79of27 Accessed 17 April 2023.

New York Times (2003b, August 15) U.S Reports Arrest of Al-Qaeda Chief for South East Asia. https://www.nytimes.com/2003/08/15/worl/45-reports-arrest-of-al-qaeda-chief-for-southeast-asia.html Accessed 17 March 2023.

New York Times. (2003a, April 22). AFTER EFFECTS: STRATEGY; Rumsfeld Denies the U.S has plans for permanent Iraq Bases. https://www.nytimes.com/2003/04/22/world/aftereffects-strategy-rumsfeld-denies-the-us- has-plans-for-permanent-iraqbases.html Accessed 17. March. 2023

Nigel S. Rodley, Torture, Encyclopedia Britannica https://www.britannica.com/topic/torture.

Nik Rahim Nik Wails, The crime of Hirabah in Islamic Law, Scribd (1996), https://www.scribd.com/doc/227589597/The-Crime-of-Hirabah-in-Islamic-Law.

Nnam, M. U., Arua, M. C., & Otu, M. S. (2018). The use of women and children in suicide bombing by the Boko Haram terrorist Group in Nigeria. Aggression and violent behavior, 42, 35-42. https://doi.org/10.1016/j.avb.2018.07.004

Noor Mohammad, The Doctrine of Jihad: An Introduction, 2 J. of L. and Religion, 381 (1985).

Nouh, M., Nurse, J. R., & Goldsmith, M. (2019, July). Understanding the radical mind: Identifying signals to detect extremist content on twitter. In 2019 IEEE international conference on intelligence and security informatics (ISI) (pp. 98-103). IEEE. https://doi.org/10.1109/ISI.2019.8823548

OKOLO, P. O., & Madu, I. T. U. (2022). Ethnicity, Electoral Expectation and Electoral Violence In Nigeria: A Prognosis Of 2011 Presidential Post Election Violence In Northern Nigeria. Ebsu Journal of Social Sciences and Humanities, 12(1).

Pooyan Fakhraei, You don't need to...., INDEPENDENT (2016), https://www.independent.co.uk/voices/you-dont-need-to-look-much-further-than-the- quran-for-proof-that-islam-is-a-peaceful-religion-a6847031.html.

Radulescu, B. G. (2020). The "Electronic Jihad" How Social Media are Used for Disseminating Terrorist Propaganda. ME. DOKMedia-Tortenet-Kommunikacio, 15(3), 89-97.

Reeder, B. W., & Smith, J. R. (2019). US strikes in Somalia and targeted civilian killings by Al-Shabaab: An empirical investigation. Foreign Policy Analysis, 15(4), 589-603.

Reuter, C., Patsch, K., & Runft, E. (2017). IT for Peace? Fighting Against Terrorism in Social Media-An Explorative Twitter Study. i-com, 16(2), 181-193. https://doi.org/10.1515/icom- 2017-0013

Rothenberger, L. (2012). Terrorist groups: Using internet and social media for disseminating ideas. New tools for promoting political change. Revista Romana de Comunicare §i Retain Publice, 14(3), 7-23.

Sadiq Reza, Torture and Islamic law, 8 Chicago J. of Inter. L. 21 (2007).

Sahabi, A., (2024, February 27). 'I take back my words'- cleric who called for killing of Remi Tinubu apologises'. Retrieve: https://www.thecable.ng/i-take-back-my-words-cleric-who-called-for-killing-of-remi-tinubu-apologises Accessed 03 April 2024.

Scheuer, M. (2006). Through our enemies' eyes: Osama bin Laden, radical Islam, and the future of America. Potomac Books, Inc..

Schulze, K. E. (2002). Militants and moderates. The World Today, 55(1), 10-13.

Shanker, T., & Schmitt, E. (2003, April 20). Pentagon expects long-term access to four key bases in Iraq. Retrieve: https://www.nytimes.com/2003/04/20/world/nation-war-strategic-shift-pentagon-expects-long-term-access-key-iraq-bases.html Accessed 30 April 2023.

Singer, M. (2018). Militant Islam's War against the West. Begin-Sadat Center for Strategic Studies, Mar. 1, 2018, pp. 1-4, JSTOR: resrep16876.1

Sky is the Limit, https://www.youtube.com/watch?v=n1AyhM9SEw8.

Stern, J. (2003) Terror in the Name of God. New York, NY: Harper Collins Publishers, pp. 365. ISBN 0-06-050532x

Terrorism and Human Rights (Emam Attalla, ISBN 978-80-87927-08-3, 2015).

The Conversation. (2016). Don't Rush to blame Molenbeek for harbouring Paris attacker. https://www.theconversation.com/dont-rush-to-blame-molenbeek-for-harbouring-paris-attacker-56575 Accessed: 29. March. 2023

The Islam Project, Making Sense of Jihad v. Hirabah, http://www.theislamproject.org/education/D05_Hirabah.htm.

Thuraisingham, B. (2004). Data mining for counter-terrorism. Data Mining: Next Generation Challenges and Future Directions, 157-183.

Tuitel, R. (2014). The future of the Sinai Peninsula. Connections, 13(2), 79-92.

Ulrika Sundberg, Terrorism and Human Rights, 76 Revue Internationale De Droit Penal, 319 (2005).

UNODC, Pakistan's Action to Counter Terrorism, https://www.unodc.org/pakistan/en/pact-pakistan-acti on-plan-to-counter-terrorism.html.

Vanguard. (2024, February). 'Order his arrest'-Shehu Sani, El-Rufai's son slam Muslim Cleric calling for Remi Tinubu's death.. https://www.vanguardngr.com/2024/02/order-his-arrest- shehu-sani-el-rufais-son-slam-muslim-cleric-calling-for-remi-tinubus-death/ Accessed: 03 April 2024.

Warner, J., O'Farrell, R., Nsaibia, H., & Cummings, R. (2020). Outlasting the Caliphate: The evolution of the islamic state threat in Africa. CTC Sentinel, 13(11), 18-33.

Why Islam, Human Rights in Islam, https://www.whyislam.org/islamicteachings/human- rights-in-islam/.

Wiktorowicz, Q., & Kaltner, J. (2017). Killing in the name of Islam: Al-Qaeda's justification for September 11. In Insurgent Terrorism (pp. 417-433). Routledge. https://doi.org/10.4324/9781351155564-16

Wilner, A. S., & Dubouloz, C. J. (2011). Transformative radicalization: Applying learning theory to Islamist radicalization. Studies in Conflict & Terrorism, 34(5), 418-438.

Wise, R. (2011). Al-shabab. Washington DC: Centre of Strategic and International Studies. https://www.csis.org/analysis/al-shabab

Wudil, A.H., Usman, M., Rosak-Szyrocka, J., Pilar, L. and Boye, M., 2022. Reversing years for global food security: A review of the food security situation in Sub-Saharan Africa (SSA). International Journal of environmental research and Public Health, 19(22), p.14836. https://doi.org/10.3390/ijerph192214836.

Index

N

P

Q

R

S

T

U

V

W

www.ingramcontent.com/pod-product-compliance
Lightning Source LLC
Chambersburg PA
CBHW051528030826
49217CB00003B/60
* 9 7 8 9 3 9 5 5 2 2 8 4 7 *